Dedicated to my reasons for wanting to be green –
Gillian, Chelsea and Rebecca

Contents

Acknowledgements		ix
1	It's Not Logical, Captain	1
2	Balance and the Bogeyman	17
3	The 'C' Word	42
4	Green Is Good (Publicity)	80
5	Beware Experts in Sheep's Clothing	104
6	Is Fairtrade Fair?	126
7	Perpetual Motion	146
8	Where There's Muck, There's Brass	168
9	The Organic Bounty	194
10	Sustainability's Balance Sheet	227
11	Economy Class	249
12	Pollution Versus eBay	263
13	Going McGreen	291
Notes		299
Index		315

Acknowledgements

Extract from *The Complete Yes Prime Minister* by Jonathan Lynn and Antony Jay, published by BBC Books; reprinted by permission of the Random House Group Ltd.

Thanks to the many people who have provided information, including Joe and Sarah Smith (Redlands Farm), David Hartridge, Robert Wine (BP), Richard Fisher (Swindon Borough Council), Helen Browning (Eastbrook Farm), Paul Allen (Centre for Alternative Technology), David Bellamy, Paul Irving (DEFRA), Jessa Latona, Vanessa Rhodes (Aviva), Gundula Azeez (Soil Association), Matt Austin, Scott Brownlee (Toyota), Mark Gillingham and Robert Falk (DoE).

As always, this book would not have been possible without the help and support of my editor Susanna Wadeson and my agent Peter Cox.

1

It's Not Logical, Captain

A 727 jet taxies on to the runway at Munich's Franz Josef Strauss airport on a beautiful June evening. The cabin is packed with delegates from Numismata, one of Germany's biggest trade fairs. They are a jovial group, discussing successful deals, swapping lurid and mostly fictional stories of adventures in hotel bedrooms. A few grumble about the one that got away, the great prize they almost captured, but even they are smug underneath. No one has left the fair empty-handed. And no one realizes that they are seconds away from the threat of death.

On the flight deck the atmosphere is calmer, but there are still smiles. The crew members go off shift after this sector. Away from the distorting plastic windows of the main cabin, the captain takes a moment to survey the stunning herringbone red sky that stretches out over the runway. He hears a snort of irritation from the right-hand seat. He has already agreed that the co-pilot can handle the take-off, and his junior is frustrated that the control tower has vetoed a rolling start because the previous flight hasn't had time to clear. They aren't late, but the co-pilot enjoys the quick turn and take-off of a rolling start – it's more macho.

The captain slips on his Ray-Bans to counter the low-lying sun. As the tower's clearance crackles in his headphones, he nods to his colleague: 'It's all yours.' The young pilot in charge pushes forward the throttles and hears the muffled scream of the engines far behind him. Painfully slowly at first, the aircraft begins to rattle its way down the runway. While the co-pilot concentrates on the controls, the captain glances at the load sheet, then back to the air-speed indicator. He is waiting for V1. And that's where things start to go wrong.

There are two critical speeds in aircraft take-off – V1 and VR. The first is the speed of last resort, the take-off decision speed. After V1, the plane should still be able to get off the ground if an engine fails; before V1 it has to abort. After V1 there isn't enough runway left to stop the plane without crashing. Once V1 is reached, there's no going back. VR, a slightly higher speed, is the rotation velocity, the point at which the pilot will pull back on the stick and the plane should lift off.

Both these speeds are governed by a number of factors. The weather. The air pressure. And crucially, the weight of the aircraft.

On the 727, the captain frowns. He has taken off from this runway many times before. It seems to him that they have travelled too far, it has taken too long to reach V1. Perhaps, though, it's an effect of the light. The flight engineer mutters something from behind him, but the captain doesn't catch it. Finally, the air-speed dial matches the number. 'V1,' the captain calls out to the co-pilot, readying him for take-off. And then, 'Rotate.' The co-pilot nods at the crisp instruction and pulls gently back on the stick. The plane judders, but does not leave the runway.

Now the captain is worried. They are well past V1 – no chance of stopping – but it seems something is wrong with the calculation. His eyes flick between the runway lights and the instruments. They are running out of concrete. 'Give it a couple of seconds more,' he encourages his junior. 'Hold on, we need more, hold on . . .' The air-speed indicator creeps up at a near invisible pace. 'Rotate!' This time the word is more than crisp – it is a barked command. Painfully slowly, the 727 noses into the sky, yards from the end of the runway, and lumbers off.

They had been within two seconds of disaster. In the cabin, the delegates noticed nothing. All that concerned them was the wait until the No Smoking sign went off and the drinks trolley arrived. Only the flight crew realized that they had faced death. But not why. They couldn't know that their plane was nearly brought down by a very common inability to combine the predictions of mathematics with an understanding of human behaviour.

Weighing passengers

If that planeload of people had died on take-off, their murderer would have been a routine calculation, made by a computer. We're all used to bags being weighed at check-in. This isn't just so that the airline can charge infuriatingly high rates for excess baggage, or to make the whole business of checking in even more irritating.

It's to help calculate the overall weight of the aircraft – an essential component in knowing how it will perform and whether take-off will be safe.

Much though airlines would like to do it, they don't weigh the passengers. It's thought that it would be too intrusive. Some airlines have given serious consideration to having secret weighing platforms as individuals pass through a pinch point on the air bridge that leads up to the aircraft door, collecting a realistic weight profile, but practicalities and a fear of bad publicity have stopped this idea being implemented. The airlines can't just ignore the passengers' weight, though – it makes a big contribution to the load the plane has to carry.

Instead, they resort to probability. Airline planners decide on the most likely weight for the average passenger and use that in their calculations. (This weight has crept up over the years as too many supersized fast-food meals take their toll.) It's not ideal, but it's good enough to calculate take-off speeds and safety factors. Usually. Even so, probability says that on some flights the approximation will be wrong – and that was what brought the 727 near to disaster on that summer evening in Munich.

Germany hosts the world's biggest coin collectors' festival, Numismata. Rotating around three centres – Berlin, Frankfurt and Munich – the event is a magnet for coin dealers. This particular flight out of Munich was timed precisely to catch dealers as they left the fair; almost all its passengers were coin dealers.

In themselves, dealers aren't particularly overweight. They are pretty average. But they are obsessive about their coins. They don't like to put their best buys in the luggage. They keep their acquisitions on their person, or in hand luggage. In those easy days before terrorist threats intensified airline security, the dealers had been able to go on board weighed down with coins, pushing up their average weight sufficiently to throw out the airline's take-off calculations. The 727 was nearly brought down by pockets full of cash.

All the information that was needed to prevent this incident existed. The planners understood how the passenger weight was calculated and the implications of getting it wrong, but they didn't know about the coin fair. Sales and check-in agents knew coin dealers and their habits, but weren't aware of the impact on the expected weight and safety. The scene was set for disaster.

This incident really happened, although some details have been changed. The airline has never publicly discussed it, but it was the talk of airline conferences for years afterwards. It was my introduction to the distinction between what seems to make sense at first glance and the realities revealed by good logical analysis.

When I went to work for an airline, my first job was to construct a system that would enable planners to avoid the kind of disaster that nearly happened at Munich. Here, the essence was finding a way to spot unexpected connections, to modify the generally satisfactory average weights to reflect special events like the coin fair, combining the mathematical input of the weight calculation with the human experience of how passengers behave in different situations.

This is the essence of operational research, the mix of logic and an understanding of human behaviour, in which I was just beginning to work. Sometimes taking a more logical view of circumstances involves an exploration of the incentives and emotional factors that are involved in making a decision. At other times a logical view requires the comparison of very different options, or testing causality – whether we are mistaken in assuming one event causes another – a key factor in everything from airline incidents to carbon offsetting.

Emotion and logic

We tend to see logic and human reaction as two sides of a coin. In the original 1960s *Star Trek* series, logic was represented by Mr Spock, emotional human reaction by Dr McCoy. The message of the series was that you need both. Neither one, in isolation, is enough to cope with everything the universe can throw at you. This is true, but the balance between the two is often hard to manage. When we consider a subject as emotionally loaded as the environment, the Dr McCoy 'feely' side totally overwhelms the Mr Spock logic. That's why, I suggest, we need some ecologic. Getting sensible answers about the environment requires both numbers and human reaction; it's not enough just to go with your feelings.

In principle, the environment should be a no-brainer. No one wants to destroy the world. We all – even the much-maligned heads of corporate giants – hope that our children will have a good life, not one that's blighted by an earlier generation's greed. Yet in practically every green area we are either failing to take the essential steps to prevent such blight, or we are being deceived – often by ourselves. By using the dissecting scalpel of ecologic, it's possible to open up the reality beneath the layers of confusion and deception.

Before exploring how this can happen, I want to tell another story that illustrates why such logical analysis is so necessary when understanding human behaviour. As in the opening example, I'm staying away from green issues for the moment. When I'm not writing books, I help organizations be more creative. Over the years I've discovered that it's important to start off with examples that aren't directly connected with the issue at hand, because otherwise participants concentrate on the details of the example, not the process. The purpose of what follows is to demonstrate how we humans deceive ourselves. These events haven't occurred yet, but there is no reason why they shouldn't.

The lottery deception

To celebrate the New Year, the National Lottery has decided to run a double event. Two draws on the same day. Two chances to become a millionaire. As usual, stacks of tickets have been sold. Millions of people are holding on to the hope of having their lives transformed. Of course, they know it's unlikely. They probably won't win. But there's a tiny chance that they could soon be living the celebrity lifestyle, and that's what makes spending the money worthwhile.

The first draw goes much as any other week. Out come the numbers, one after another, a random string of possibilities and hopes. This particular lottery uses six numbers from a possible forty-nine. There's a bonus ball too, but that's for losers. Let's watch those six big numbers: 24 – 39 – 6 – 41 – 17 – 29. It's over for all but the lucky few. There's nothing exceptional. Although the announcer tries to inject wild excitement into his voice, it has been done a thousand times before. It's not news.

Then the second draw begins. Let's pick up the commentary. 'They're using the machine they call Delilah for the draw tonight, started by none other than a former member of Blondie. Here comes the first number and . . . what are the chances of that? The first number is one. Okay, next choice. Well, would you believe it? Two. That's incredible. And the third number's coming through now. Hey, is this a joke? The third number is three . . .'

And so it goes on until the draw is complete: 1 – 2 – 3 – 4 – 5 – 6. All neatly in sequence. There is uproar. The payout is suspended while the draw machine is overhauled and checked. A trickle of demands for a refund soon becomes a torrent. Questions are asked, all the way up to parliament. Yet no one can find anything wrong. How could this be? How could such an incredible result happen?

That simple lottery draw exposes a strange, disturbing reality. Our world has many random elements in it, where probability is the only guide. Whether you are running an environmental campaign or you are a quantum physicist, probability is an essential contributor to what's happening in your world. Yet human beings are incompetent when it comes to handling the outcome of chance. We just don't get probability. It seems unnatural, and it fools us all the time. There really was no reason to be surprised by the lottery draw: 1 – 2 – 3 – 4 – 5 – 6 is just as likely to come up as 24 – 39 – 6 – 41 – 17 – 29. It has *exactly* the same chance. Yet to our probability-blind brains there is a huge difference between the two results.

It might seem strange that we can't cope with probability if it's so important, but evolution often produces a compromise, where one capability is sacrificed to make another strong. The ability that makes it impossible for us to handle probability well is pattern recognition. We depend on patterns. They provide our interface with the real world. So strong is our need for patterns that we frequently make them up where they don't exist. Where there is no pattern, where probability rules a sea of randomness, we are lost.

This is why the lottery result takes us by surprise – and why so many people bother to buy lottery tickets in the first place. When we see a draw like 24 – 39 – 6 – 41 – 17 – 29 our probability blindness conceals just how unlikely it is that a particular combination of numbers is going to be drawn. It is only when a pattern is imposed and we see 1 – 2 – 3 – 4 – 5 – 6 that we realize just how improbable the whole thing is.

Living a pattern

Why are patterns so important to us? Because they help us make sense of a complex world. If we didn't deal with patterns, we would collapse under the strain of information overload. I don't hold in my brain the exact instructions for flipping the light switch in the lounge. It would involve too much detail. Exactly where to stand, where to position my finger, where to press and at what angle, how much pressure to use, how far the switch moves before I can stop pressing . . . It's too much, and it's too specific. Even if I could hold all this detail, then

I'd have to learn all over again how to switch on the lights in the kitchen. Instead I have a broad pattern that says, 'This is what light switches are like, this is how to turn them on,' and until I get to America and find their switches are the wrong way up, I can get along pretty well.

We use patterns all the time without even realizing it. When I pass someone in the office corridor and recognize them, I'm using pattern-matching. If I had to collect every detail of a face and compare it with the data on everyone I knew, I'd be lost. What's more, I would only have a chance of recognizing a person if I saw them from exactly the same angle, with the same lighting as when I first stored their details away. As soon as they changed their hair or put on glasses or gained a wrinkle I would have to start all over again. This is why the biometric systems now being introduced to identify individuals at airports using fingerprint identification, retinal scans or face recognition are so hit and miss. It's a difficult job. The eye/brain combination that allows us to recognize people (and do a host of other things) doesn't work like a camera, breaking a picture down into a grid of pixels – it picks up patterns and shapes, which enable us to be much more flexible in recognizing what we see.

This is also why computers find it so difficult to come close to the human ability to recognize objects and text. We can see that **word**, *word* and **word** all say the same thing, because we are working with patterns, not using exact matching. We can even use patterns to see what isn't there.

In the example overleaf, it's very clear that the top word is 'bank' despite significant parts of the letters

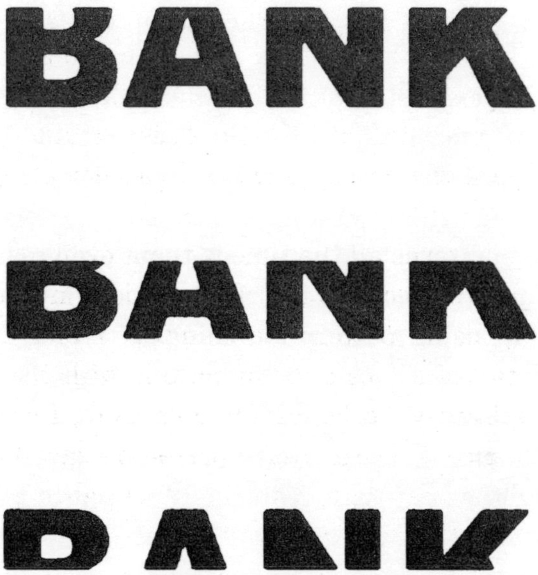

Figure 1 Breaking the bank.

being missing. Even the second example, with a full half of each letter missing, is readily identifiable. It's only when we introduce ambiguity that our pattern skills fail – does the bottom word say 'bank' or 'rank'? There's no way of telling.

Such is our dependence on pattern that it is frighteningly easy to jump to a whole set of false conclusions based on an over-simplistic picture. We might just be starting from a single word, like that half-glimpsed BANK sign, but immediately our pattern-building brains begin to construct a whole network of links and associations that may not have as much validity as we believe. All through this book you will find examples of how we take the implications and linkages of words and other patterns to make incorrect deductions.

The environment as comfort blanket

Here's an example. A recent edition of the *Ecologist* magazine featured an article entitled 'Age of Awakening', describing ancient spiritual wisdom provided by an ethnic wise man. Ecology is a science (the clue is in the 'ology') and this magazine carries a reasonable number of scientifically based stories, though admittedly with a particular message in mind. But at the same time, it also carries touchy-feely stories like this one with little or no scientific basis. The inclusion of such an article in a magazine with an apparently scientific theme demonstrates how easy it is to deceive ourselves, confusing the 'feeling' of being green (all natural, warm, hand-knitted and such) with the actual science of saving the planet.

To be effective in solving environmental issues we have to cut through the patterns and self-deception – that's the role of ecologic. Warm, cuddly feelings are great when we are trying to get people enthused, encouraging them to join in a campaign, but they are a tool of marketing, not a practical guide to making things happen.

That emotional response – which tells us that 'natural' is better than 'chemical', for example – is a common cause of misunderstanding. A pinch of the purely chemical substance sodium chloride (I'm using 'chemical' in the way it is often misused to portray something unnatural) will do us much less harm than a pinch of the entirely natural deadly nightshade or the devastatingly poisonous castor bean plant containing the neurotoxin ricin. The things that frighten us are often not the greatest dangers we face. Many people fear flying, for instance, not because it is more dangerous than other modes of transport, but because it is more scary. We let emotion influence our weighting of what's important.

Take the word 'organic'. When we hear it, all sorts of associations spring into being, apparently fully-formed. Tasty food, perhaps. Healthier eating. Produce that is grown sustainably. Natural rather than artificial. No chemicals. Good animal welfare. A concern for the land. This could well all be true – but we can't assume that the pattern holds just because it's what we expect. We need to bring in ecologic to test that pattern.

Irrational acts

Although operational research, the basis behind my ecologic approach, is mathematically based, delving into ecologic doesn't require sophisticated calculations. The numbers will rarely get more complicated than $1-1 = 0$, and often it's more about gaining an understanding of why people take a particular action even when it doesn't make sense. We need the guidance of a logical viewpoint because as human beings we tend not to act rationally.

A good example of this can be seen in the Ultimatum game. Before I describe this, answer a simple question. If I were to offer you £1 – no strings attached, nothing to be done, all you have to do is say yes – would you accept? It's not a trick question. Be clear what you would answer.

Now imagine you were taking part in the Ultimatum game. You play with one other person. I offer the pair of you £100. The other person has to decide how the cash is split between you. Your part in the game is to decide whether or not you will accept the split. If you say 'yes', the cash is split between you the way the other person decides. If you say 'no', neither of you gets any money. There is no negotiating; it's just a one-off, yes-or-no decision. The other person decides to keep £99 and give you £1. Would you accept?

Rationally, this is exactly the same choice as before. All you are really being asked is if you would accept £1 for doing nothing. However, the majority of people would say 'yes' to the first question and 'no' to the second. They feel hard done by if the other person takes almost all the money. It's not fair.

Experiments have shown that unless the person splitting things makes it at least 70:30, the choice will tend to be rejected. There is more than one influence at play. We can afford to punish the other person if the amount is relatively insignificant. £1 is a small enough figure for most of us to ignore. If the amount being split were £100 million, I suspect far fewer would turn down the £1 million on offer just because the other person was getting £99 million. Even so, there's something strange at work in this decision.

Rationally, taking the money is the only sensible thing to do, however small the portion you are awarded. But we have evolved to cooperate, and so strong is the need to feel fairness and reciprocal support that we flip into punitive mode, even though we suffer as well as the person dividing the cash. However, we can't afford to take a similar, irrational, 'cutting off your nose to spite your face' attitude when making decisions about the environment. We have to overcome our social conditioning and emotional reactions to take the logical, rational choices that will help save the planet.

Which caused what?

Another aspect of our natural make-up is our limited ability to think outside the here and now. Only in the last 50–100,000 years – a moment in the evolutionary timescale – have we had the ability to think about the future. Not only does this make us bad at long-term planning – we all put much too much weight on the present – it has also left us pathetically poor at getting to grips with why things happen in a particular way. We can find it surprisingly difficult to match up cause and effect. We are often tricked into assuming false causality simply because two events are close together in time or space.

For several years after the Second World War the rate of pregnancy in the UK closely followed the number of bananas imported into the country. More bananas, more babies. Fewer bananas, fewer births. Just looking at the numbers, it's easy to assume a link, but anyone who suggests that the bananas directly caused the pregnancies is imagining a false causality (and is due a few refresher lessons in biology).

In practice there are many ways in which this apparent relationship could have been caused. There could have been a reverse causality (more pregnancies caused an increased demand for bananas), a mutual causality (both the pregnancies and the urge to buy bananas were caused by the same surge of post-war enthusiasm) or a total lack of causality (coincidences happen).

Such misunderstandings of causality are easy to make. We see apparent linkages ('correlations', in maths-speak) and assume that the environmental equivalent of the bananas was the driving force behind the green 'pregnancies'. We are not helped by the way the media present information to catch our attention rather than making sure we really understand what is going on. As we will see, we need to be constantly on our guard against misinterpretation.

2

Balance and the Bogeyman

So dependent are we on patterns that we find it easy to see them when they aren't really there. This is the bogeyman effect. The world seems a dangerous place, particularly in the dark. Our senses are ready to spot and identify a predator. So we imagine a strange shape under the bed or in the corner of the room. It's caused by something quite ordinary, but our pattern recognition goes into overdrive and we are scared out of our wits.

It becomes harder to be scared by shadows as we get older, but we don't lose that frisson of fear – and we have a whole new set of environmental bogeymen, thanks to the media. Writers for newspapers and TV journalists are always looking for a hook – something that will catch the audience's attention. Broadcaster Andrew Marr wasn't far from the truth when he called journalism 'industrialized gossip'. Few hooks are more effective and visceral than fear, so the media regularly pick up on dangers and magnify them in order to achieve ratings. It's a bit like the way children exaggerate to get attention.

Biased 'balance'

This doesn't mean that every media scare story is wrong, or even biased towards the scary side. Sometimes, thanks to another dangerous media word, 'balance', the media will play down a story that really needs bringing out. For several years, for instance, the BBC attempted to give balance by putting up both sides of the argument when it came to man-made causes for climate change. Unfortunately, it continued to do so long after there was any significant scientific doubt about the existence or the causes of global warming. As environmental campaigner Jonathon Porritt put it at an event in 2007 organized by the Royal Society of Arts, 'As the science gets harder, the politics gets softer . . . flakier.' While the scientific results on climate change were firming up, politicians and the politically minded broadcasters were becoming less effective. With its tendency to bring in someone to speak against climate change to 'balance' the scientific consensus, it was as if the BBC were reporting on one of Richard Branson's publicity stunts and, after announcing that he intended to fly round the world, then brought on a representative from the Flat Earth Society to say that it's not possible because the world isn't round.

This is not saying that balance is a bad thing. It's perfectly reasonable to bring in two opposing views if both are held by appropriate people in the relevant fields of knowledge, and if the two viewpoints hold similar degrees of substance. But the attempt to provide balance at all times, particularly when dealing with a piece of science, is a guaranteed way to confuse the audience.

The MMR madness

When a bogeyman comes along, balance both good and bad goes out of the window. Perhaps the strongest bogeyman card the media can play is danger to children. When children are put at risk, our sense of balance and fairness is abandoned. Sadly, the media quite often raise the public's awareness of a bogeyman with insufficient evidence – and because we don't wait for detailed evidence in dealing with a bogeyman, we go straight into panic mode.

This was all too obvious in the MMR scare, started in 1998 by Dr Andrew Wakefield. For nearly ten years the suggestion that the measles, mumps and rubella vaccine could cause autism in children resulted in worry and confusion in the public. Yet the fuss was largely based on a study of twelve individuals by one semi-amateur. Rather than listen to the many different experts who had undertaken vastly larger, more conclusive studies, the media sparked fear by picking up on the scare stories of one man, based on little more than anecdote. And once a bogeyman has been raised, it is very difficult to put down. In 2007, even after Dr Wakefield's claims had been conclusively discredited, there were still occasional bursts of MMR panic in the media, despite outbreaks of measles among those not inoculated, including at least one death.

Part of the problem is that the news media are very unwilling to reveal their mistakes. Science often advances by learning from error. But when contrary results show that a scare story was based on false evidence, as happened with the MMR panic, this is not usually reported by the media in anywhere near as much depth as the original story – if it's covered at all. What typically happens is that someone pre-announces some research before a peer-reviewed paper comes out. The media pick up on this and make a big splash, terrifying everyone. Then either the paper isn't published, or later work shows that it was an error. And the media respond with silence. We don't get to hear of the new research. We certainly don't hear, 'Sorry, we scared you unnecessarily – we got it wrong.' The reality is just ignored.

Coping with clusters

One of the biggest bogeymen out there fits comfortably into the world of green issues – the impact on human beings of electromagnetic radiation, whether it is from mobile phone masts or, more recently, from wireless networks.

There were two main triggers for fears: clusters of cancer cases, and individuals who were convinced they got headaches and other symptoms as a result of being exposed to this radio frequency output. Each has been repeatedly picked up by the media, feeding the bogeyman. I want to concentrate on the 2007 concerns about wireless networks, which have been based primarily on the second type of trigger, but it is worth exploring clusters first, because they are a repeated cause of concern.

The argument is simple. When there is a cluster of a particular type of illness – for instance several outbreaks of the same type of cancer – in a particular place, then the chances are that anything suspicious about that place was the cause of the cancer. It might be a phone mast, a nuclear power plant or a local factory, but the two rapidly become connected.

Unfortunately, there has been a leap of imagination in drawing this conclusion. Anything that happens randomly will tend to occur in clusters. Imagine dropping a whole box of ball bearings on the floor. It would be incredibly unlikely that the metal balls would be evenly spread across the floor so that they formed a nice, regular pattern. If they did fall this way you would suspect some sort of cause – a series of magnets under the floor, perhaps. Instead you would expect there to be parts of the carpet with lots of ball bearings in a small space, and others where there is a sizeable gap.

It's just the same with outbreaks of a non-contagious disease like cancer. What would be really strange is if cases *were* evenly spread across the country. This would imply that something (some *real* bogeyman) was causing this unnaturally even spread. A truly random distribution would have some clusters of cases and other areas with gaps. Clusters don't imply a local cause; they are a natural phenomenon.

This doesn't mean, of course, that every cluster *is* random. New evidence suggests there may be a link between cancer clusters and some nuclear plants (though possibly not as a result of radiation). And the unusually high incidence of asbestosis in workers at a factory in the northern town of Rochdale was certainly no coincidence. The factory was part of Turner & Newall, the world's biggest asbestos producer, and clear evidence of the connection exists. It is possible to use statistical methods to look at how often a cluster coincides with, say, the locality of a phone mast to see how confident we can be that the masts are responsible for the clusters.

With the number of mobile phone masts around, there is no doubt that there will be some coincidences of masts and cancer outbreaks, but statistically a causal link is yet to be demonstrated.

However, statistics don't make good TV, whereas worried parents do – so the media are likely to pick up on their concerns and the result is only to strengthen the bogeyman. This phenomenon is nothing new; it is just the culprit that has changed. At one time, if there was an outbreak of disease in a confined area someone in the village would be accused of being a witch. Now it is the mobile phone mast that gets blamed.

I know how difficult it can be to accept clusters, even for something trivial. I sell copies of one my books, *The First Scientist*, which is out of print, through Amazon's Marketplace. On average I sell a book every couple of months. One day, however, I sold three in as many hours. I was convinced there had to be a causal link producing the cluster – perhaps my book had been cited in some course or other. I emailed each of the purchasers, only to find that there was no link. It was a purely random chance, but I found it hard to accept. How much harder it must be if you are dealing with cases of serious illness.

Another way to look at the reality of clustering is the 'shock percentage' effect. Percentages can sometimes give a misleading slant on information. Company human resources departments like to keep a check on when people are taking sick leave, in case they are taking a day off when there's nothing wrong. It seems reasonable that this might happen more often near a weekend, and some people are genuinely shocked if in a particular company *40 per cent* of sick days are taken adjacent to a weekend. This seems too much to be a coincidence – until you remember that two work days out of five, Monday and Friday – 40 per cent in all – sit next to the weekend. Similar self-deception can occur over clusters.

Because of the nature of statistics, about half the towns and villages in the country will have above-average numbers of cancer cases. Many of these will have a phone mast or something else to blame. Remember, we're talking around half of *all* the places in the country. That's a lot of locations in which to find some significant cause for a cluster. Again, it would be surprising if a good number of these above-average locations didn't coincide with a suspected cause. You can make the silliness of this more obvious by saying that (for instance) practically every small town with above-average cancer levels has a pub. Suspicious. Perhaps having a pub nearby causes cancer.

The radio-controlled bogeyman

Phone masts have been regular triggers for bogeyman scares for a long time, but 2007 saw an outbreak of a related but different kind of fear – the risk from wireless networks. To understand how bogeyman fears are generated, the best place to start is the media portrayal of the problem. Here the sources are particularly rich, but I am taking two – an article in the *Ecologist* and an edition of the BBC's flagship current affairs programme, *Panorama*.

The *Ecologist* is a broad-church magazine, as we have seen, so it is not always clear if an article is based on science or feelings. The December 2007 issue carried a piece by Mark Anslow called 'The Gathering Brainstorm', which featured an impressive list of studies and enough technical content to reassure the reader that it was more than an emotional response.

It begins by giving the background to Wi-Fi, the short-hand term often used for wireless networks or wireless LANs. These computer networks using radio signals to connect computers are now common in schools, in public places and in homes as an alternative to trailing wires all over the building. The first thing that's noticeable about the article is the term used for the radio signal that links your laptop or other device to the network.

Electromagnetic radiation (no relation to nuclear radiation) covers a vast spectrum, from radio through microwaves and ordinary visible light to X-rays and gamma rays. Although all electromagnetic radiation, such as the sunlight we see with, consists of a stream of particles called photons, it is often referred to as a wave as it has wave-like properties and historically was thought to be a wave. The normal way of referring to what's used in Wi-Fi is 'radio waves', but Anslow's article repeatedly refers to them as 'microwaves'.

This is a loaded term, one of the common components of an intentional media bogeyman trigger. Microwaves are an arbitrary chunk of the electromagnetic spectrum, sitting between radio and the visible. Microwave ovens cook via a particular set of microwave wavelengths, around 1 centimetre in length, so 'microwaves' as a term suggests a form of electromagnetic radiation that could fry your brain, where the more accurate 'radio waves' is neutral.

Much of the article is a collection of anecdotes of protests against Wi-Fi. It makes note of the *Panorama* programme, of which more detail follows. It also covers a range of bodies involved in the dispute, and attempts to discredit a particularly interesting study by Essex University, to which we will also return. Anslow places a lot of weight on what he describes as 'the battery of research built up over the past decade demonstrating very clear health risks from exposure to mobile phone masts [that] could now be translated almost exactly into the risks faced by exposure to Wi-Fi equipment'.

This 'battery of research' comes from thirteen studies, named in the article though with no details of where they were published or whether they were peer-reviewed – an essential if a scientific paper is to be given any weight. Some of these, summarized, were as vague as 'residents . . . reported significantly higher occurrences of headaches, memory changes, dizziness, tremors, depressive symptoms and sleep disturbances than a control group' – which seems little more than anecdote. The author lists none of the many studies with findings other than those he wants to show – a highly unscientific approach.

Even the studies listed that were from respectable sources could be a little lacking in persuasive evidence. For example, the first, by Santini et al. in 2002, is the result of analysing a questionnaire. There is a big problem with this approach. First, just asking people how they feel suffers from all the problems of potential questionnaire bias (see page 131). And even if the questionnaire is perfectly worded, the people know too much. For a medical study to be worthwhile, it has to be double blind.

This is the method of scientific testing used in medical trials and means that both the people taking part and the researchers are ignorant of who is taking the medication and who the placebo (sugar pill). Otherwise there are surprisingly strong biases, because with knowledge of what's expected of them, people react differently. An impressive parallel with the mobile phone mast example is the 'nocebo' effect. When drugs are tested, they come with a list of potential side effects. Test subjects who have taken a placebo and are also given the list of side effects regularly appear to suffer the problems that go along with the medication – headaches, dizziness, nausea and so on. This kind of reaction – exactly the reaction supposedly generated by phone masts – is easily self-generated by a harmless placebo. So the only effective trial would be one where the people in question didn't know whether or not there was a mobile phone mast nearby.

The *Ecologist* has a clear editorial standpoint, so its approach should be no surprise. Significantly more worrying was the *Panorama* programme, as the BBC is expected to take an unbiased view on such issues. *Guardian* columnist Ben Goldacre has ruthlessly dissected the programme's flaws.

Panoramic Wi-Fi

Like the article in the *Ecologist*, *Panorama* reporter Paul Kenyon used a bogeyman term for the radio signals from Wi-Fi, though rather than microwaves he repeatedly referred to them as radiation – a total of thirty times throughout the programme, according to Goldacre. While this is technically an accurate label – Wi-Fi signals are electromagnetic radiation, just as the light you are using to read this book is electromagnetic radiation – when used alone 'radiation' is usually associated with nuclear radiation or radioactivity, that indubitably hazardous stuff produced by nuclear power stations and nuclear bombs (and, less well publicized by the anti-nuclear movement, by granite rocks such as those in Cornwall and parts of Scotland).

Goldacre rightly discards a horrendously unscientific scene in which Kenyon walks around the streets with a meter measuring 'Wi-Fi radiation' and sounds shocked when the meter goes 'well into the red'. We have no idea what 'into the red' means, or even what this meter, designed and sold by Kenyon's companion in the film, does. The companion is Alasdair Philips from the anti-phone and Wi-Fi campaign group Powerwatch (one of the sources recommended by the *Ecologist* article), which also sells a range of protection gear, including a mesh helmet to keep off microwave exposure.

The school *Panorama* filmed in when testing Wi-Fi 'radiation levels' refused to take further part when they heard about the unscientific approach being adopted. Tests were made by Philips with a hand-held meter, positioned about a centimetre away from the screen of a laptop downloading a large file (not a typical use); it produced readings that were claimed to be significantly higher than in the 'main beam' of a phone mast.

As Goldacre points out, it is quite remarkable that the BBC, an organization that employs many radio engineers, had to bring in a man who makes money out of selling anti-electromagnetic radiation equipment and heads a campaigning pressure group to provide a 'fair' assessment of the signal levels in the school – without the public being made aware of this. Other experts used on the programme (significantly more for than against its proposition) have been publicly derided for using 'vague, deceptive and suggestive language' and speaking outside their area of competence.

Later in the programme, Kenyon looks at 'electro-sensitivity' – people who claim to be able to detect the influence of electromagnetic radiation, proving that it has an effect on the body (though not necessarily that it is harmful). *Panorama* resorted to the classic non-scientific approach of anecdote. Just one person was shown, who it was claimed had correctly identified whether a signal was present two times out of three. On its own, this proves nothing. I can toss a coin three times and correctly predict the outcome on two of those tosses. It doesn't mean I'm detecting anything; that's just how statistics work. What's needed again are double-blind trials, and in this particular case they exist in abundance. Goldacre lists references for thirty-one trials of people who believed that their headaches and other symptoms were caused by electromagnetic radiation. The results were hugely supportive of there being no such thing as electrosensitivity.

Of these studies, twenty-four found no effect; two had positive results that the authors of the study were unable to reproduce (and lack of reproducibility strongly suggests error); three seemed to be based on mistaken statistical assumptions; and the remaining two were mutually inconsistent. This is a very strong indication that the whole concept is imaginary. It doesn't prove that phone masts or Wi-Fi are safe, but it does destroy one of the more significant pieces of evidence against them.

It might seem surprising that in some of the trials scientists got the statistics wrong, but most of those undertaking these studies are not themselves statisticians, and the statistics of trials can be particularly misleading. Here's why.

Getting the numbers right

Imagine you went for a test for a medical condition. Say the test is 98 per cent accurate for false positives. That means that 2 per cent of patients are told there's a problem when there isn't one. What's the chance, if you get a positive test result, that you have the medical problem being tested for? The vast majority of people would answer 98 per cent. It's practically certain that you've got the illness. If you think that's the case, you could be very wrong.

Say the test is administered to one million people a year, of whom 1 in 1,000 have the particular problem. To keep things simple, we'll also assume a 98 per cent accuracy for false negatives, where the test misses the fact you've got the problem.

So 1,000 of the people tested have the problem, and of those 980 will be told they have it. But remember that 2 per cent of the million people tested will be told they have a problem when they don't. That's 20,000 people. With these particular numbers, if you get a positive result from a 98 per cent accurate test, the chances are 20:1 that you *don't* have the medical problem. This is the sort of statistical complexity anyone analysing the results of a test that looks for cause and effect has to watch out for.

This is why it's so important to rely on peer-reviewed studies, and any responses to them in the journals, rather than on an individual study or, even worse, an anecdote. Paul Kenyon in *Panorama*, rather than using the wealth of existing data, interviewed one individual who had taken part in the University of Essex study that was attacked by the *Ecologist*. When *Panorama* made the film, this study was incomplete, but its final verdict would show no significant evidence for electrosensitivity. By associating the subjective views of one individual with the study, *Panorama* made it seem that those opinions were supported by the research.

The Essex study has been attacked because a number of alleged sensitives dropped out, as did a number of the control non-sensitive people. It has been argued that the individuals dropping out were the most sensitive, and so most likely to be ill, but if this meant the study failed, it would imply that the remaining forty-four individuals who claimed to be electrosensitive were wrong – and as the only basis for the existence of electrosensitivity is people's perception that they are, this would indeed be damning for those believing in it. Six more sensitives dropped out than controls, but this has no effect on the analysis of the results.

It has also been said that the numbers were insufficient for a statistically significant result – not the case with forty-four sensitives and 120 controls taking part. The reduction in numbers did inevitably increase the chance that the study could be wrong – but that is true of every statistical study and doesn't change the outcome. Perhaps the most bizarre complaint about the Essex study is that the researchers didn't screen the people who said they were electrosensitive for the known symptoms; they just took their word for it. But given that there are no known symptoms for electrosensitivity – it is dependent on individuals' belief that electromagnetism is causing their problems – this is a meaningless complaint.

Environmental concerns can never simply be ignored. No one is doubting, for instance, the seriousness of the symptoms in the case of some 'electrosensitives' – merely the unfounded assumption that exposure to electromagnetic radiation is the cause. Similarly, there have been many cases in the past where individual or corporate greed, or simple ignorance, has put the population at risk. For thousands of years lead was used in white cosmetics that women applied to their faces. There is now no doubt that it resulted in disease and premature deaths.

Yet the mere existence of environmental threats does not mean that we can assume that every concern is valid. Where there is strong scientific evidence that a technology is safe, as is the case with the level of electromagnetic radiation from phone masts and Wi-Fi, it makes sense to accept the technology while continuing to probe for possible problems.

Balancing risk

All of life is about balancing risk. Would any of us accept the introduction of a technology that would kill 3,000–4,000 people a year in the UK alone? I doubt it. Yet that's exactly what we do with road transport. We know there is a risk involved, we try to minimize it, but in the end we decide it's more important to get around than to stay at home in a cotton-wool cocoon. Despite those numbers of deaths, the chance of being killed on a particular car journey is only around one in ten million (slightly better than the chance of being killed on a particular plane journey, which puts paid to the old chestnut that flying is safer than travelling by road). There is a risk, but we can put it in proportion.

It's important with any technology that we assess the risk, if any, and continue to monitor it. But what has to be avoided is the bogeyman effect. The media have a unique responsibility to avoid such inflammatory presentations of information, and particularly to avoid the habit of pre-announcing. Even the UK's current-affairs flagship radio programme, *Today*, doesn't usually report on the results of studies or reports: it features them the morning before they come out and guesses what they are going to say. This just won't do for scientific results. The media must wait until we have facts rather than deal in anecdote and speculation.

It would be ideal if we could all take responsibility for checking the facts before reacting. Whether it's a story about that discredited link between MMR and autism, or a story of petrol shortages that results in horrendous queues at the filling stations, a knee-jerk reaction to a bogeyman story will only result in disaster. But few of us have the time or the facilities to do this. The journalists who broke the MMR stories with insufficient scientific evidence should feel a personal responsibility for those who have suffered or even died as a result of catching measles. They should be ashamed. And the same goes for all those who set environmental bogeymen on the loose without a careful scientific basis to rely on.

Playing with our emotions

Images and associations are widely used to sell green ideas and products. We are sold organics and free range, for example, on the back of rosy images of traditional farming and the warm goodness of the countryside, rather than the cold clinical nature of agribusiness and factory farming. This doesn't mean that traditionally farmed food *isn't* better than the product of factory farms, but we shouldn't be basing our decisions on warm rosy feelings – an issue we will return to again and again.

It's easy to see the danger of this by taking a more abstracted example. What would you rather put on your food: chemically produced sodium chloride, mined salt or sea salt? The natural inclination is to prefer the sea salt, with all its associated images of the wild, natural sea over mined salt. Mining is somehow dirty and mechanical. On the other hand, the mined salt is a natural mineral, as opposed to that disturbing sounding chemical.

In terms of purity, this picture is entirely reversed. The chemically produced salt is to all intents and purposes pure. Mined salt will inevitably have some impurities (unless it is refined – another word with confusing negative connotations), while sea salt will be packed with impurities. If we're lucky these will be health-giving minerals – but they could also be heavy metals and other undesirables.

This isn't saying we shouldn't use sea salt – I do because it looks pretty in the grinder – but rather that we mustn't be led astray by the *feel* of the words. Every foodstuff, from the simplest inorganic product like salt to the complexities of a side of beef, is chemical in nature. And there is nothing inherently good (or safe) about something being 'natural'. Many of the most dangerous neurotoxins are natural. A deadly poisonous toadstool is just as natural as a tasty organic mushroom.

Small is not beautiful

This may seem to be an obvious and easy trap to avoid, but equating 'natural' and 'safe' is still a regular fact of life. In January 2008, the Soil Association, one of the organic certification bodies in the UK, banned nano-particles from organic products. Nanoparticles are ultra-small particles of *anything*, provided the substance is divided up into pieces that are just a few nanometres (billionths of a metre) across. But the Soil Association specifically banned only man-made nanoparticles, claiming that natural ones (like soot) are fine because 'life has evolved with these'.

This is just not an acceptable argument. If a nano-particle is dangerous because of its scale – entirely possible, because the physics (rather than chemistry) of particles of this size is quite different from the objects with which we are familiar – then that danger is just as present whether it's natural or not. Even where scale isn't the only factor, natural nanoparticles can be dangerous because of the way they interact with the body. Viruses are natural nanoparticles and, like soot, aren't ideal for health.

The Soil Association defends its position by drawing a parallel with carbon dioxide in the air: there is no problem with natural carbon dioxide, only with the man-made extra contribution. This is a specious argument, both because carbon dioxide is carbon dioxide, and if levels are too high it doesn't matter where it's coming from – and also because there is no comparison between CO_2 and a nanoparticle that could be directly physically dangerous to humans.

To make matters worse, the Soil Association also says that it can't control natural nanoparticles present in the environment – they're just there. But the Soil Association isn't an environmental control group. It is discussing what goes into organic products, and there is nothing to stop a manufacturer putting natural nanoparticles into a product either by accident or intent. You might as well say we don't mind a manufacturer putting salmonella into organic food because it's natural. If the Soil Association believes nanoparticles are a bad thing, it should ban all nanoparticles from a product that gets its seal of approval, not just artificial ones.

In summing up, the Soil Association lets slip the reason it takes this strange attitude: '[T]he organic movement nearly always takes a principles-based regulatory approach, rather than a case-by-case approach based on scientific information.' In other words, theirs is a knee-jerk reaction to concepts rather than one based on genuine concerns about the dangers of various products. In the end, although there is much that conventional farmers can learn from organic experts, the Soil Association is an accreditation body – it's a marketing vehicle for selling the rosy glow of feeling good about buying natural – and it is probably unfair to expect anything else from it.

Dirt means fresh

It's not only organizations with a vested interest that make such illogical connections. A surprising number of people like to buy vegetables with soil on them. The people who do so are almost all enthusiastic about their green credentials. They believe that they are doing the right thing by getting such 'earthy' products, rather than the artificially clean and scrubbed vegetables that line the supermarket shelves.

Unfortunately they are fooling themselves, and giving the planet a minor kicking at the same time. Every clod of earth sticking to your carrots and potatoes has to be transported from the field to your home. Unless you pick the produce yourself and take it home on foot or in the pannier of your bike, transporting that soil will have a negative environmental impact.

The chances are that the purchaser will then wash the vegetable with copious amounts of water to get it clean enough to eat. Unfortunately, just as a dishwasher is more eco-friendly than washing up by hand, a commercial vegetable-washing plant, which should recycle water, is significantly greener than doing it yourself, plant by plant, in the sink. And don't get me started on the ridiculous enthusiasm for transporting Brussels sprouts attached to more than their own weight in stalk.

The Alar panic

Food concerns regularly raise bogeyman reactions out of proportion to the risk. As we'll see later (page 200), pesticide residues on food are often cited as a reason for preferring organic produce, even though the amounts present are microscopic, and one of the most dramatic examples came in the way the chemical daminozide, marketed as Alar, was withdrawn in the US.

This chemical was widely used to regulate growth, increase shelf-life and improve colour in apples. In the early 1980s it was shown that daminozide in large quantities was carcinogenic for lab animals. In itself this isn't surprising – the same goes for many things we consume, such as coffee, but we don't take them in these dangerous concentrated doses (though we drink a lot more carcinogens in coffee than in Alar – see page 204). But US legislation required that chemicals that caused tumours in lab animals even in high doses should be avoided, so the Environmental Protection Agency was considering withdrawing daminozide and it began to be phased out by growers.

At this point, encouraged by a study from an environmental group called the Natural Resources Defense Council (NRDC), the influential US television show *60 Minutes* took on daminozide. Emphasizing the dangers to children, who eat more apples than adults, the programme left its viewers with a stark message: buying apples amounted to 'supermarket roulette'. Following this, rather than submit its study for peer review, the NRDC released it direct to the public through a PR agency.

Within days, actress Meryl Streep was announcing the formation of 'Mothers and Others for Pesticide Limits' and the story was splashed across the American media. Apple sales collapsed. It was only by disposing of stock exposed to daminozide and immediately stopping its use that the American public was weaned back on to eating apples.

Unfortunately, there were some serious problems with the NRDC's study. It wasn't primary research, but was based on selecting results from other studies relevant to the NRDC's case. If only studies that give the right message are included, then the data will be strongly biased. The study then used two figures, one for the risk of getting cancer on exposure to daminozide and the other for the amount of apples and apple juice children consume. Both these figures were compromised.

The dangers of daminozide were taken from a twelve-year-old study which the Environmental Protection Agency later called 'fundamentally flawed' and 'useless for assessing carcinogenic risk'. It involved feeding lab animals 266,000 times the quantity of daminozide to which humans might be exposed. At the same time, the estimate of apple and apple juice consumption was based on a relatively small survey, which suggested that a toddler consumes more than thirty-one times the apple juice relative to his or her weight than is drunk by an adult. This figure was pretty much plucked out of the air.

The result was an assessment of risk that was much larger than any reasonable number. Risk assessment is inevitably an inexact science – it's educated guesswork – but it can be a lot more rigorous than this. As a result of the campaign, for a significant period of time a considerable proportion of the US population reduced its consumption of fruit and vegetables. This possibly had a significantly bigger negative impact on their health than anything daminozide residues might have done.

Apart from that unfortunate reduction in healthy eating (something the NRDC admitted regretting), it's arguable that the daminozide scare did no harm: the chemical was likely to be removed from use soon anyway and the industry was moving away from it. Yet what happened was not a controlled, sensible response but the environmental equivalent of a lynch mob, taking action on unreliable information without concern for its consequences. The bogeyman was hard at work.

Genetically modified fear

Perhaps the ultimate environmental bogeyman has been created by the use of genetically modified organisms. While GM is common in the US, Europe, led by campaigns in tabloid newspapers (rarely a good sign of sense winning through), has clamped down heavily on it. However, this is yet another example of being over-influenced by the feeling that 'natural' has to be better. The fact is that all the food we eat is genetically modified. If you doubt that we've been busy with genetic modification for thousands of years, consider a few simple examples.

First take a look at a chihuahua and a Great Dane alongside each other. Both dogs were bred from the same basic wolf stock – but they are far more bizarre in their modification than practically anything that a GM scientist can dream up. Then take a look at sweetcorn (maize) and a cauliflower. Sweetcorn has been so modified from wild maize that it is no longer possible for its huge seedheads to propagate. Cauliflower is a mutant cabbage, where the flowers have grown out of control and fused into a useless lump – again it can't breed naturally.

This doesn't mean we don't have to be careful with GM. There are dangers with introducing elements into a genome that will spread to the wild (as is happening with non-GM oilseed rape, which can be seen escaping fields all over the country). Yet the dangers of GM have been hugely overstated, providing the technology is used responsibly. It probably needs significantly more restrictions than currently apply in the US, but more freedom than it is given in Europe.

The whole GM debate is complex enough to fill a book in its own right, but it has certainly been subject to the same misuse of information that we see in attempts to deny the significance of global warming. A genetically modified variant of rice, called Golden Rice, that was designed to help counter vitamin A deficiency was dismissed by the environmental organization Greenpeace, which claimed that to obtain the required amount of vitamin A would require 'seven kilograms a day of cooked Golden Rice'. The actual amount is 200 grams or less. Many trying to show concerns about GM point to a study showing that rats fed GM potatoes had damage to their immune systems – but this study was condemned by the Royal Society, which said that the work was flawed and no conclusions should be drawn from it – something we somehow don't hear so often.

Although GM has been pilloried and kept out of Europe largely by fear, it is possible that environmental necessity will make it more acceptable. Major developments are under way at the moment to produce plants that are more able to resist the impact of global warming – drought-resistant strains of maize, for example, or rice that is better able to cope with higher salt levels as evaporation leaves water more saline. As always, there are genuine concerns – for example, it's possible that the salt resistance could spread to wild rice variants that could then clog up estuaries and disrupt the natural ecosystem. But, as global warming proceeds, it may be that we will have to take more risk with GM, just as we have in the past with 'natural' genetic modification.

To keep the bogeymen at bay, throughout this book it will be necessary to hold the heart in check and make sure that the head agrees. And of all the bogeymen we've come to recognize from a green standpoint, carbon has to be public enemy number one.

3

The 'C' Word

Forget the old 'C' word. We've a new obscenity for the twenty-first century – carbon. It's easy to forget that carbon is essential for life. We need other chemical components too, but it is carbon's unique flexibility that makes life possible in the first place. All life on Earth is carbon-based, and though some writers have speculated there could be silicon-based life somewhere in the universe, the chances are that if there *is* other life out there, it will be based on carbon too. Yet too much carbon in the atmosphere is a disaster.

Carbon now has its own happy baggage of terms, without which any enthusiastic environmentalist would seem naked. We should check our carbon footprints and reduce them, aiming for the Holy Grail of becoming carbon neutral. If we must do something that produces carbon, we should find a way to reverse our impact by carbon offsetting. And there's the prospect of carbon trading, something our pet environmentalist is probably a touch wary of, as it smacks of making money out of emitting greenhouse gases.

We don't make carbon

Let's get something straight immediately – there's a blatant error in the previous paragraph. We get so used to moaning about carbon that it's easy to make the mistake of labelling our carbon footprint as the carbon we *produce* (or, more significantly, that's produced on our behalf by the goods we manufacture and by our use of goods). Let's make it clear here and now that, apart from a few nuclear scientists, none of us produces or consumes carbon. The carbon on this planet has been here since day one. It has been on the planet over four billion years and it's going to be here for billions of years to come, whatever measures we take to save the environment.

The atoms that make up the Earth – and you – can be traced back to the Big Bang, which at current estimates was around 13.7 billion years ago. After things settled down enough for atoms to exist, pretty well everything was hydrogen or helium, the lightest elements, but with the formation of stars, these atoms were gradually cobbled together to make heavier matter. Stars alone, though, weren't enough of a cosmic crucible to forge the really heavy elements, which were assembled in the great stellar explosions we call supernova.

The carbon that makes up a fair part of your body, and is found all over the Earth, is stardust. So nothing we do 'makes' carbon. Instead, what a carbon footprint refers to is the amount of carbon we are responsible for converting from harmless, usually solid, forms – whether it's the relatively pure carbon in coal or the complex carbon chain molecules in a living animal or plant – to the threatening greenhouse gas carbon dioxide.

The essential CO_2

Carbon dioxide, like carbon itself, gets an unfairly bad press. This colourless, odourless gas is not a bad thing in itself. Although oxygen-breathing animals like us can't live in a carbon dioxide atmosphere, we need a small amount of CO_2 in the air to trigger their effective processing of oxygen. This is why someone who feels faint or is having a panic attack is recommended to hold a brown paper bag, or a cupped hand, over their mouth and nose. When hyperventilating – the physical action underlying the panic attack or faintness – your body is getting too much oxygen and not enough CO_2. By re-breathing exhaled air you are taking in a higher concentration of carbon dioxide and this overcomes the hyperventilation.

For plants, carbon dioxide is even more important. In essence, for them, it's food. Plants depend on it, extracting the carbon from the gas to build their structures and giving off the oxygen that we need to breathe. Let's be clear about that: without carbon dioxide in the atmosphere, the plants would not be able to grow and would not give us oxygen.

Unfortunately, excess carbon dioxide in the atmosphere has a more worrying function. It is, as we all know, a greenhouse gas – a gas that contributes to the greenhouse effect. This is a well-understood physical phenomenon that prevents some of the energy that the Earth receives from the sun being reflected back out into space. This isn't a bad thing in itself. If there were no greenhouse effect, the Earth would have average temperatures of −18°C, around 33 degrees colder than it actually is. But living in a gaseous greenhouse can be equally troublesome.

Carbon dioxide and other gases – like water vapour and methane, which we'll come back to later – act like a kind of one-way mirror in the atmosphere. Most of the incoming sunlight shoots straight through, but when the energy heads back into space as lower-energy infrared photons, some of it is absorbed by the gas molecules in the atmosphere. Almost immediately the molecules release the energy again. A portion continues off into space, but the rest returns to Earth, further warming the surface.

Having a degree of greenhouse effect is essential to make the planet viable for life, but too much carbon dioxide (and other greenhouse gases) inevitably produces excess global warming. There have been arguments about how much man-made greenhouse gases are contributing to that warming, but no one doubts that the greenhouse effect exists, or that carbon dioxide is a greenhouse gas. (Strangely, the greenhouse effect is *not* how greenhouses work – their warming is largely a matter of trapping air and avoiding heat loss by convection – but the atmospheric effect and greenhouses were originally thought to depend on the same mechanism.)

The usual suspects

When getting excited about carbon emissions, we shouldn't overlook the fact that carbon dioxide isn't the only greenhouse gas. The most significant contributor to the greenhouse effect in our atmosphere is in fact water vapour. It tends not to be mentioned because we are not contributing to a significant change in its levels – but water vapour will always be an important consideration in evaluating what's happening to our climate.

Methane is another greenhouse gas that is often over-looked. There's less of it around than CO_2, but methane – another simple gas CH_4 – is twenty-three times as powerful a greenhouse gas as is carbon dioxide. In West Siberia lies a huge peat bog, around a million square kilometres in area (the size of France and Germany put together). The partly decayed remains of ancient moss and vegetation, peat is a rich source of methane. Methane from the bog has been frozen in place by the permafrost – a solid ice/peat mix that never melts. At least, until now. That permafrost is liquefying, discharging a huge quantity of methane into the atmosphere. By 2005 it was estimated that the bog was releasing 100,000 tonnes of methane a day. That has a more warming effect than the entire daily direct man-made contribution of the United States.

Despite its impact, methane is frequently pushed aside in the panic response to carbon. In a five-page article on peat bogs and their potential impact on global warming in the February 2008 edition of the *Ecologist*, carbon dioxide appears in every other paragraph, while methane is mentioned only once in a sidebar referring to the Siberian bog. There is no mention of the methane emitted by all bogs – so called 'marsh gas'; the focus is purely on carbon dioxide.

Just how significant the other greenhouses gases are – demonstrating very clearly why concentrating purely on carbon is a serious mistake – can be illustrated by taking a walk through a farmer's field under the flight path of an airport. As you stroll alongside the green crop and look up at those ravenous beasts pouring out CO_2 as they fly overhead, it's easy to curse the planes and wonder why we can't forget them and get back to the green world. But in fact, the farm is the bigger threat of the two. Farms produce more effective greenhouse gases than planes. Worse than that, agriculture produces more than all the planes, trains and automobiles put together – and you can even throw in shipping for good measure. The contribution made by cow burps is now reasonably well known – there's plenty of methane there – but the overwhelming agricultural contributor to warming the planet is nitrogen.

Living with nitrogen

Like carbon, nitrogen is essential for plant growth and, as crops are cultivated and harvested, that nitrogen needs to be replenished. As we'll see elsewhere (page 229), there are three ways to do this. You can use a nitrogen fertilizer, or animal faeces and rotting vegetable matter, or you can give your field over temporarily to certain plants (clovers or peas, for instance) that have the ability to extract the abundant 'raw' nitrogen from the air and pass it back to the soil.

It's not nitrogen itself that is the problem, it's nitrous oxide (N_2O). This is a greenhouse gas that is significantly weaker in effect than carbon dioxide, but that has a dirty trick up its sleeve. Nitrous oxide hangs around in the atmosphere much longer than CO_2, which is heavier than air and tends to sink down and dissolve in water. Over a hundred-year period after emission, a tonne of nitrous oxide will have 300 times the impact on global warming than the same weight of carbon dioxide will have.

Whatever we do, nitrous oxide won't go away entirely. It's a natural by-product of bacteria digesting rotting organic material, and there is currently over seven times as much N_2O going into the atmosphere from natural sources than there is from human activity – but, as we've seen before, greenhouse gases aren't a bad thing per se. It's just having too much that's a problem – and that man-made contribution is part of what's pushing us over the edge.

One way to reduce the impact is simply to use less fertilizer. (This includes making less use of nitrogen-fixing plants like clover and legumes – as they enrich the soil, the bacteria churn out more N_2O.) The organic standards in the UK, for example, limit the amount of nitrogen that can be applied to around 170 tonnes per hectare, and this can come down to as low as 50 tonnes for some standards. This has the double benefit of reducing greenhouse gas emissions and lowering the quantity of pollutants that leaches into watercourses – fertilizers, both natural and organic, may be good for crops, but they become pollutants if they get into our water.

GM for greens

There is also, however, a more controversial option that will reduce greenhouse gas emissions from farms. One of the problems with the green agenda is that some of the solutions to environmental problems upset the campaigners. The best covered of these is nuclear power. This isn't a technology totally lacking carbon footprint, as CO_2 is produced in mining fissile materials, building the plants and some elements of their running, but even so, some environmental experts like James Lovelock have argued forcibly that nuclear power is the only relatively short-term option that will enable us drastically to reduce emissions from power stations.

We'll get on to nuclear and the other power sources later (see page 154). Nuclear power is, without doubt, a green bogeyman. But in recent years it has been less contentious than a major contender for reducing nitrous oxide emissions – genetic modification. A US company, Arcadia Biosciences, has been working on plants that require less fertilizer for successful growth.

Usually there's a clear polarization between environmentalists and bio-companies, but Arcadia is run by Eric Rey, a member of the US environmental group the Sierra Club, who believes that it may be necessary to give a little on resistance to GM in order to reduce the global warming impact of fertilizer. Not only would using less fertilizer reduce the N_2O emitted, it would also cut down on CO_2, as the processes involved in producing nitrate fertilizers generate a lot of carbon dioxide.

Like all GM developments, it's a move that has to be made with care. Forgetting the 'Frankenstein food' scaremongering, there is a risk, for instance, that such plants could spread genes to the wild, producing some sort of superweed. In principle any plant can be a weed if it's growing somewhere it's not wanted, and either the crop itself or the wild plant crossed with the relevant genes could push out more fragile species and upset the environmental balance.

Even so, this is an application of genetic modification that is worth serious consideration. Early GM crops could easily be portrayed as bogeymen because their benefits were purely commercial. One of the first examples was making crops Roundup resistant. Roundup (glyphosate) is a popular commercial herbicide but it kills crops as well as weeds; there were therefore plenty of commercial benefits in developing a glyphosate-resistant crop. First, herbicide manu-facturers sold more glyphosate. This benefited several companies, as the patent expired in 2000 and, though only Monsanto makes Roundup, there are now other glyphosate brands. Second, Monsanto got a double bonus: they produced not only Roundup but Roundup Ready seeds with built-in resistance to the herbicide. And finally, the farmer could kill off his weeds safe in the knowledge that his crop wouldn't be damaged.

However, consumers saw less to get excited about. Glyphosate is toxic, so any residue on food is worrying and the product is damaging to the bacterial systems in soil. There was also the worry that the Roundup-resistant gene would spread to wild plants. This may have happened: Roundup-resistant weeds have been recorded in the US, though this could have been a natural mutation.

In principle there were small benefits for the environment that partially offset the negatives. Monsanto promised that Roundup-resistant crops would result in reduced use of herbicide, but there is mixed evidence of how much this happened. Using herbicide has the advantage of minimizing soil disruption prior to planting, as there's no need to till to dislodge weeds. It is accepted that the less you disrupt the soil, the better for the environment, in terms of both soil erosion and release of natural greenhouse gases, though a recent paper suggests these savings are relatively light.

Genetic modification of crops so that they require less fertilizer brings much clearer benefits, provided there aren't 'escapes' into the environment. Arcadia plans to make a change to the plants that will enable them to absorb significantly more nitrogen from a given amount of nutrient, slashing the requirement for fertilizer and the subsequent damaging run-off of nitrates. To see how significant this could be, reducing fertilizer use by one-third would have the equivalent effect on greenhouse gases of all of us stopping flying altogether. This would be, admittedly, only a 1.5 per cent reduction in global emissions, but is still significant.

Following in the footprints

Our consumption of agricultural products is just one of the many aspects of our 'carbon footprint' – the measure of the carbon emissions produced by what we do and what we consume. A footprint is a useful image to help us think through how we, as individuals, influence the planet and there is now a wide range of online calculators – for instance the UK government's actonco2.direct.gov.uk – that can be used to add up our personal impact. These tend to concentrate on items around the house and on travel, but a true carbon footprint needs to consider the indirect carbon emissions associated with everything we consume and purchase.

It's easy when thinking about carbon footprints to believe that 'I'm so small I don't matter', but it's not that simple. While it's true that there are billions of people out there also doing their bit to warm things up, and that a single business or power station is going to do much more to increase CO_2 levels in the atmosphere than an individual family, this doesn't stop each person being responsible for 10–12 tonnes of carbon per year in Europe and as much as 20 tonnes in the US and Australia.

A big step forward can be made by hitting your home heating bills – the energy you pump into heating is responsible for well over a tonne of a typical carbon footprint. The good thing about reducing this is that it helps your pocket as well. However altruistic we are, a spot of self-interest never goes amiss; only the enlightened few are ever going to cut their carbon footprints out of feelings for the planet. Their actions are set against the sort of backlash demonstrated by individuals such as Jeremy Clarkson, presenter of the BBC's hugely popular *Top Gear* show, who openly sneers at people who want to reduce emissions to 'save the planet' as spoilsports and purveyors of the nanny state. From the ecologic point of view, while such short-sightedness is not itself logical, neither is it logical to expect human beings to give a lot of weight to long-term measures. We aren't programmed to think that way. Even preventing the huge damage that climate change is expected to bring is too wishy-washy and disconnected from everyday life. It's still not obvious in the here and now.

This means that, however much we tell people to think about their children and their children's children, it's much better if we can produce an argument that is about the present. If we can get effective financial incentives to go green that hit the wallet right now – like reducing our heating and lighting bills – then we can get millions of families to buy in. And that means our small individual contributions start to make a lot of difference.

While some green campaigners want everyone to suffer the environmental equivalent of sackcloth and ashes, this isn't the way to encourage change. The carrot is more effective than the stick.

You can legislate on certain items – banning incandescent light bulbs, for instance – but it is much better to incentivize. Initially, low-energy bulbs were very expensive, making the buyer wait years to see a financial payback. Now the price of long-life, low-power bulbs has come down significantly and they are selling much better. It would be better still if incandescent bulbs were much more expensive than low-energy bulbs, making the decision a no-brainer without having to use the heavy-duty weapon of a ban.

Blinded by the light

We ought, in passing, to clear up the long-running light-bulb argument. Few existing low-energy bulbs are the ideal replacement for traditional bulbs. Early versions were very slow to reach full light output and even now they take a while, giving the impression that they are dimmer than the equivalent incandescent bulb. Low-energy bulbs are also rather more dangerous than traditional bulbs in landfill because of their mercury content.

Finally, there is the power issue. The big selling point for low-energy bulbs is that they give out the same amount of light as a traditional incandescent bulb but use less power. Where did that extra power in the old bulbs go? Into heat. And what does that do? It warms your house, reducing your heating bills. This is true, but is advantageous only at times of the year when you need to heat the house (and the better designed the house, the less this is the case). What's more, the ceiling isn't the ideal place from which to source heat, and even in winter there may be times when you want light but not heat.

The green credentials of the low-energy bulb are more than greenwash – adding up the pros and cons, everyone ought to switch. It's probable, though, that we should regard the current low-energy technology as a temporary solution. There are better options still – LEDs, for instance, which use even less power and don't contain mercury. These alternatives will eventually replace the current low-energy bulbs, but are yet to be viable in most applications.

It's relatively easy to deal with light bulbs by legislation, because they are replaced on a regular basis, but it's much harder with other aspects of personal energy use and that's where we need more effort to make the alternatives attractive, using the power of incentives to encourage us all to go green.

Green cars – red tomatoes

Sometimes the way of reducing carbon emissions isn't obvious and we need help to spot it. Cars provide a good example. An average UK driver switching from a petrol car to a hybrid petrol/electric car like a Toyota Prius would save around 0.8 tonnes of carbon a year. The figure is higher in the US, where the owners of inefficient, gas-guzzling vehicles would save around 2.5 tonnes annually by switching to a hybrid. (Note this is a mythical 'average' driver who does a lot of urban driving. For other road-users, hybrids are not the best option.

See page 258.) Also, a UK motorist who usually changes his car every year could cut down enormously on emissions by keeping each car for three years, because building a new car results in 3–5 tonnes of emissions. There are now some incentives to buy a lower emission car, but where are the tax breaks to encourage us to buy new cars less often?

Be wary about some of the apparently obvious ways of cutting a car's emissions. In principle, switching off the air conditioning should be good for the environment, as running the air conditioner consumes power from the engine, meaning more fuel burned and more CO_2 emitted. But assuming you are running the air conditioning because it's unpleasantly hot, the alternative of driving with the windows down is even worse – the extra drag on the car results in even more fuel consumption than the air con.

Similarly, it might seem tempting to take the car out of gear and leave the engine idling as you roll down a hill to minimize fuel use. This might have been worthwhile once upon a time, but a modern car with fuel injection recognizes when there is no need for fuel input and effectively shuts off fuel consumption when driving downhill. It will therefore use less fuel in gear (assuming your foot is off the accelerator, which you can consider a fuel/pollution-level switch) than coasting out of gear.

Turning away from cars, the greenest way to buy commercially grown food is not always obvious. Minimizing the distance that food travels before it reaches your plate ('food miles') is a good thing, but it isn't the only factor. This becomes clear when you learn that Spanish tomatoes are generally more environmentally friendly for the British consumer than those from UK greenhouses. Spanish tomatoes are grown in a climate that doesn't need artificial help. British greenhouses need heating and the result is that, despite lower food miles, British tomatoes take a lot more energy and water, and pump out around three times as much CO_2 as the Spanish alternatives. Having said that, there is significantly more use of pesticides on the Spanish outdoor crops . . . If you really want to be green, grow your own on the windowsill.

Going neutral

For many, the absolute measure of achievement in carbon terms is to be carbon neutral. The insurance company Aviva proudly states in its advertising that it is 'committed to becoming the first insurer to go carbon neutral worldwide'. European broadcaster Sky, part of News Corporation, announced in May 2006 that it had become 'the world's first CarbonNeutral® media company, reflecting significant work across the business to measure and reduce our CO_2 emissions'.

The idea of being carbon neutral (or even CarbonNeutral®) is a simple one. It implies that our activities do not add to the carbon dioxide levels in the atmosphere. This can be achieved by a combination of reducing our own CO_2 output and the practice of carbon offsetting, where actions are undertaken to balance our personal output by helping either to reduce carbon dioxide output elsewhere or to take CO_2 out of the atmosphere. If, for example, I am personally responsible for the production of 5 tonnes of carbon (more on what this means in a moment), I could change my ways of doing things and bring this down to 3 tonnes. In addition, I could contribute to a charity working to switch energy production in India from coal to wind turbines, which would result in another two tonnes not being emitted, and also contribute to planting a forest of trees, where my contribution would take another tonne out of the atmosphere. Such carbon offsetting involves making a payment to a project that reduces carbon emissions. The cost of the project is divided across the emissions saved, giving a cost per tonne, though, as we shall see (pages 59–67), it can be difficult to ensure that offsetting is effective.

What carbon neutral *is*, then, provides no problems. What is less obvious is the *why* of being carbon neutral. It's true that by being carbon neutral we do no harm in terms of adding carbon dioxide to the atmosphere, but equally we do no good. Very few of us set out to be money neutral. That, presumably, would be earning just the money we need to live on for that week or month. Instead, we want to earn enough money to buy what we want, to put some aside for future big purchases and disasters, and to leave something for our children. Why would we possibly want to be carbon neutral?

Out in the real world, plenty of others are still churning out CO_2, and greenhouse gas levels are already so high that we are undergoing dangerous climate change. We don't want to be carbon neutral; we want to be carbon negative. Economist Tim Harford, when asked how he got to an environmental conference so that the organizers could offset the carbon he produced and so make the conference carbon neutral, said, 'I came on an anthracite-powered steamer from Australia.' His idea was, if it was worth offsetting the small amount of carbon dioxide he actually produced, how much better it would be to offset even more.

Harford also wondered why the meeting was worrying only about being carbon neutral. What about being sulphur neutral, for example? Or lead neutral? Or, bearing in mind its much greater impact as a greenhouse gas, methane neutral? It's hard not to suspect that aiming for carbon neutral is more about being seen to do the right thing than any real thinking about what's best for the environment. Arguably, the best way to help the environment would have been not to have held the conference at all, but to have arranged some form of video conference, or to have held a virtual conference using social-networking software.

Harford points out that the problem is that, as long as we are making judgements on a moral rather than an economic basis, it is highly unlikely that a bunch of enthusiasts will change the world. What is essential is to get good information on how what we buy, use and do impacts on the environment – the full impact – and to take economic action to counter that impact.

When making such measures it's important to be clear what the units are, as there is some confusion and loose language over measures of carbon dioxide. For convenience, other greenhouse gases, like methane, are usually converted into carbon equivalents, but be aware that a tonne of carbon is not the same thing as a tonne of carbon dioxide. Each molecule of CO_2 contains two atoms of oxygen to one of carbon. Those oxygen atoms weigh 16 units each to carbon's 12. So to save (or emit) a tonne of carbon, you need to deal with around 3.66 tonnes of carbon dioxide. It doesn't matter which unit you use, but you need to stick to the same one, and it's very easy to get the two confused: many sources refer to a 'tonne of carbon' where they mean a 'tonne of carbon dioxide'.

Offset to offload guilt

The approach to dealing with carbon emissions much beloved of rock stars and others with plenty of cash to spare is carbon offsetting. The concept, as we have seen, is simple. Instead of cutting back on your own carbon output, pump out as much carbon as you like and pay someone else to deal with it. Put like that, some would find it morally dubious. For those with more active consciences, a preferred description is something like 'I will do all I can to reduce carbon emissions, but where there is, for example, essential business travel, I will off-set that.'

This can be done on the personal level or on a larger scale. When Germany hosted the World Cup in 2006, they attempted to offset the estimated 100,000 tonnes of CO_2 generated by travel associated with the matches by buying 'carbon credits' that were invested in wind-power projects in the developing world. (This meant that a sum of money corresponding to the cost of removing a tonne of CO_2 from the atmosphere was paid for each tonne of CO_2 emitted.) Such offsetting lies behind the attempts to be carbon neutral in everything from the 2012 Olympic Games in London to the flights of British politicians. It has become the fashionable thing to do among the chattering classes.

There are three issues to consider when deciding whether or not carbon offsetting makes sense under the spotlight of ecologic. The first is whether or not the action taken really provides the benefit that is ascribed to it. The second is how the amount of carbon to be offset is calculated – including the bigger issue described above of whether or not you should aim to be carbon neutral or carbon negative. The third is how individuals and companies can make this happen.

Coming down from the trees

Offsetting can involve either removing carbon dioxide from the atmosphere, or reducing CO_2 emissions elsewhere. It might mean planting trees to soak up CO_2, paying to shift energy production from fossil fuels to wind farms, providing low-energy light bulbs or even building scrubbers that can directly remove CO_2 from power-station emissions or from the atmosphere at large.

The most common mental picture conjured up by offsetting is a forest of newly planted trees. It's a lovely image – countering a dirty action like a plane journey by making the planet greener with a natural, biological factory for taking carbon out of the atmosphere and storing it in solid form. Unfortunately, it is also by far the weakest option for offsetting, often amounting to little more than greenwash – so much so that some carbon-offsetting bodies no longer consider it a viable mechanism.

The idea is simple. Trees absorb CO_2 as they grow, turning the despised gas into the long chain carbon molecules of life. So calculate how much a tree will absorb, and by planting that tree you are offsetting that amount of emissions. Unfortunately, trees aren't as predictable as machines. Some trees will fail to grow at all – and some tree-planting schemes have been plagued with problems such as mass failure of trees planted in an unsuitable environment.

Even if the tree does flourish, its absorption of carbon will take place gradually over its lifetime. So you are balancing an emission of carbon *now* with a tree slowly absorbing carbon over tens or hundreds of years. Unless the balance is set quite low – say to the amount of carbon the tree can absorb in five years – the offsetting will be left much too far behind the emitting. By the time the offsetting has had much effect, the world could already be in crisis.

If that's not bad enough, the worst thing about trees is that at some point they *will* die. Once they do, whether prematurely in a forest fire or at the end of a natural lifespan, they become carbon emitters. As they rot, the carbon sequestered away in the tree will be pumped back out again. So trees don't permanently remove carbon from the system; they temporarily set it aside.

Perhaps the worst problem of all with offsetting using trees is that it's not enough to point to a newly planted tree and say that this particular tree is offsetting your carbon emissions. There needs to be a clear link between the person doing the offsetting and the tree being planted. A commercial grower recently planted a stand of trees in a field near where I live. If a carbon-offsetting company were to claim those trees as an offset for a payment they received it would be a fiction, because the trees were going to be planted anyway. Claiming them as carbon offsets would not benefit the environment one bit. Trees can be carbon offsets only if they are *additional* to those that would be planted as a matter of course.

There's also the 'sponsor an animal' effect to watch out

for. Zoos and animal charities frequently ask donors to sponsor an animal, often in return for pictures and correspondence 'from' the animal. They are quite happy to allow many more people to sponsor a single lovable animal than they need to raise the cash to support it. 'Why not?' they would argue. All the funds are used for good purposes, and it's easier to get people to sponsor a panda (say) than a skunk. But you can't do the same kind of thing with offsetting. If a tree is planted as part of the offset of your plane journey, it can't also be the offset for someone else.

This isn't just a hypothetical problem. For example, the CarbonNeutral company, previously trading as Future Forests, enabled everyone from the Rolling Stones to Volvo to offset their guilt by buying into the planting of woodland at Orbost on the Isle of Skye in 2002. But the company did not plant a single tree. It bought the rights to claim the carbon in trees that were being planted anyway by the Highlands and Islands Enterprise Board. The trees would have been planted whether or not that 'offsetting' took place. Nothing happened as a result of the spend, except some good publicity for the companies making the purchase and an excellent profit for Future Forests (they took £10 per tree from their clients and paid the Enterprise Board 54 pence per tree for the rights). CarbonNeutral still uses Orbost as an offset project, but claims that they are now funding additional planting.

These are just the problems that arise without including the possibility – sadly all too easy to contemplate – that an organization could take your money for doing the offsetting then take no action at all. Guilt money at its best. There can be no absolute certainty about carbon offsets, but the best ones have some form of government certification that increases the likelihood that your carbon emissions really will be offset. The best known is the Gold Standard, which tries to ensure that the off-setting will be new as a result of your action and that it will be environmentally positive. Because of mixed feelings about the effectiveness of tree-planting, this is excluded from the scheme.

How much do I owe?

Working out how much CO_2 is produced by your journey (or whatever else you want to avoid feeling guilty about) is apparently simple, using one of the many online calculators (some of them provided by companies that will be happy to take your cash to arrange the offsetting for you). And it's a much easier calculation than a true footprint of your journey, which would involve much more than carbon. But even so, there are problems. Let's take a straightforward example of a long-haul plane journey – an excellent source of guilt. We'll use a return trip between London and San Francisco.

The first problem is what to put into the mix. Do you consider only the fuel burned by the aircraft, or also the journeys to and from the airports? Then there's the CO_2 produced in building your bit of the plane – take enough bums off seats and one less plane needs to be built. And at the extreme, the CO_2 output of all the rest of the air-line and airport infrastructure. Get enough fliers out of the skies and we could shut down a few less favoured operators. Even worse, planes, producing CO_2 and other emissions high in the sky, make a greater contribution to the greenhouse effect than the same emissions on the ground. Some (but not all) calculators increase the carbon emission two- to threefold to cope with this. I was advised by a range of online calculators that this journey would produce between 1.9 and 6 tonnes (rising to 9.6 tonnes for flying first class).

That little twist at the end is not available from many calculators, but it's worth noting. Allowing more tonnes for a first-class flyer is not a punishment for conspicuous spending, but reflects the fact that the more people you pack into a plane, the less carbon is emitted per person in the journey. This is the reason car-sharing is good, and public transport is usually better than cars. It is also why private jets are so iniquitous from a CO_2 standpoint; you can, with some confidence, place anyone who says 'I care for the environment' and then uses a private jet firmly in the 'hypocrite' camp.

The numbers above show the variation in calculation of your impact on just a single flight. Imagine the complexity of attempting to calculate all the impacts of something on the scale of the World Cup or the Olympic Games. (For the World Cup they simply gave up and estimated only the extra flights caused by the event.) And when the amount of carbon has been settled, there is the need to make something happen. Most opt for paying someone else to do this. There is also a huge variation in the cost of carbon offsetting from different sources, ranging from around £2 to £20 a tonne.

Is it enough?

Even if the methods of offsetting do deliver the desired reduction, the inevitable question is whether we should regard these actions as sufficient. The whole idea of offsetting suggests that the world would be okay if only I could cancel out my CO_2 emissions. But what about the offsetting provider? Who offsets them? If, for example, the offsetting is achieved by converting power production in a developing country from coal to wind, shouldn't that be happening anyway – and I should still do without the CO_2 emissions caused by my holiday flight to the Seychelles?

Many offsetting schemes – typically the sort where you pay a little extra to an offsetting company to compensate for your flight – are at best ways to push aside personal guilt. However, there are better programmes, such as that run by the Converging World organization, which has devised what it calls 'second-generation offsetting'. It works something like this. Individuals and companies do their best to reduce carbon emissions and calculate what remains. They then make a donation to the Converging World charity and this money is used to build wind turbines in the developing world. These turbines feed the local grid, reducing the need for polluting power generation. The carbon credits (see carbon trading, page 69) from the turbines are withdrawn from circulation – so the carbon isn't passed from place to place but taken out of the system. The money raised by use of the turbines is split between investment in more turbines and in a local non-governmental organization providing direct benefits to the region in sustainable developments. Money is also spent on carbon-reduction schemes in the UK. And by building the turbine in a developing country there is a significantly higher actual reduction in carbon output – typically twice the amount – than would be the case in the West, as the generating capacity it puts out of use is more polluting than the Western equivalent.

Some do argue that this kind of approach is Victorian and paternalistic – that Western organizations like Converging World shouldn't interfere in other countries, and that anyway the result will simply be more power used in the developing world rather than a reduction in the use of dirty power sources. However, the better organizations, of which Converging World seems to be one, work directly with local, on-the-ground organizations – they aren't imposing their ideas from the outside. Furthermore, if there is any imperialism here, it is surely from those who say, 'You people in developing countries should not be allowed the access to electricity that we have – we want to keep you undeveloped to reduce the impact you will have on the planet.'

A more valid objection to this kind of offsetting is the issue described in economic circles as 'moral hazard'. The implication here is that I can pay to get what I want and then I don't have to worry about it – I can go on emitting just as much carbon as I ever did without feeling guilty. It's a genuine problem. However, the better offsetters, like Converging World, do insist that you do your utmost to reduce emissions first and use this approach only to deal with what remains.

Even at best, then, while offsetting is preferable to doing nothing, it is likely to be a half-hearted measure that will probably only ever have a small percentage impact on carbon emissions, and in many cases is more about appearances and making a point than truly saving the planet. Converging World is proud that their scheme was set up by local activists in an English village – concerned people got together and made something happen. Realistically, though, such an approach will not touch many of us. Only if this sort of activity were to become an essential part of every individual's and every business's day-to-day use of emission-generating activities would it make a real impact.

Permits to pollute

Offsetting may nibble at the edges, but a larger-scale way to control carbon – and one that has the economists cheering – is carbon trading, or more precisely, cap and trade. This approach can cause concerns, because its less pretty label is 'permits to pollute'. It combines strict limits on the amount of carbon that can be emitted (the cap) with permits to emit that can be traded between businesses (or, technically, individuals).

The 'paying to pollute' idea may sound morally dubious, but in practice it provides a much more cost-effective way to control emissions than taxing them – and that means it is a mechanism that businesses will buy into, rather than fight. We're back to the importance of incentives. This business support is essential, as the decision to adopt cap and trade will typically be made at national government level where big business has powerful lobbying capabilities – arguably more than environmental groups, which tend to have more clout at the transnational level.

Provided a trading scheme is set up properly, this is about the only practical way to make big enough reductions in carbon emissions to have a significant impact on the environment. Being set up properly means good, transparent mechanisms for establishing the pricing of permits – auctions seem to work best; having good monitoring of outputs; and ensuring careful setting of the allowed levels and their rate of reduction. Carbon trading can also be combined with a large-scale form of offsetting, where permits are available at a reduced price for companies actively reducing carbon levels.

Sadly, although carbon trading is a powerful tool, one of the most effective parts of pollution control by permit trading is being omitted from most carbon-trading schemes, including the current EU scheme. Auctions are a very powerful mechanism for revealing information and making trading work effectively. Arguably just to avoid such transparency, carbon businesses have strongly resisted the inclusion of auctions in carbon trading – a pressure that has been successful in the EU and is likely to be equally so in the US. The alternatives – either giving away permits for free, or setting an arbitrary price – simply lack the same economic leverage.

The ironic thing is that with a good carbon-trading scheme companies can actually be more enthusiastic about regulation than governments. At the 2007 Bali conference on climate change there was the odd sight of big businesses supporting the EU proposal to have a target of between 25 and 40 per cent cuts in emissions by 2020 compared with 1990, and to have total global emissions peaking within fifteen years and halved by 2050. What seemed particularly odd was that this proposal was vetoed by the US government – usually a business-friendly regime.

As often seems to be the case, the apparently capitalist-driven US was in fact voting for protectionism, an anti-market stance that rarely makes economic sense. The American government succumbed to isolationism, and the quaint concept that by not regulating it would help business. By contrast, many blue-chip companies want to be regulated, as it gives them a clear playing field rather than a murky, uncertain future. Provided there are appropriate economic tools in place to trade, having clear aims makes much more sense than vague directions.

It would be foolish to pretend that carbon trading won't have an impact on the consumer. It has been estimated, for example, that including air travel in the European carbon-trading scheme would add between 50 and 80 per cent to the cost of a flight. This may seem extreme, but at the moment air travel benefits from a number of hidden subsidies that give it an unfair advantage over alternative means of transport.

Such large-scale changes are not the only way that carbon trading can bring about changes. It can also have a more personal impact.

I'll trade if you'll trade

To date, carbon trading has usually been applied at national or industry level. It's not that it shouldn't work for individuals, but the practicalities of bringing in such a scheme across every person in a country are intimidating. There is a personal alternative, though, which still has some of the aspects of true trading but works in local networks. It's called Carbon Rationing Action Groups, or Crags.

The idea is that a network of individuals gets together to help reduce carbon emissions. The group sets a target level, usually beginning with a practical reduction on the typical average. If that average is around 5 tonnes a year for air travel, car use, household heating and electricity (the four categories on which most such schemes concentrate), then the group might set a ration level of 4.5 tonnes for the next year.

Through the year, each member of the group sends details of their usage to a 'group accountant' (not necessarily literally an accountant) who keeps track of how this translates in carbon emissions. Now the stick/carrot bit. At the end of the year comes a grand reckoning. Anyone who goes over their ration is fined at an agreed rate per kilogramme. That fine is either re-distributed to all those who didn't go over their ration (more attractive to the economist) or to a suitable charity or green project (more appealing to the ethically minded).

As an effective scheme, Crags suffers from a number of problems. Although self-organizing networks are a very good way to get things done for a small percentage of the population, they will never exist on a big enough scale to bring in most of a country. Despite significant publicity for the concept, in late 2007 there were only 160 people in Britain taking part in Crags. Not 160 groups, 160 *people*.

Schemes that operate in this manner are also very open to misuse. If the financial benefits are sufficient to encourage cheating, it's worth noting that there are no measures in place to prevent someone failing to register a flight – except peer pressure, which will be more effective among a group of friends than in a virtual network.

The final, and perhaps biggest, concern is that the scheme is hugely oversimplistic. Just taking those four items exposes only a tiny fraction of the carbon footprint of an individual. There's no allowance for the huge potential for carbon emissions from the manufacture of goods and foods consumed – so you would see a similar consumption by someone who lived on vegetables from their allotment and hadn't bought any manufactured goods since 1984 and someone who had all their food airfreighted from 3,000 miles away and threw away the entire contents of their house and replaced them every year.

What really happened, or what's easy to measure?

There is always a compromise in taking measurements. It's rarely possible to be absolutely accurate. Many of the statistics we rely on are a compromise between what it's practical to measure and what will produce an acceptable result. Each year, as an author, I get paid a small amount of money by a body called the Public Lending Right (PLR). In theory, they pay me an amount for every copy of one of my books that is borrowed from a UK public library. This amount was 5.98p per loan in 2008. In case that sounds as if authors should be rolling in it, of the 34,000 authors registered, over 10,000 got nothing and another 17,000 got less than £100. Only 359 were in the maximum band of £5,000–6,000.

Ideally, the PLR people should list lendings at every library, tot up the total and arrive at an accurate figure. It's what a company like Tesco does in its sales monitoring. But the systems aren't there to do this, so PLR monitors a number of 'representative' libraries and scales up the numbers to come to a set of figures.

This isn't ideal – there will, for instance, be clustering (see page 20), which means that a book may have most of its loans spread across very few libraries – and those libraries may not fall into the sample – but the approach is practical. An even more obvious case of such pragmatic sampling is the statistics on migrants in and out of the UK. The figures we see trumpeted on the news, dealing with hundreds of thousands of people, are based on the work of the International Passenger Survey, a small band who interview people on ferries and at international stations and airports. Because most people they stop aren't migrating, their figures are based on as few as 600 or 700 people a year. It's a best guess, given the practicalities of discovering just why thousands of people each day are travelling.

Let's go back to those Carbon Rationing Action Groups. It's reasonable to expect them to stick to what can be measured reasonably quickly, but as yet not enough is included to make the exercise worthwhile. A parallel to the way they operate would be if the International Passenger Survey ignored everyone except people coming into the international passenger terminal at St Pancras station in London. The existing survey is very broad brush, but to ignore everywhere but St Pancras would make the process useless. At the very least, to ensure that they have any real meaning, Crags should make some attempt to deal with the carbon footprint involved in items bought (and any offsetting as well). Crags are well intentioned, but need a considerable amount of tweaking if they are to deliver a realistic and effective result.

Force feeding

We are used to the argument that we should reduce carbon dioxide levels to minimize global warming, but there is another, more insidious, reason why too much carbon dioxide is a bad thing. More CO_2 doesn't just mean a stronger greenhouse effect; it also influences the way that plants grow, and this could have major implications for feeding the world – an aspect of rising carbon dioxide levels that is almost always ignored in the furore over global warming.

This won't be a surprise to many farmers using greenhouses – many of them boost levels of CO_2 inside their glasshouses. The result is dramatic, producing bigger yields more quickly and reducing the need to fertilize, as less nitrogen is taken from the soil. Some have suggested that this effect may even counterbalance the impact of global warming on crop growth. But enhanced-carbon growing has its dark side.

According to a press release from the University of Hohenheim, as a result of increased CO_2 levels baking bread will be impossible, beer will no longer foam and French fries will be *exotisch* (I have seen this translated from the German as 'poisonous', but I suspect the implication is that they would be a rarity). Since issuing this, Professor Fangmeier, the scientist responsible, has admitted a bit of exaggeration – he hasn't tested these outcomes, but from chemical analyses of plants raised in high carbon dioxide atmospheres he rather expects that there will be an impact on these food products.

The reason for this concern is that, although high CO_2 levels improve yields of starch and sugars, they decrease the amount of protein produced, hence the reduced need for nitrogen, which is involved in protein synthesis. This might be particularly significant for grazing animals that rely on plant leaves as their sole source of protein. It's not an insuperable problem – by boosting nitrogen levels (that is to say, extra undesirable fertilizer) it should be possible to offset the reduction. But this is a problem for developing countries where fertilizer is in limited supply – and runs contrary to the desire to reduce the amount of nitrogen spread on the land.

Alongside the reduction in protein levels comes a shift in the chemical make-up, with less gluten proteins (used to store nitrogen in wheat) – hence Fangmeier's concerns about baking bread, which depends on those gluten proteins to establish the dough. Fangmeier also noted at least 50 per cent reduction in vitamin C levels in potatoes, and other essential nutrients experienced significant reductions. This may be particularly worrying where, for example, soya is used to substitute for milk products, as there appear to be large reductions in calcium levels in soya beans.

Overall, it seems this is one more reason to be concerned about increased levels of carbon dioxide in the atmosphere. Not only does it result in global warming, it may also reduce the food value of our crops – at a time when climate change is already devastating some food production – and though there is some offset in increased yield of carbohydrates and sugars, the overall effect is negative. Carbon, like every green issue, turns out to be more complex than it first seems.

Clarkson's dream – recycling carbon

Despite its effects on plants, though, there may still be something to celebrate when it comes to carbon in the atmosphere. Carbon itself, as we've seen, is a very useful element. Without it there would be no life, and were it not for suspicions that supplies are running out, hydrocarbons – molecules made up of hydrogen and carbon – make very effective fuels and raw materials for production. Hydrogen is in plentiful supply in water, so why not recycle the carbon from carbon dioxide in the atmosphere to make new fuel? It might seem like heresy to fanatical greens, but that way we could keep our petrolheads happy and save the planet all at the same time.

Chemically speaking, the process is quite simple. Split one of the oxygen atoms off CO_2 to make carbon monoxide, mix it with hydrogen, feed it over the right catalyst, and out pours a liquid hydrocarbon that can be used to fuel a car or manufacture plastics. The only problem is providing the energy to split off the oxygen atom and produce the hydrogen. Here's the clever bit. Do that with sunlight and you've found a way to translate solar energy into a form of energy that can easily be stored and distributed. And while you're at it, you have taken carbon out of the atmosphere.

Unlike biofuels, which also effectively convert solar energy to liquid fuel and take carbon out of the atmosphere, this approach has the advantage of not competing with food crops for viable land – factories can be sited in areas that are unsuitable for agriculture. And although it isn't hugely efficient, CO_2 recycling is around ten times more efficient than biofuels when you take into account all the energy used in growing, harvesting and processing. To be even more efficient still, the excess sunlight from a CO_2 recycler could be used for direct power generation.

It will be a few years before the technology for recycling carbon dioxide is widespread, but prototype equipment is under development in the US and Europe, and it seems it may be only a matter of time before we can reduce fossil-fuel use, replacing a portion of it with hydrocarbons from recycled greenhouse gas.

Hiding the carbon under the rug

More immediate than recycling are technologies that are the carbon equivalent of landfill (though without its negative connotations). Collectively they are known as carbon capture, and the idea is simple. If carbon in the atmosphere is bad, take it out. In principle trees do this; but, as we have seen, they are slow to do so and have a tendency to release it back into the atmosphere. Good carbon capture takes it out and it stays out.

There's a parallel between the different approaches to carbon and slimming. The worthy approach is to eat less and exercise more. This is the equivalent of cutting back on our carbon footprint. But most of us would secretly prefer it if we could eat whatever we like. There's always a tinge of envy when older people say of a youngster, 'She can eat what she likes and never puts on a pound.' There isn't (as yet) a magic pill that enables us to do this, but if there were it would make the manufacturer billions. Carbon capture is a bit like this. You can indulge in all those guilty pleasures, like driving cars, and not worry, because the carbon is going to be taken away.

In such a system, carbon dioxide is removed from the output of power plants (or cars), then stored away somewhere it is not going to get into the atmosphere. In principle this can be done in the sea, provided it's not near the surface, where the carbon dioxide will simply bubble out again like a fizzy drink. The problem is that it increases the acidity of the sea water, which can be uncomfortable or even dangerous for sea life and corals.

And even if injected low in the ocean, the carbon dioxide will gradually escape to the atmosphere.

A more effective approach is to pump the CO_2 into underground fissures or old oilfields. Carbon dioxide is heavier than air and, combined with appropriate capping, such underground stores could keep the carbon out of the atmosphere for thousands of years. There is a price attached, however. When the expense of extraction, transport and storage are added on, the cost of energy production can be double that of using the same power plant without capture and storage.

The most worrying aspect of carbon capture is that the idea is being used as a means of procrastination. Everyone agrees, for example, that producing electricity by burning coal in the traditional way is a powerful contributor to CO_2 emissions. Yet the continued use of coal – rapidly expanding in China, for instance – is justified as acceptable because carbon capture and storage is coming along to make it all clean.

There is often government backing for this beguiling but dangerous concept. In October 2007, for example, UK business minister John Hutton said that by 2030 up to a third of Britain's energy could be generated from burning coal accompanied by carbon capture and storage. But this seems to be an aspiration with little practical backing. At least two major carbon-capture projects have been cancelled because of a lack of government funds. In mid-2007, BP dropped development of a carbon-capture plant in Scotland, where the captured material would have been stored in a disused North Sea oilfield. Then, in January 2008, the US government reneged on an agreement to contribute $1.3 billion to the FutureGen project, a coal-fired power station designed from the ground up to emit practically no CO_2, using carbon capture and storage. At the same time, the EU has made it clear that there is no possibility of significant funding for carbon capture from the EU budget.

Arguably the energy companies should be responsible for cleaning up their own mess, yet to kick-start the process it seems reasonable for governments to contribute to clean-energy projects. The withdrawal of the US from support for FutureGen hardly sends the right message on carbon capture.

Crystal healing

The trouble with much carbon capture, whether it's operating on car exhausts, your domestic boiler or a power station, is that the processes involved can be energy intensive. The exhaust gases are bubbled through a liquid solvent that reacts with the CO_2, pulling it into the liquid. You then either have to dispose of the solvent wastefully and dangerously, or use a considerable amount of energy getting the carbon dioxide back out of the solution so it can be stored away.

Over at the University of California, Los Angeles, a location all too familiar with car exhaust gases, they have been developing new carbon-capture materials. These zeolitic imidazolate frameworks are collections of tiny crystals like CO_2 lobster pots. The crystals have pores into which the carbon dioxide molecules can slip, but from which they find it difficult to escape. Because the CO_2 has not undergone a chemical reaction, it can be extracted from the crystals simply by dropping the air pressure, leaving the crystals fresh to be re-used. The team at UCLA hopes to be able to test the crystals live in a power station within a year or two.

Some approaches to carbon – trading, recycling and capture, for instance – seem legitimate from an ecologic viewpoint. Others, like carbon neutrality, are arguably more about posturing than about saving the planet. Such an 'appearance is more important than reality' approach is a worrying aspect of environmentalism that is all too evident in the media's celebrity-obsessed version of being green.

4

Green Is Good (Publicity)

Back in the 1980s, Michael Douglas's character in the movie *Wall Street*, Gordon Gekko, proclaimed, 'Greed is good.' Now the fashionable sentiment for the celebrity being driven to the latest premiere in their Toyota Prius (the private jet, SUV and limo are hidden away round the back of the mansion) is *'Green* is good.' At least, it's good publicity. Yet there is a worrying irony about the way in which rock stars, arguably the most environmentally damaging creatures on the planet, were used in 2007's fundraising concert Live Earth to sell the idea of preventing climate change.

When we see such consumption-hungry celebrities promoting going green, we are witnessing the 'David Cameron effect' writ large. In his early attempts to put across a green image, Cameron, then newly leader of the opposition, cycled to work. This looked great until it was noticed that a big car followed with his papers. The message that came across was that there is no need to change behaviour so long as you get it right for photo opportunities.

Some celebrities are quick to leap on the green

bandwagon as just one more way to keep their faces in the public eye. While some may be genuinely concerned about the environment, they are also not shy about making the most of the opportunities that involvement in green issues can offer. This is typically the case in the big charity fundraising efforts like Live Aid, Band Aid, Comic Relief and Children in Need. There's no doubt that most of those participating have an interest in making things better – and these events wouldn't raise the money they did were it not for celebrity involvement – yet it's hard not to feel that in the end they are motivated as much by the fact that it is good personal publicity.

In the 2007 Comic Relief fundraiser Ricky Gervais gave what initially appeared to be one of those heart-tugging broadcasts from Africa, but which rapidly descended into self-serving parody as it was revealed to be a studio-based sketch. This wicked satire was hilarious, perhaps in part because it did reveal that less palatable side of celebrity involvement in issues of this kind – a side that is clearly present when the most blatant consumers on the planet try to sing along to the environmental hymn sheet.

Drink rats' milk!

Just how badly this can backfire was illustrated in late 2007 when Heather Mills, the then soon-to-be-ex wife of Paul McCartney, attempted to get the message across that we should stop drinking cows' milk to reduce global warming. Mills has an undeniable track record as an animal rights activist, but the me-too feeling of this leap into the green agenda (admittedly coupled with a rarely equalled media dislike of Mills) resulted in a highly negative response.

The message itself – become vegan, because meat and dairy products cause huge damage to the environment – was not one that was likely to engender a lot of enthusiasm, even though agriculture *is* responsible for a fair chunk of the emissions of climate-changing gases. Mills didn't point out that much of this comes from use of fertilizer and other crop-related activities rather than from cattle, but in carbon-emission terms livestock are a very inefficient way to produce protein. Her campaign was then given a touch of the ludicrous by the suggestion that Mills is alleged to have made that we should drink rats', cats' or dogs' milk instead. And they would live on what, precisely? They're not exactly efficient either.

This led to headlines like 'DRINK RATS' MILK AND SAVE THE WORLD, SAYS HEATHER'. But the killer blow was the suggestion that, while Mills was delivering her speech, 'her gas-guzzling Mercedes 4×4 sat with the engine running and piles of Selfridges carrier bags in the back'. We all tend to be guilty of green hypocrisy, but no one is more fairly open to the allegation than a celebrity who preaches one thing and does another. The caption to a photograph of Mills says it all: 'Earnest plea or milking the limelight?'

Brands as celebrities

If your only reading matter were the tabloid newspapers and glossy magazines, it would be easy to assume that the only people setting out to impress us with their green credentials were media celebrities, but there are other celebrities that have just as much intention of looking good by appearing green. They are the brands. Brand names are non-human celebrities. Just like any other celebrity, brands are marketed to keep their name in the press and to fit tightly to a particular lifestyle and ethos.

In an earlier era, when respect for authority tended to overwhelm the interests of the individual, big business could get away with practically anything. Anyone who questioned the ethics of a large company's operations would be sent away with the sentiment, 'Don't worry your little head about it. We know what we're doing. We'll take care of it.' But that approach no longer holds water.

One of the essential contributors to this change of viewpoint was marine biologist Rachel Carson. Her book *Silent Spring* (published in 1962) energized awareness of the dangers of artificial fertilizers and pesticides. Carson was concerned about the impact of the pesticide DDT (dichloro-diphenyl-trichloroethane) on wildlife and human beings. Introduced during the Second World War, DDT had proved very effective in dealing with insect pests. Not only was it widely used in agriculture and the home, it was a major weapon in the control of mosquitoes carrying diseases, like malaria, which were responsible for millions of deaths. DDT was sprayed anywhere and everywhere, with a casual disregard for any side effects it might have.

Silent Spring uncovered the potential dangers of DDT, suggesting that it was responsible for the death of many birds, could cause cancer in humans, and that its dangers were being covered up by a conspiracy in the chemical industry. It was the first of many campaigns against chemicals used in agriculture and resulted in the banning of DDT in the US, the UK and much of the world. Of itself, the campaign had mixed benefits because of the reduced defence against malaria. Banning DDT has probably killed many more people than it has saved, and Carson's campaign has spread an unnecessary fear of pesticide residues in the informed population (see page 200). But the important thing here is that Carson was in the vanguard of a new generation who would be prepared to stand up to big business and create such a stir that the corporations had to take action.

Green wish or greenwash?

In recent years we have seen a swathe of companies promoting their green status. Yet the public cannot easily be won over by simply proclaiming how green you are as an organization, or by publicizing green actions. Fine words have to be accompanied by a clear perception in the minds of consumers that yours is a trustworthy company. This is highlighted by a survey of opinion on the tendency of high-profile companies to use greenwash. Undertaken in September 2007 in the UK, the survey was sent to 1,200 UK journalists, sustainability experts and political groups. Some doubt has to be placed on the validity of the response, given that only ninety of those polled responded (see comments on surveys on page 131), but what was said still provides an interesting insight into how these companies' green credentials were perceived at least by some people.

Not surprisingly, there was a degree of cynicism. The main reasons that it was thought companies tried to promote a green image were: to protect their reputation; as a response to consumer pressure; and because it made good business sense. Just one per cent of those polled – with a poll this size, that means one person – believed that the companies had a genuine concern for the environment. Yet not all companies were seen in the same light. And those that were most visible in their green efforts weren't necessarily the ones considered to be most genuine in intent. In fact, two out of the three most visible campaigners, oil company BP and supermarket giant Tesco, were also considered the worst greenwashers – guilty of spreading disinformation to appear environmentally responsible. The third highest on the greenwashing list was British Airways.

BP and BA were almost inevitably going to be criticized, both being in businesses that have a direct negative impact on the environment. Tesco's position is more subtle. As a retailer, it doesn't have to be one of the bad guys. Another large UK high-street name, Marks and Spencer, came out top of those considered to be making a genuine green effort, well ahead of any other company. The key differences would seem to be that Tesco is a giant of a company, known to be highly voracious, while at the same time more orientated to cost-cutting than Marks and Spencer and so is seen by outsiders as more likely to cut corners on green expenditure.

BP – beyond petroleum?

I asked BP why they made a visible effort on green issues. Their spokesman told me that what they were taking was 'a business approach, not a "green" approach'. As a company with customers and shareholders, he said, they need to operate in a way that addresses the concerns of governments, the public, suppliers, staff and investors. (It wasn't made clear how you can do this when the concerns of these different stakeholders pull in totally different directions.)

BP announced back in 1997 that they intended to take action on climate change. At the time, the company's contribution to global warming, both from their own direct action and through the use of their products, was around 95 million tonnes of carbon a year. A huge amount, though they downplayed this by saying it was only one per cent of total human-generated carbon dioxide emissions. The aims they set out at the time were to monitor and control their own emissions, to fund research into reducing impact on climate change, to look at the opportunities for technology transfer and to help with development of alternative energy sources.

How well BP has done at these goals in the ensuing eleven-plus years – not as well as many campaigners would like – is reflected in the high greenwash score they received in the survey. However, BP has reduced its own emissions (which contributed about 5 million of those 95 million tonnes) and grown their alternative energy business, including a big expansion in solar and the addition of a wind-power business. As their spokesman said, 'Nowadays we think of ourselves as an energy company, not an oil and gas company.'

At first sight, the oil companies seem to have a strong argument. We do need energy, and they are the experts in providing it. By gradually moving to more and more environmentally friendly sources, they are keeping the energy flowing while reducing their environmental impact. The trouble with this argument is that, as yet, however much they label themselves 'energy companies' rather than 'oil companies', these organizations' share prices are totally dependent on their oil reserves (as was observed recently when various companies had to revise down their estimates).

Environmental campaigner George Monbiot argues that the subtle repositioning that saw BP change the meaning of its initials from 'British Petroleum' to 'Beyond Petroleum' is a dangerous one. In the past Monbiot has accused the oil company ExxonMobil of funding groups that put forward the message that climate change doesn't exist. BP and other oil giants like Shell, Monbiot says, have rather tried to persuade us that they are big cuddly giants who have seen the error of their ways and are now as green as you can get.

As we have seen from the response from BP above, this is partially achieved by pushing their green energy investments like wind farms, and also by suggesting that with carbon offsetting it is possible to overcome any negative impact of their industry – we can drive guilt-free once more. As Monbiot puts it, 'They have created the impression that a large and growing oil industry is compatible with preventing runaway climate change. BP in particular now looks more like an environmental pressure group than an oil company.'

There is no evidence that taking on wind farms and other green sources has led to a reduction in the amount of oil the companies produce – and without such a reduction, their claims are highly suspect. Other companies have in the past proved that corporate leopards really can change their spots, but it is going to take more than fancy adverts and mission statements to change the nature of the oil giants.

Words aren't enough

The message for companies is clear. There is no point pushing your dubious green credentials if your business is inherently damaging to the environment. A strong majority of the respondents in the survey believed that it was better for big business to own up to not being green, and to show willing to make changes, rather than to try to trumpet their greenness against a backdrop of carbon emissions. BP, for instance, was berated for trying to put across a friendly image with its green sun/flower logo that bears no resemblance to its major role in oil production. Equally, there's no point trying to look green if you have a reputation for being avaricious. Until you put that particular house in order, you might as well forget the green side of your business.

The survey recommended that companies fold their green message into their wider communications, rather than have specific high-profile green campaigns. Encouragingly for the companies, over 75 per cent of the respondents believed that it was possible for business and green interests to converge. There is hope for business – which means hope for the rest of us. But what is needed is a shift in the way companies see the world.

It was interesting to learn from insurance giant Aviva that they 'aim to recycle as much waste as possible (88% in 2007)'. They told me that 'in the UK, we recycle 14 waste streams, helped largely by having binless offices. We have water reduction techniques in place and colleagues in Aviva India have been harvesting rain water for grey water use.' This, to be honest, is much more convincing than their advertising tag-line of being the world's first carbon neutral insurance company. Aviva says that they have 'never entered into any corporate responsibility projects with a view to gaining publicity. In fact we tend to understate our involvement rather than seek to gain from it.' That seems to be the case from the recycling information – but it then gets spoiled by that advertising boast.

With all too many companies, the tendency is to stick 'be green' into the goals and mission statement, to throw around a bit of green publicity and a few token stunts like installing a high-visibility wind generator, and to fail to make any significant changes, because profit-ability remains the number-one goal. Until companies have a goal of being profitable within the limits imposed by environmental concern – essential for long-term profits – there won't be a significant change.

It is easy to see how difficult this will be from the public's reaction to energy companies telling us they want to help us reduce our energy use. There is some-thing very strange about companies that make their profits from selling energy trying to persuade us to use less to help the environment. The collapse of the energy giant Enron, which resorted to fraudulent practices to hide its financial mismanagement, demonstrated just how far some will go to keep the bottom line inflated. So what are the energy companies up to? Can we trust them? Can they satisfy their shareholders and at the same time help us reduce our consumption? Would they be encouraging us to fit cavity wall insulation and use low-energy light bulbs if they weren't under immense pressure from government?

A 2004 report showed just how big a gulf these companies have to cross. It found that consumers have 'a high level of cynicism about the motives of energy suppliers to promote energy saving and generally low levels of trust in their advice; a deep cynicism about the motives of energy companies promoting energy efficiency measures' and 'a strong dislike for any feedback concept which compared their energy use with average, other homes like theirs or other homes in their neighbourhood'. It takes ecologic to see how we can move away from this suspicion and get consumers to take energy-saving seriously while at the same time helping the energy companies survive in a changing world.

The price/consumption equation

This problem of maintaining a commercial existence while encouraging environmentally sound action on the part of their customers is one that is increasingly recognized. In February 2008, energywatch, the UK's consumer energy body, argued that it was time for energy companies to take a different approach. Allan Asher, chief executive of the group, said, 'Nothing's going to change unless we reinvent the way that firms produce, distribute and derive profits from energy.'

Asher asserts that fundamental to this is breaking the link between price and consumption. At the moment, no matter how green the energy company's credentials, the more domestic energy we use, the cheaper per unit it is.

This is an economic vehicle that has only one purpose – to make it attractive to use more energy. Hardly the weapon we need to cut back consumption. Pricing structures need to change, and quickly.

This part of Asher's case is impossible to argue against. However, he also says that there's a serious problem because a third of energy bills are estimated, and if we don't have accurate metering we can't expect consumers to control their energy consumption effectively. This seems something of a red herring, especially when he argues that accurate metering and billing would encourage people to buy more energy from renewable sources or to install their own micro-generators.

Now, there *is* some evidence that having a monitor that brings your consumption (averaged up as a monthly spend) in front of your eyes does encourage you to switch off more. The UK government intended to make use of this effect to encourage us to cut power use by insisting that energy companies provide such monitors for free – but under pressure from the industry, in April 2008, the government backed down and let the suppliers choose whether or not to provide the monitors. That the energy companies applied this pressure is another example of why consumers are cynical about their intentions.

However, even if there is a benefit from visual displays of consumption, there seems little logical connection between better metering and our consumption of greener energy. Estimated bills are certainly irritating because they delay the facts, and without monitors or smart meters we can't say just how much we are spending at any moment, but getting that information doesn't encourage anyone suddenly to switch to a power company that uses only wind power.

Similarly, the obstacles to micro-generation are a combination of problems with household locations – we don't all have somewhere to put south-facing solar cells, or to mount a turbine – and financial barriers to putting micro-generation in place. If energy companies (or governments) really wanted to increase the use of green micro-generation, they would install the equipment for free, pay for it out of the electricity fed back into the grid and, when it went into profit, reduce the householder's bills.

Many more of us, I believe, would happily have micro-generation at home if we weren't spending any more than our existing energy bills – we could even be given a 10 per cent discount for contributing to the scheme – and knew that at some point in the future we would have significantly reduced bills (while doing our bit to save the planet as well).

I hope, but doubt very much, that when the government next does a cost-benefit analysis of building a new power station, it will compare that with the benefits of spending the same money on installing free micro-generators in homes with this kind of pay-back scheme. The householder would benefit in reduced bills, and even greater reductions in the future. The government would have installed the equivalent of a very large renewable energy resource, tailored to local conditions, spread across the country so less susceptible to local weather variations and without the planning and ecological worries generated by large-scale power plants.

Grow your own fuel

As customers become increasingly aware of environmental issues, some companies are changing their products to make them more green. Yet this approach can be fraught with problems. A good example is biofuels or agrofuels. The idea is simple. Burning fossil fuels uses up a scarce resource – if those who trumpet the cause of peak oil are right, a declining resource – and pumps tonnes of unmitigated carbon into the atmosphere. But if, instead, your fuels are produced from growing crops, you have a resource that is renewable on a practical timescale, and the crops while alive will take carbon out of the atmosphere, balancing some of the CO_2 produced when the fuels are manufactured and burned.

There are two common ways to do this. Bioethanol is ethyl alcohol produced from fermenting sugary or starchy crops like sugar cane or maize. The alcohol in alcoholic drinks is bioethanol – rum, for example, contains bioethanol from sugar cane. But the drinks are not pure alcohol – just as well, as a relatively small amount can kill you. Bioethanol is refined until only the combustible ethanol is left. Car engines can be converted to run on bioethanol, or an ordinary petrol engine can take additions to the petrol of around 10 per cent of bioethanol without serious impact on performance.

The alternative is biodiesel. This is produced from vegetable oils – palm oil, for example – which have been processed to make them suitable for diesel engines. As an ideal, a converted diesel engine can be run from used cooking oil from your local takeaway but, realistically, most biodiesel will require purpose-planted crops.

It seemed such a great idea that the EU was quick to

jump on the bandwagon, as was the US. Even George Bush, no friend to environmental groups, could see the wisdom in encouraging biofuels. It's possible to argue, of course, that his enthusiasm is more about national benefit than saving the planet. In his 2007 State of the Union address, Bush stated an aim to reduce gasoline usage in the United States by 20 per cent over ten years. When that was the case, he told the nation, 'we will have cut our total imports by the equivalent of three-quarters of all the oil we now import from the Middle East'.

The US may not be able to compete with the Middle East in oil production, but it has much more capacity for growing biofuel crops and to switch from oil to biofuel would enable the US to be less dependent on outside sources – not a bad thing with doubtful future supplies and constant turmoil in the Middle East. However, bio-fuels are not a magic bullet to solve our energy problems. Jean Ziegler, the UN special rapporteur on the right for food, has called them a 'crime against humanity'.

Ziegler, in his 2007 report to the General Assembly, pointed out that the number of people suffering from hunger had increased to 854 million, and had been rising every year since 1996. According to Ziegler, more than six million children die each year from hunger and hunger-related causes before their fifth birthday. The concern that underlies this report is that biofuels are grown in direct competition with food. The crops used to produce biofuels – maize, wheat, sugar and palm oil – are foodstuffs themselves (though of doubtful value in the case of sugar and palm oil) and, more importantly, take up agricultural land that would otherwise be used to grow food crops. If land can produce a relatively modest income from food or a higher income from fuel, it is hard to blame the farmer for switching away from food production.

Ziegler suggests that, instead of using food crops, biofuels should be made from non-food plants (presumably growing where food crops can't thrive, or the distinction is irrelevant) or from plant and agricultural waste. This is a strong argument, where crops from a particular location could sensibly be feeding people in need. To produce sufficient biofuel to fill a car tank once requires enough maize, for example, to feed a person for a year – around 200 kilograms.

As always, we need to be careful that our reaction to biofuels isn't pure knee-jerk. Cuba's Fidel Castro remarked that it is a 'sinister idea to transform food into fuel'. But this statement, creating an image of food being snatched from the mouths of the hungry and being used to power unnecessary cars, is exactly that: a knee-jerk image. There's nothing magical about maize that means it can only be put to a single use. Bioethanol and biodiesel don't turn food into fuel, they turn a plant into fuel.

As has often been said, the world doesn't suffer so much from a food shortage as a food location and distribution failure. Where biofuels are grown and used in an environment where food production wouldn't make any difference to world starvation, there is no inherent problem with the concept, unless the biofuels drive up the prices of relatively scarce food crops. However, what is unpalatable is when biofuels are grown in a developing country that is short of food, at the expense of producing foodstuffs. While this picture doesn't fit the US, it does apply to some of its neighbours in the southern part of the continent – a worrying thought when Latin America seems set to be one of the world's biggest sources of biofuel.

The UN report blames the shift in maize production in the Americas from edible to industrial varieties for the Mexican food riots in February 2007, when the price of maize tortillas rose by over 400 per cent. Similarly, it points to the danger of forced eviction for those living on desirable, potentially cultivatable land, and the same sort of deforestation that has already been seen to make way for soya plantations in the Amazon basin.

A telling quote comes from Eric Holt-Gimenez, executive director of the FoodFirst Institute for Food Development Policy in Oakland, California: 'I think a lot of environmentalists got caught with their pants down. They were thinking of biofuels in a local, non-industrial way. When agro-industry and oil companies got ahold of it, they turned it into something that is by no means sustainable.' It's that old green problem raising its ugly head again: ideas that are based on fuzzy warm feelings ('Hey, we could grow a crop in the back garden to power our moped') rather than the logic of the real world.

Do biofuels do what it says on the tin?

Even if it were possible to plant enough crops for biofuels, it has been argued that the effort required in producing the fuels outweighs the value of the product. If you add together all the energy input of a biofuel crop – planting, tending, fertilizing and protecting, harvesting, transporting and processing – it is greater than the amount of energy that comes out in the engine. According to Tad Patzek of the University of California,

Berkeley, and David Pimentel of Cornell, around 27 megajoules of input on a bioethanol crop produced only around 21 megajoules of usable energy.

This argument is less convincing than the environmental impact. It's normal to lose efficiency when converting energy from one form into another. That extra energy is effectively being used to make the output storable and portable. It's not ideal, but is a fact of life because, despite the attempts a hundred years ago by electrical experimenter Nikola Tesla, we can't broadcast usable power over the air waves.

However, what is more significant is that the majority of the energy input into growing the biofuel will itself involve emission of CO_2 and other greenhouse gases and this will offset, or even entirely wipe out, any environmental benefit from using biofuels. This takes us back to President Bush's statement as the only truthful reason for deploying biofuels – they enable countries with a big capacity for agriculture to reduce their dependence on fossil fuels, whether it's oil from the Middle East or gas from Russia.

Biofuels are politically expedient in a dangerous world, and for that reason may be valid in some circumstances, but they should not be trumpeted as a major environmental saviour. This makes the current UK and EU plans to increase dependence on biofuels for environmental reasons, with the EU aiming to have 10 per cent of road traffic fuelled by biofuel by 2020, unsound. We may still decide we want some biofuel proportion in our fuel mix to offset supply risk, but the reasoning should be clearer, and it's essential we make sure that it is grown appropriately without putting further stress on the environment.

As is often the case with environmental issues, there are potential technological solutions to the problems – but as is also often the case, they aren't here yet. It is possible to produce biofuels more effectively, by deriving ethanol from a plant material called lignocellulose. This can be extracted from agricultural waste and un-fertilized plants on otherwise useless land, taking away the threat to food and reducing the environmental impact as no fertilizer and less external energy are required for production. But this process is currently only at the experimental stage, and isn't clearly sustainable in the long term.

Fuel from the oceans

Another alternative is to make use of algae. It's easy to dismiss these tiny floating plants found in the sea and fresh water as insignificant, but that would be a serious misreading of their importance. We're used to the rainforest being labelled as the lungs of the planet, but really it's just the emergency respirator. Even before fires and human devastation turned the Amazon rainforest from a net carbon sink to a carbon source, the rainforest was outclassed by algae as a way of locking away carbon and producing oxygen. Three-quarters of the photosynthesis activity on the Earth takes place in algae.

Greg Mitchell of the Scripps Institution of Oceanography at the University of California, San Diego, has suggested using algae as a source of biofuels. Vegetable oil can be extracted from algae, while the carbohydrates in these microscopic plants can be fermented to produce alcohol-based fuel. According to Mitchell, algae in ponds covering around 20 million acres would be enough to provide for all the US's transport needs. This sounds a lot of ponds – and there are water-shortage implications, of course – but those 20 million acres need to be put alongside the 900 million acres of agricultural land currently in use in the US. Such algae can feed on sewage, making the ponds dual use, and there's a lot of interest in algae-sourced biofuels from both oil companies and the US defence agency, DARPA. Like the use of lignocellulose, this approach is currently experimental and would require a much bigger change in approaches to agriculture – but algae can in principle hold out more hope for biofuels than any other source.

Who will buy my green solutions?

There might be a lot of concern about the way energy companies vie to be seen as the most green, but a more subtle perversion of what we need to do to be environmentally effective also comes to us from celebrities and brands. Here, instead of selling themselves as green paragons, we are given examples of green living that are designed to sell the celebrity's latest book, or encourage us to buy a brand's supposedly greener product. This is the world of green consumerism, where we can assuage our guilt by buying the right products – or buying into the right lifestyle.

Green consumerism tells us that we don't need to pull on a hair shirt; we can keep consuming away to our hearts' content, provided we subtly change direction. Buy organic cotton rather than those nasty natural fibres. Get a new Prius every year instead of a new 4×4. Make sure your second home is built out of environmentally friendly materials and insulated with sheep's wool instead of glass fibres. Unfortunately, the real environmental message should be don't buy new clothes at all until your old ones wear out; get a good efficient car if it's necessary but keep it for years; and don't have a second home.

The green-lifestyle celebrities tell us we should all be out there starting *Good Life*-style smallholdings in our surburban back gardens, producing our own preserves and baking our own bread – ideal for those who don't need to work for a living or have enough money that they can employ someone else to do the less fun chores, but not realistic for many.

It's interesting to look at the advertising in a magazine like the *Environmentalist*, aimed firmly at those green consumers – here you will find words like organic and natural and green bandied around endlessly, but very little that does more than greenwash the surface. As environmental activist George Monbiot has commented, 'no political challenge can be met by shopping'. It's not nice or jolly that taking a serious approach to the environment probably does mean cutting back and doing things differently – but to pretend that we can get away with simply shifting our rampant consumption to different suppliers with a nicer attitude and paper bags instead of plastic ones is facile.

Recycling the Andrex puppy

There is plenty of pressure on manufacturers to bring out products that will appeal to those would-be green consumers – and no business is going to turn down such an opportunity. Being seen to be green is now such a good thing in a commercial sense that companies go to quite surprising lengths to promote what can often be a relatively low level of environmental friendliness. A good example is recycled toilet paper (not, as the name worryingly suggests, used toilet paper that has been recycled, but toilet paper made from recycled sources).

The best option with any disposable product is not to employ it at all – and we could all use less toilet paper (and other paper products like kitchen roll) – but seeing 'recycled' on the pack isn't a certain indicator that you have made the best possible purchasing decision to save the planet. Worse still, the vast majority of toilet paper and kitchen roll isn't recycled at all, with recycled usually coming in as a more expensive, less attractive-looking option.

In one sense, less attractive-looking is a good thing. The ideal is that the toilet paper shouldn't be bleached (which involves significant use of unnecessary chemicals) or coloured. In the end this makes no difference to the functionality of the product, but a lot to the environment. It's just a matter of thinking of grey as a fashionable colour in toilet paper, as it has become in cars. If the paper has to be bleached, oxygen-based bleaches will be more environmentally friendly than the chlorine-based equivalents.

That apart, it's that recycled label we're liable to look for. After all, not only does recycling reduce the number of trees needed to produce Europe's 22 billion annual rolls, it also cuts both the energy and the water used in production. However, not every recycled roll has the same amount of recycled content (toilet paper can't be 100 per cent recycled, as recycling paper reduces the fibre strength, so some fresh pulp has to be added), and the pulp may not be from a sustainable source. (Some 'recycled' material is waste wood pulp, so not strictly recycled at all.) Some products are quite forthcoming in the details of their 'recycled' content; others don't bother to say. It's only fair to assume the worst if you aren't told any different.

We need to take all green consumerism with a huge pinch of low-sodium salt. If you are going to buy the product anyway, yes, it's a good idea to minimize the environmental impact of what you buy – at least as much as you can with such a bewildering array of possibilities under the 'recycled' banner alone. However, if we really need to make a difference, reducing un-necessary replacements of products, from cars to mobile phones, will have a much bigger impact than changing our brand of toilet tissue.

In choosing the right products, information is essential. But when dealing with human interactions, the type of information required to understand an issue is often less obvious than the sourcing of raw materials. We need to know the incentives that make people act. Unless we understand, for example, that most people have incentives to avoid recycling, it's impossible to take action. Some of these are in the open, visible to all who look for them, though few bother to do so. Others are more carefully concealed.

If we are really to understand why whole nations have fought attempts to manage climate change, and why it is that we *still* hear 'there's no proof that climate change is man-made', we need to cut below the surface and examine the true incentives that drive those who seem determined to push the world to the brink of disaster.

Why has respected scientist David Bellamy called man-made climate change 'poppycock'? Why do some apparent experts claim that climate-change scientists are 'deeply divided over the causes of climate change' when this simply isn't true? Where better to bring ecologic to play than on the experts who are wolves in sheep's clothing.

5

Beware Experts in Sheep's Clothing

We all love experts these days. Where would a news bulletin be without hearing that expert witness evidence has been given in court, or that an expert tells us the FTSE 100 index has just plummeted for some apparently trivial reason? We need experts because the world is so complex. It's not possible for all of us to understand every role and field that's available. And that's a good thing. Most of us would prefer to have an expert flying the plane we're in, or operating on us, rather than someone who has picked up a few ideas from the internet and wants to try them out. Yet experts have significant limitations.

One problem is that experts have tunnel vision. They are so focused on their own field that they often don't understand other areas that might have an impact on what they are involved in. This can lead to a common difficulty when trying to solve a problem – experts are very good at telling you what *isn't* possible. The best ideas often come from someone who is ignorant of what you can't do. This isn't equating ignorance with a magic ability to get things right: most of the ideas that are born out of ignorance are either poor or need significant development. But the fact remains that experts often can't see beyond what they know.

This type of tunnel vision can lead to an expert giving misleading evidence, as we will see later in the case of Henrik Svensmark and the impact of cosmic rays on climate change. But it can also be the case that an expert deliberately misuses statistics, information and expertise (or lack of it) to further a personal goal. When that's the case, we need to look out for the incentives that drive them.

Incentives to act

It is by examining incentives that we can see why some people seem determined to go against the huge scientific consensus supporting climate change. The obvious sources of opposition to the findings of environmental science are companies benefiting from products and services that threaten the environment. It's not a simple equation. The executives of these companies are human beings with children, who may well personally want to help the environment. Yet history has shown that organizations are very good at ignoring the negative aspects of their products until forced to take them into account. The history of cigarette manufacture makes it clear that companies are prepared to ignore evidence until the last possible moment, and to try to manufacture opinion that supports their business objectives.

This same combination of ignoring evidence and trying to counter expert views has come time and time again from those who have a motive for suppressing the bad news about climate change. Often third parties are used – organizations and individuals set up to present the anti-global-warming message in an apparently independent manner, but whose funding can be traced back to energy companies and other businesses that find climate change a commercially irritating concept.

In early 2007, Senator Barbara Boxer, chair of the US Senate's Environment Committee, had a meeting with the head of the Intergovernmental Panel on Climate Change (IPCC), the body set up by the World Meteorological Organization and the UN to provide scientific evidence to governments around the world. She was given an unequivocal message that climate change was real and that there was a very high probability that the burning of fossil fuels was a major contributor to the problem. As Boxer left the meeting one of her staff pulled her to one side. She was told that a conservative organization, funded by an oil company, was offering scientists $10,000 to write articles that attacked the IPCC report and the models that had been used to produce its gloomy predictions. Boxer commented that she realized it wasn't just a matter of winning voters over – there was an active movement to suppress the realities of climate change.

This was organized resistance. Former senator Tim Wirth, one-time Democrat environmental leader, drew a parallel with the tobacco industry at its height. 'Both figured, sow enough doubt, call the science uncertain and in dispute. That's had a huge impact on both the public and Congress.' The result has been that until recently there has been significant doubt and confusion in the public mind. The message the public has received is that scientists and science were divided on whether or not there was human-caused climate change.

Those who feel that the whole idea of a covert alliance attempting to dismiss global warming smacks too much of conspiracy theory might be shocked to learn that, as long ago as 1998, a group including representatives of well-known organizations that argue against global warming met with oil company Exxon at the hardly unbiased American Petroleum Institute to discuss a campaign to train twenty scientists to become media representatives for their viewpoint (a campaign that was dropped when memos from the meeting were leaked).

ExxonMobil seems finally to be losing its will to push on with fighting its cause. After being rapped over the knuckles by the US Senate for spending over $19 million on anti-global-warming organizations producing, as one senator put it 'very questionable data', the company has publicly announced that it accepts the risks posed by climate change. These could be weasel words, and there are still senior Republican politicians who have been so indoctrinated with the anti-global-warming view that they can't shake it off – but the US seems finally to be turning the corner on climate change.

The great global warming swindle

In March 2007, *Daily Mail* columnist Peter Hitchens commented on the recently screened Channel 4 documentary *The Great Global Warming Swindle*:

If you were worried about those snaps of polar bears clinging to melting ice-floes, sentenced to a slow death by global warming, you may now relax. They'll be fine. Channel 4 has paid in full for its recent misdemeanours by screening, last Thursday, the brilliant, devastating film *The Great Global Warming Swindle*.

Nobody who watched it can continue to pretend that the case is closed, or that scientists don't disagree about the causes of climate change. It should be repeated, soon, and made available to schools.

And, if your child's school has been panicking young minds with claims of impending doom, lobby the teachers to get a recording of this programme and show it. I bet they resist.

The documentary pulls no punches. We are told not to be worried about the impact of climate change because it's not true. 'You are being told lies,' it states. What follows are attempts to counter the science, just as happened in the US campaigns mentioned above. Everyone who appeared in the film spoke negatively about global warming. This wasn't a surprise from eight of the interviewees, linked to American right-wing think tanks. But it did also include some legitimate experts – and many of these feel they were misrepresented. Ocean circulation and climate expert Professor Carl Wunsch later commented:

> I am angry because they completely misrepresented me. My views were distorted by the context in which they placed them. I was misled as to what it was going to be about. I was told about six months ago that this was to be a programme about how complicated it is to

understand what is going on. If they had told me even the title of the programme, I would have absolutely refused to be on it. I am the one who has been swindled.

The film wheeled out the well-exercised and equally well-disproved counters to climate change that have proved so popular with those US think tanks. These are arguments that the Royal Society has got so used to countering that it has a website section listing them all and showing why they are misleading or useless – yet the documentary presented them as unarguable fact. Wunsch again:

In the part of the 'Swindle' film where I am describing the fact that the ocean tends to expel carbon dioxide where it is warm, and to absorb it where it is cold, my intent was to explain that warming the ocean could be dangerous – because it is such a gigantic reservoir of carbon. By its placement in the film, it appears that I am saying that since carbon dioxide exists in the ocean in such large quantities, human influence must not be very important – diametrically opposite to the point I was making – which is that global warming is both real and threatening in many different ways, some unexpected . . .

What we now have is an out-and-out propaganda piece, in which there is not even a gesture toward balance or explanation of why many of the extended inferences drawn in the film are not widely accepted by the scientific community. There are so many examples, it's hard to know where to begin, so I will cite only one: a speaker asserts, as is true, that carbon dioxide is only a small fraction of the atmospheric mass. The viewer is left to infer that means it couldn't really matter. But even a beginning meteorology student could tell you that the relative masses of gases are irrelevant to their effects on radiative balance. A director not intending to produce pure propaganda would have tried to eliminate that piece of disinformation.

A political message

What this illustrates is that it isn't just those in the pay of big oil who are prepared to do whatever it takes to knock the accepted view on climate change. There is no suggestion that director Martin Durkin was influenced by energy companies. He has been refreshingly explicit about what he was trying to do: 'I think it will go down in history as the first chapter in a new era of the relationship between science and society. Legitimate scientists – people with qualifications – are the bad guys.' It appears that this is chip-on-the-shoulder political film-making from someone who takes the post-modern but highly unrealistic view that it's what you believe is true that matters, not the science underneath.

It's equally important to see what is happening on the opposite side of the argument with misrepresentation from the Al Gore bandwagon. There seems little doubt that Gore, an ex-vice president of the US, has genuine beliefs about the dangers of global warming, and that his high-profile status has enabled him to spread these beliefs to the world. His book and video, *An Inconvenient Truth*, have been widely consumed and Gore's stance is clear. But there have been problems with his presentation of the arguments. This led to the 2007 case at the High Court in London, where the judge identified nine errors in Gore's video and supported the need for teachers to have guidance notes pointing out these errors if the video is to be shown in UK schools.

The problem here is not with science itself; it's that politicians are, to some degree, incompatible with a scientific approach. It's worth remembering a seminal quote from one of the few individuals with science training to reach high office, Margaret Thatcher, holder of a chemistry degree. In 1980 she famously said, '[T]o those waiting with bated breath for that favourite media catchphrase, the U-turn, I have only one thing to say: You turn if you want to. The lady's not for turning!' In politics it is much more important to have certainty and conviction than it is to worry about the detailed facts, scientific or otherwise, which might require a change of direction.

When a politician has a message to get across, he or she uses the information available in the way that will best support that message, rather than in the way that best gives an accurate scientific view. If that means showing an image of a cute polar bear, apparently stranded on an ice floe, to emphasize that global warming is already having an effect, then fine. It is taken as no more than the scientific equivalent of kissing a baby. The fact that the message is almost entirely wrong (polar bears aren't cute, the bear wasn't stranded, and the lump of ice wasn't the remainder of a habitat wasted by global warming) is considered beside the point, because the aim is to swing opinion using gut feel, not to put across clear, scientific facts.

An inconvenient inaccuracy

This explains Gore's approach, even if it doesn't excuse some of the errors in his presentation. These flaws have become armament for those who wish to attack the perfectly legitimate science involved. It isn't necessary to work through all the errors, whether the judge's original nine, or the extra twenty-six that others with the opposite agenda to Gore have suggested are present, but it is worth highlighting two to see what has happened.

A typical example was the statement that a rise in sea level of up to 6 metres could be caused by the melting of either the West Antarctic or Greenland ice sheet. Gore does not say this will happen soon, which is just as well. The IPCC reckon it would take several thousand years of melting to produce this kind of rise. However, Gore is not being totally alarmist here either. As Jim Hansen, director of the Goddard Institute for Space Studies and George Bush's top in-house climate modeller, graphically put it, '[Greenland's ice is] on a slippery slope to hell.' By 2000, the rate at which the ice sheet was melting had accelerated so much that it was already losing vastly more than had been estimated just ten years before. The assumption had been that the ice would gradually melt from the surface downwards, trickling its way to the sea as run-off water. But what is actually happening is startlingly different.

Lakes of water are forming on top of the ice sheets. These sheets aren't always uniformly solid. If there's a crack in the ice below a lake, the water can rush down, opening up the crevasse further as it flows until it has passed through the entire sheet to the bottom, where the water flow can eat away from beneath, enabling huge swathes of the ice sheet to float off the land. '[If] the water goes down the crack,' says Richard Alley of Pennsylvania State University, 'it doesn't take 10,000 years [to reach the base of the ice sheet], it takes 10 seconds.' If the entire Greenland ice sheet were to end up in the ocean, it would raise sea levels by 7 metres. And this is without considering the impact of the melting Antarctic ice cap, which is on land, so also contributes to sea level.

There is, then, a mechanism by which Gore's predictions could come true in our lifetimes. This isn't currently accepted as the most likely future, but there is nothing wrong with describing the possibility. However, Gore should have made it clearer how opinions were divided on this, and where there are relatively low probabilities.

A stronger example of getting the facts wrong is Gore's assertion that, in the last four interglacial periods of warming, changes in carbon dioxide levels caused the change in temperature. As shown elsewhere (see page 122), this is not the case. In fact, the mechanism was unrelated to the climate change we are currently experiencing, so the example is helpful neither to Gore nor to his opponents, but the inclusion in the film was highly misleading.

Al Gore was doing nothing more than other politicians do: spinning the facts to get across to the public at large a message that he genuinely believes is important. However, this approach is not appropriate to good science. It ought to be pointed out that this spinning works both ways. In a response to the Gore film by Lord Monckton, published by the Science & Public Policy Institute (an organization that promotes climate change scepticism), similar approaches are used to attack Gore.

For example, Monckton (also a politician) makes the bizarre statement that the atmosphere, not the sun, warms the Arctic ocean. He points out that Gore says that the ice-melt in the Arctic allows the sun to heat the ocean more than it otherwise would. Monckton's report comments that 'The ocean emits radiant energy at the moment of absorption and would freeze if there were no atmosphere. It is the atmosphere, not the Sun that warms the ocean.' This is a very strange statement: no one is doubting that the atmosphere keeps the temperature of the planet up, but to suggest that the heating is *caused by* the atmosphere rather than by the sun is ludicrous.

The chilling stars

It's less easy to see why some respected scientists persist in holding out against the consensus on climate change. Some are defending a very specific theory, and as a result of that can make statements that are more confusing than helpful to an overall understanding of the issue. In 2007, scientist Henrik Svensmark and science journalist Nigel Calder wrote a book called *The Chilling Stars*. In this, they do not deny the existence of global warming, but ascribe it to astronomical influences – a combination of cosmic rays, causing changes in cloud patterns, and the sun's magnetic field, which varies how much impact cosmic rays have as its field waxes and wanes.

The idea is that cosmic rays – streams of high-energy particles from outside our solar system (or more precisely, the secondary particles that are generated when the cosmic rays impact the atmosphere) – act as triggers for cloud formation. When there are a lot of cosmic-ray particles getting through, there are more clouds; when there are fewer cosmic rays, there are fewer clouds. This is significant for climate change because low clouds cool the planet.

In putting this theory across, Svensmark and Calder are simply publicizing an interesting idea. Most scientists do accept that cosmic rays have some impact on the weather, though the general feeling is that they are relatively insignificant. The book's theory could well provide an explanation for some of the cycles of heat and cold that have happened in the Earth's past, but cosmic-ray climate change cannot be used in an attempt to dismiss the major contribution of human-caused global warming.

Unfortunately, the book takes a bitter approach to conventional climate-change scientists, who are portrayed as having a vested interest in showing that carbon dioxide levels are the only driver of global warming. Worse, the book was used as part of the basis for Durkin's TV documentary, which made it seem as if an interesting but ultimately unlikely theory was a serious challenger to the reality of human-caused climate change.

Seriously sceptical

Better known than Svensmark is another Scandinavian climate-change maverick, Bjørn Lomborg. In publishing his book *The Skeptical Environmentalist*, Lomborg attacked the unthinking acceptance of human-caused climate change, dismissing the Kyoto Protocol and managing to irritate many climate scientists along the way.

(It probably didn't help that he isn't a climate scientist himself, but a statistician.) He doesn't totally deny the impact of climate change, or that there is any man-made component, but he pours doubt on the scale of the impact, believing there are other and more important things to worry about.

Lomborg examines a much wider range of environmental issues, but his concern throughout is the misuse of numbers. He points out that the models used to predict the impact of climate change are hopelessly over-complex and riddled with unknowns, such as the contribution of clouds, that threaten to overwhelm the useful data that can be extracted from them. Lomborg certainly has a point that making accurate forecasts can be difficult: he himself falls into this trap when dismissing suggestions that natural resources like oil and foodstuffs like wheat are in increasingly short supply.

Back when Lomborg wrote his book, in 2001, he was able to laugh at earlier suggestions of an oil crisis:

> Even though oil prices have doubled since the all-time low in mid 1998, the price in the first quarter of 2001 is on a par with the price in 1990, and the barrel price of $25 in March 2001 is still way below the top price of $60 in the 1980s. Moreover, most consider this spike is a short-term occurrence, where the US Energy Information Agency expects an almost steady oil price over the next 20 years at about $22 a barrel.

Not quite. The price of oil passed $110 a barrel in February 2008. Although prices subsequently fell sharply in the 2008 global slowdown, they peaked at over $130 a barrel.

Similarly, Lomborg pooh-poohs those who see world food prices rising. The trend, he assures us, is down. In the fifty years to 2000, world wheat prices fell steadily from around $18 per bushel to under $4 a bushel. Admittedly there was a sharp peak in the 1970s when it nearly got back to the $18 mark, but that was soon corrected. Nothing to worry about? In February 2008 the price was $24 a bushel. Even allowing for inflation since 2000, this is a big, big rise. It could be another blip – but could equally well show a marked change in the trend.

Lomborg is right to treat the climate models with caution, but he ought to have shown similar concern about his own modelling. We need to make best guesses about the future, but we should never forget how uncertain some of those predictions are.

The climate change denier

With a similar viewpoint but a much stronger line on climate change, and more visibility in the UK, is scientist and broadcaster David Bellamy. Bellamy has been attacked widely as being a 'climate change denier', a label that seems to put him on a par with those who deny the Holocaust. The unfortunate thing is that the way he has been treated is all about knee-jerk reactions and nothing to do with science.

Before getting to grips with Bellamy's arguments, how they have been treated and both his and his detractors' motivations, it's worth taking a step back from green issues to look at what happened to another scientist who regularly strayed from mainstream thinking – the astrophysicist Fred Hoyle. This is important, because it emphasizes how Bellamy's treatment has been very different from what might be expected.

Fred Hoyle was a versatile scientist, who put his hand to writing science-fiction books and the twice-made TV series *A for Andromeda* alongside his work in astrophysics. He is best known for developing the now universally held theory of how the elements, apart from the very lightest, were forged in stars.

In Hoyle's younger days, there was much debate in astronomical circles about the mechanism by which the universe originated. Until the 1960s there were two main opposing theories. One, originated by Hoyle and his colleagues, was the Steady State theory, which suggested that matter was constantly being created and flowed into an expanding universe that need have no particular beginning or end. The other, which Hoyle sarcastically labelled the 'Big Bang', only to have the name stick and be used less critically, involved a specific start point for a universe that grew from a tiny, dimensionless speck.

Over the years, the Big Bang theory gradually pushed Steady State aside as more and more evidence was accumulated that pointed towards a single point of emergence. Eventually there was strong consensus among cosmologists that Big Bang was the best current theory to support the evidence (about as strong as science can get) and that there was nothing going for Steady State. But Hoyle clung on to the theory, frequently tweaking it in an attempt to get it to fit better with the new data. It was a theory that he had helped bring to birth and, like many scientists, he was reluctant to let his baby go. Most of his colleagues would say he was wrong – but they always listened to him with interest and continued to test his ideas against the best evidence. At no time was Hoyle labelled a 'Big Bang denier' or personally attacked for his theories. He was simply a scientist with a view that differed from most of his colleagues.

Contrast this with the near-vilification of Bellamy by some sources. Bellamy too has acknowledged expertise in his field. As he pointed out to me, he 'taught Ecology at Durham University for 22 years, supervised 23 PhD students, tutored 124 MSc students, and over 1,000 BScs. [His] research expertise was in wetlands including coral reefs and human ecosystem interaction.' And like Hoyle, Bellamy now supports a theory that is not mainstream.

Compared with cosmology, green issues have a greater emotional impact, a more direct influence on our lives, and much wider media coverage. Instead of accepting that Bellamy is simply putting forward alternative scientific theories that should be considered alongside other interpretations of the evidence, he has been treated extremely poorly.

Admittedly, he has sometimes brought this on himself by adopting a pugnacious attitude to those who disagree and by using emotive language. In 2004 he wrote an article for the *Daily Mail* (a newspaper that delights in anti-science stories) entitled 'Global Warming? What a Load of Poppycock!' But he is not just a crank who can be ignored – his reasons for coming up with this stance have to be examined. At the heart of his view is a genuine scientific concern.

He says that our worries about future problems arising from climate change are based on computer models – which do have a wide range of possible outcomes.

It's arguable that these are so wide that we can't place much credence on the models, especially as some of the variables involved, like the impact of clouds, are so unpredictable. However, this doesn't mean that the evidence that man-made global warming exists is dependent on modelling. That is much firmer science. It is only the predictions of the future that are, as always, educated guesswork at best.

Bellamy observes that our climate is always experiencing ups and downs, and that it is an unnecessarily large jump to go, as the media often does, from a particular climate high to the assumption that we are experiencing global warming. He points out that in 2007 snow fell in Portugal for the first time in fifty-two years and three US states had their lowest ever recorded temperatures. This is playing the media at their own game: not only is it citing specifics rather than giving an overall picture, but it attacks the simplistic concept of 'global warming' rather than the more subtle one of 'climate change'. None of Bellamy's serious opponents suggest that the world is going through uniform warming – in fact, all the evidence is that for some locations climate change will mean both worse droughts and wetter times, while in others there will be more extremes of cold at the same time as higher and higher summer temperatures.

Bellamy says that he is not a 'denier' because he bases his argument on facts, whereas deniers do their best to ignore and cover up the facts. He argues that 'there are no facts linking the concentration of atmospheric carbon dioxide with imminent global warming . . .' He cites 'the most reliable global, regional and local temperature records from around the world' as displaying no distinguishable trend up or down in the last century.

Fighting the arguments, not the man

The arguments Bellamy presents are interesting, and not seen enough.

The last peak temperatures were around 1940 and 1998, with troughs of low temperature around 1910 and 1970. The second dip caused pop science and the media to cry wolf about a catastrophic ice age just around the corner. Our end was nigh! As soon as the temperatures took an upward turn in the 1980s the scaremongers changed their tune switching their dogma to imminent catastrophic scenarios of global warming all based on computer models . . .

I used to discuss climate change with my undergraduates and point out that there was much good scientific evidence that the latest of a string of ice ages had affected the climate and sea levels around the world. Thank goodness it began to come to an end a mere 18,000 to 20,000 years ago. The Romans grew grapes in York and during the world wide medieval warm period when civilization blossomed across the world, Nordic settlers farmed lowland Greenland (hence its name) and then got wiped out by the Little Ice Age that only started to wane around 1850.

Back to the data: how can a sixty-year cycle of changing temperature give any credibility to claims that carbon dioxide is causing an inexorable march towards a climate Armageddon? The concentration of carbon dioxide in the atmosphere has risen throughout this time frame, yet the temperature has gone up and down in a cyclical manner. How can this be explained unless there are other factors in control overriding the effect of this greenhouse gas? There are of course many to be found in peer-reviewed literature, solar cycles, cosmic ray cloud control and those little rascals El Niños and La Niñas all of which are played down or even ignored by the global warming brigade.

This is fighting talk. It is true that the concentration of carbon dioxide has risen fairly steadily – a pattern that the global temperature has failed to match over this period. However, no one is arguing that CO_2 and the greenhouse effect are the only contributors to climate change. The other factors Bellamy mentions are involved – and there are also cooling factors. It has been widely described how levels of particles in the air, responsible for global cooling, rose through to the 1960s and then reduced as emission controls were put in place – an influence which neatly matches the observed temperature changes but which Bellamy doesn't mention.

Of course, he could be right. This might be just one of those little fluctuations that the temperature cycle goes through from time to time. It could be that the impact of CO_2 – and Bellamy would not deny that CO_2 is a greenhouse gas – is not significant enough to make the change we are observing, and that our efforts to cut carbon emissions will have negligible effect. We can't know that for certain until it's too late to act if we turn out to have been wrong. Arguably, even though there may be some doubt, it is worth taking the preventative measures.

Bellamy also puts forward the argument, commonly used by those who doubt global warming, that carbon dioxide levels historically tended to rise *following* warming rather than the other way around. This reflects the fact that at warmer temperatures more carbon dioxide is pumped into the atmosphere from natural sources.

This is not the strongest of arguments. We know that many of the historic warmings, particularly those following ice ages, were caused by changes in the Earth's orbit round the sun. And as a result of those warmings, CO_2 was released – so that was the causative order. But it didn't stop the released carbon dioxide contributing further to the warming in the spiral of positive feedback. However, the current warming cycle does not seem to be linked to orbital changes.

In one of his few peer-reviewed papers on the subject (he points out that it is very difficult to get anti-global-warming papers published because of the current climate of stridency), Bellamy makes an interesting case that the predicted impact in CO_2 levels will not have as great an effect on warming as suggested, though it must be stressed that he does *not* deny either the existence of man-made CO_2 or that CO_2 is a greenhouse gas and results in temperature increases. Instead he advances the point, rarely made but worth considering, that increasing shortages in fossil fuels will make it hard for us to achieve the levels of carbon dioxide that some predict. However, this statement is based on just the sort of modelling that he generally does not like: there is considerable uncertainty over the level of fossil fuel reserves and recent reports have suggested that 'peak oil' may be further away than first thought.

Much of David Bellamy's work on climate change has been simply a matter of providing a sceptical balance, if in a rough-and-tumble way. It did, however, include at least one significant error, picked up by one of the thorns in Bellamy's side, environmental campaigner George Monbiot. In a letter to *New Scientist* in 2005, Bellamy commented that 555 out of the 625 glaciers under observation by the World Glacier Monitoring Service have been growing since 1980. Monbiot checked with the WGMS, who responded in robust terms that this was 'complete bullshit'.

On investigation by Monbiot, it seemed that Bellamy had taken his data from a dubious source – a website linked to organizations that appear to have business reasons for promoting anti-global-warming messages. There also seemed to have been a typing error on Bellamy's part – the original website said that 55% of the 625 glaciers were advancing. Monbiot points out that '%' is on the same key as 5 on the UK keyboard, and Bellamy has admitted this may have been a technical error.

There seems little doubt that in this particular case Bellamy's attack on climate change was based on dubious data. Because of the position he has been put in, he resorted to taking more of a political stance than a scientific one, resulting in the sort of trouble Al Gore got into in putting the opposite message. This is, however, a relative rarity in Bellamy's work.

David Bellamy's treatment is based on fear and publicity rather than on proper scientific analysis. This doesn't say that he is right. There are many more scientists, and lots of evidence, suggesting that we are undergoing global warming and that it has a man-made component. But Bellamy's viewpoint is one of a respectable scientist coming up with alternative theories, and should be treated as such.

*

However you view the way some individuals have presented climate change and green issues, it's essential to avoid knee-jerk labels. From an environmental viewpoint, trade is often considered one of the bad guys, but it is oversimplistic to equate trade with damage to the environment. And it is worth giving more thought to the thorny aspect of ethical shopping. Can trade ever truly be fair?

6

Is Fairtrade Fair?

Fair trade and ethical purchasing are complex issues, and, as we'll see, it's not uncommon to use polls and surveys to understand public opinion on these matters. However, these tools, so popular in business and politics, need to be extremely sophisticated in their application of statistics, and are dangerously easy to manipulate. Before looking at fair trade itself, let's take a moment to appreciate what can go wrong with polls and surveys, as they crop up in many of the chapters in this book.

According to a recent poll . . .

Statistical sophistication is required to ensure that the usually extremely small sample of people surveyed is a reasonable match to the wider population being studied. To use a very simple example, if you take a poll at a Vegetarian Society meeting on the impact of cattle on the environment, you will get a very different result from using exactly the same survey on exactly the same sample size but asking members of the Federation of

Master Butchers. Not surprisingly, neither will represent the views of the country at large.

This is not just an issue with polls. The same effect is seen on television, when a 'spokesperson' for a particular viewpoint or community airs their opinions. Often these opinions are not truly those of the community at large. Such spokespeople tend to be used because they are readily available and known to the broadcaster, not because they necessarily provide a good indicator of feeling in the wider population.

Of course, few of those undertaking a poll would pick quite such an obviously biased group as those above – at least not unless there was malicious intent to mislead. But the selection of a group can be a tricky job, even for a professional. The survey-taker cannot necessarily control who responds; what's more, the distinctions between individuals aren't always clear. Even if you allow for regional variations, different cultural inputs and so on, there is always the self-selection problem.

This can result from where, when and how the poll is conducted. Take a poll on a high street at 11 a.m. and you won't get many full-time workers. Take a telephone poll and you won't get anyone who doesn't have a phone. And to make matters worse still, the people who tend to answer polls and surveys are, by definition, the sort of people who like (or at least don't mind) answering polls and surveys. And that is a subset of the population as a whole.

We ask the questions

Equally, it is possible to manipulate the response that is given in a poll from the way the questions are phrased. This can be down to the wording of an individual question, or even the way a series of questions leads up to the key one that will be publicized. This technique is described beautifully by the character Bernard Woolley in Jonathan Lynn and Antony Jay's book *The Complete Yes Prime Minister*. Here a poll has suggested that the public wants to bring back National Service, an idea the armed forces hate:

[Sir Humphrey] was most interested in the party opinion poll, which I had seen as an insuperable obstacle to changing the Prime Minister's mind.

His solution was simple: have another opinion poll done, one that would show that the voters were *against* bringing back National Service.

I was somewhat *naïf* in those days. I did not understand how the voters could be both for it and against it. Dear old Humphrey showed me how it's done.

The secret is that when the Man In The Street is approached by a nice attractive young lady with a clipboard he is asked a *series* of questions. Naturally the Man In The Street wants to make a good impression and doesn't want to make a fool of himself. So the market researcher asks questions designed to elicit consistent answers.

Humphrey demonstrated the system on me. 'Mr Woolley, are you worried about the rise in crime among teenagers?'

'Yes,' I said.

'Do you think there is a lack of discipline and vigorous training in our Comprehensive schools?'

'Yes.'

'Do you think young people welcome some structure and leadership in their lives?'

'Yes.'

'Do they respond to a challenge?'

'Yes.'

'Might you be in favour of reintroducing National Service?'

'Yes.'

Well, naturally I said yes. One could hardly have said anything else without looking inconsistent. Then what happens is that the Opinion Poll publishes only the last question and answer.

Of course, the reputable polls didn't conduct themselves like that. But there weren't too many of these. Humphrey suggested we commission a new survey, not for the party, but for the Ministry of Defence. We did so. He invented the questions there and then:

'Mr Woolley, are you worried about the danger of war?'

'Yes,' I said, quite honestly.

'Are you unhappy about the growth of armaments?'

'Yes.'

'Do you think there's a danger in giving young people guns and teaching them how to kill?'

'Yes.'

'Do you think it wrong to force people to take up arms against their will?'

'Yes.'

'Would you oppose the reintroduction of National Service?'

I'd said 'Yes' before I'd even realised it, d'you see?

Humphrey was crowing with delight. 'You see, Bernard,' he said to me, 'you're the perfect Balanced Sample.'

While this may be going a little too far for many pollsters, there is no doubt that those who are employed to produce surveys can and do try to provide the message that the organization sponsoring the survey wants.

At the very least, unlike scientific research, the survey will never be published if it comes up with the 'wrong' results. But there is clear evidence that questions are sometimes selected with a client's message in mind, and this is where we get into the field of ethical trading.

The question below appeared in a survey on green Christmas presents by an online market research company. The respondents were being asked to tick the box for the statement they most agreed with. Along with 'I want to buy ethical presents but just don't know where to find them' and 'Some brands claim to be environmentally friendly that aren't' came this innocent-looking statement:

Ethical presents are a fad (for example, saving an acre of rainforest).

Unfortunately, someone at the agency preparing the poll decided this was in danger of producing the wrong outcome for their client. Instead of deleting the statement, he or she added a comment – and the poll went out with both the question and comment in place:

Ethical presents are a fad (for example, saving an acre of rainforest) **could we take this out as it conflicts with the brand**

Rather unfortunate.

Surveys to waken the bogeyman

Of course, this use of polls only happens to have been applied to ethical trade – it could have (and probably has) been used for practically any area covered in this book, from organics to carbon trading. In Chapter 2 we looked at the bogeyman at work. Surveys – especially surveys commissioned by an organization with a message to get across, whether it's a commercial one or an environmental one – are highly fruitful ways of waking the sleeping bogeyman in us all.

Careful selection of questions is just one of many ways that pollsters can, and frequently do, bias the result. In the book *Tainted Truth*, Cynthia Crossen points out a number of worrying examples. One survey, for instance, found that 'ninety percent of college students say Levi's 501 jeans are "in" on campus'. What the commissioners of the survey (Levi Strauss & Co.) failed to point out is that in the survey's very limited set of options, there was only one example of blue jeans – Levi 501s – put against less likely selections like long-sleeved hoodies and unfashionable neon-coloured clothes.

A more dramatic example of the biased survey is one where the numbers are used misleadingly to give a false impression. Imagine this. We take a survey and announce the shock result that 70 per cent of shoppers say that conventional fruit and vegetables taste as good or better than organic fruit and veg. That would be really worrying for organic farmers.

Now let's look at the numbers in this (imaginary) survey, sponsored by the imaginary Down With Organics Foundation. We find that 30 per cent of those polled said they preferred organics, 10 per cent preferred conventional, and 60 per cent said they tasted the same. Three times as many people preferred organic than preferred conventional. Yet it is entirely factual, though hugely misleading, to say that 70 per cent of shoppers preferred conventional or had no preference.

Another easy way to bias polls is to make sure that the people you select are going to be sympathetic to your cause. If you asked a hundred drivers whether a hybrid car helps save the planet, you might get quite a mixed response. Ask a hundred Toyota Prius drivers and you will get a much more positive outcome. This technique is regularly used by pollsters, through accident, laziness, when their cross-section of people to be polled is not selected well enough, or intentionally.

An example of accidental bad sampling is likely with any online poll concerned with the use of technology. The people who fill in online surveys are self-selecting. If they hated technology and never touched it, they wouldn't be filling in the survey. More devious were a number of campaigns by US car companies based on small surveys of customers. In one example, comparing Chryslers to Japanese cars, the individuals surveyed were all selected as people who don't currently own a foreign car – hardly an unbiased sample. In another, customers were asked to choose between a new Dodge saloon and the new version of their own cars. However, they were allowed to drive only the new Dodge – so in practice compared a new Dodge with their old car.

Fair trade is not the same as green

So let's get away from the survey (and treat any survey information we meet in the future with a high degree of suspicion, particularly if the survey was commissioned by people with a vested interest) and make the fair trade picture a little clearer. Note that I am going to use 'fair trade' to indicate the philosophical concept of trading fairly, and 'Fairtrade' to indicate specific schemes that brand their products as being ethically traded.

The first assumption we need to bust is that fair trade can be equated with being green. This is an easy assumption to make because environmental issues and fair trade tend to be pushed by the same people. You'll find both splashed all over a magazine like the *Environmentalist*. Both fair trade and good environmental practice involve taking an atypical approach to business, but one doesn't imply the other.

You can have, for example, Fairtrade products that are damaging to the environment. The idea of Fairtrade is simple. More of the money you spend on the product goes to the (usually) poor original producer. Less of it goes to one or more of the middlemen. So when I buy Fairtrade coffee, more of my cash goes to the coffee-grower. However, this does not in itself stop that coffee-grower from hacking down and burning the rainforest to plant his coffee. In fact, arguably, the poorer producers are more likely to cause environmental damage than those who can afford to do it the right way.

Of course a good Fairtrade organization will try to make sure that their growers aren't environmentally irresponsible – but there is no guarantee that by buying Fairtrade we are helping the environment. Help the poor, yes. A good thing? Yes, if done correctly. But, as always, you need the full picture.

We expect to pay a little more for Fairtrade products. It makes sense. If the middlemen are paying the producers more, either they take less profit, the super-markets make less profit (now that's likely, isn't it?), or the consumer has to pay more. However, economics is not just about relative amounts. It's about absolutes. Not just 'more' but 'how much more?'.

Using Fairtrade to identify big spenders

If you are selling something and making a profit, in principle you're okay. But you would be a poor business person (and an even poorer economist) if you didn't recognize that some people will *voluntarily* pay more than others. And you would be even worse at your job if you didn't try to give those people the chance to pay more. We may not all have the lifestyles of the rich and famous, but if they are happy to pay large amounts for a piece of clothing just for the label, or for a particular champagne for the name, or to eat food like caviar that is expensive because of its rarity value but disgusting tasting, who are we to stop them?

Unfortunately for retailers, it's not always easy to dis-tinguish the people who are willing to pay more. If you run an exclusive restaurant it's no problem, but in an ordinary shop you will get a mix of customers and so need to find, if possible, a way for those who have more flexibility with their spending power to self-select. Supermarkets, as we will see elsewhere, do this by using labels like 'something special' or 'best ever' or 'taste the difference' to imply a touch of class, or by using 'organic' or 'free range' as a way of singling out those who aren't on too tight a budget.

Coffee shops traditionally use luxury to single out the more generous spenders, but a while ago the Costa

Coffee chain found a different way to part people from their cash. Fairtrade. Like most coffee shops, Costa offers Fairtrade as an option, and for a number of years charged 10p a cup extra for choosing it. This seemed reasonable. More was being given to the growers – the coffee supplier CaféDirect paid a premium of around 50p a pound to their producers – so Costa charged the customer more too. Yet the numbers don't add up.

The extra cost to Costa of each cup of coffee was less than 1p a cup. All the rest of that 10p went in Costa's pockets. Of course 10p isn't much on the price of a cup of coffee. Costa could have simply put their prices up by 10p without any contribution to Fairtrade – but they would have put some buyers off. This way they got the best of both worlds (from their point of view). Those who wouldn't pay extra still bought coffee at the profit-making standard rate. Those who would pay more did so, and got Fairtrade.

Costa doesn't do this any more – when word got out, it looked a little unfortunate. Yet we shouldn't really blame Costa, because all they were doing was using the vehicle of Fairtrade to identify those who weren't too fussy about price. All shops do this, whether through premium brands or through 'basics' lines that are visually un-appealing. The look is enough to put off those who can afford a bit more, while they still manage to take the cash of those who wouldn't otherwise spend.

The last resort

It is reasonable to ask why it is necessary for us to give Fairtrade status specifically to (say) coffee-growers or banana-growers. We don't expect to buy Fairtrade petrol, or Fairtrade DVDs to watch while we drink our coffee and eat our bananas (or Fairtrade mugs to drink that coffee out of). Equally, shouldn't we look at Fairtrade milk, for instance, when we know that many dairy farmers in the UK were forced out of business by price pressure from the supermarkets?

In economic terms, Fairtrade is a last resort because it distorts the market. In that sense, Fairtrade is not fair trade. The fairest form of trade is one without the sort of tariffs and barriers that the EU and the US erect to prevent developing countries trading fairly. Yet the Fairtrade mechanism can have some positive effect on products that are easy to get into producing, particularly if they are easier to grow in poor countries than rich (rich countries' produce is more likely to be protected by trade barriers).

Such easy-to-grow crops will inevitably result in poor earnings for the producer. Should there be a shortage of the crop, then the price will start to rise steeply, and other people from poor countries will move in to undercut the pricing. Remember, we're talking about a product that's easy to get into in poor countries. This doesn't imply a cushy life for the growers. Farming coffee or bananas is hard work. But there are plenty of others who want to do that work, and it's relatively easy for them to start doing it – so the price remains low.

Where this is the case, Fairtrade is useful in making the trade more ethical, but we should be clear that it will never pull those farmers out of poverty. We are locking in the status quo. Until the bottom end of the entire world has been lifted financially, there will always be others to step in. Fairtrade will never fix the world but provided it is operated reasonably, it can help some individuals right now, and even economists see that isn't a bad thing.

Practical solution or marketing tool?

However, in February 2008 the Adam Smith Institute came out with a report that suggested that reasonable operation was not the norm. While there needs to be a certain amount of care taken in interpreting any results from this institute – it is a fanatically free-market organization – the report does make several telling points. It suggests that the Fairtrade logo is more a brand-marketing exercise than one to help the world's poorest people.

The arguments are those we've already seen. Fairtrade distorts the market. This is definitely true, but the Adam Smith Institute report argues that the result is harmful. Although the small percentage of growers who are in the Fairtrade scheme will benefit, they argue that all their neighbours who aren't involved will suffer because purchasing will shift to just those few. All the other farmers are isolated from this market.

The report also claims that the 'Costa effect' is much more common than a historical event in a coffee shop. Based on a report in *The Economist*, they suggest that, on average, only 10 per cent of the Fairtrade premium goes to the producers. The rest is soaked up by the supply chain, having identified customers who are happy to pay more, or to switch to a brand because of the Fairtrade logo. In essence, if the Adam Smith Institute is right, Fairtrade is less fair than most of us think.

There are points in this report which have no significant value. The author asks, '[Why] are these farmers poor? Is it really our fault?' This is a very strange question. If you see someone knocked down in a car accident, do you walk past and ignore it because 'it's not our fault'? Fault isn't the issue here. Similarly, the report criticizes the fact that sales of Fairtrade coffee do not make up more than 5 per cent of the market in any consuming country. The implication is that it's insignificant, but that's not what this kind of process is about. The 'oaks from acorns' effect is not inconsiderable.

Other points in the report, however, are more telling. It points out that Fairtrade has a significant presence in schools. The concept of Fairtrade and Fairtrade materials are used in lessons, universally supported and positively promoted. Yet if any other brand – and in the end, that's what Fairtrade is – were promoted in our schools, we would rightly raise serious questions about the ethics of promoting that brand to students.

The report quotes the House of Commons International Development Committee: 'The rise in ethical labels demonstrates that both retailers and consumers are interested in ethical sourcing. It is important that fair trade organisations do not assume they have a monopoly on this . . .' Fairtrade is not the only ethical brand, yet it can be promoted in this way.

It is also clear that the benefits of Fairtrade are often more knee-jerk than carefully measured. It feels good to buy Fairtrade, so it must be doing good. The positive evidence demonstrating the effectiveness of Fairtrade is usually anecdotal, with stories of happy farmers getting a better life. Such stories are valuable marketing tools, but they are not evidence. As *Voodoo Science*, a book on pseudo-science, pithily comments, 'Data is not the plural of anecdote.'

One significant 'could do better' aspect is the distribution of Fairtrade agreements. There are more than twelve times as many Fairtrade producers in Mexico (51) as there are in Ethiopia (4), despite average salaries being twelve times greater in Mexico. If the result of this is trade going to Mexico rather than Ethiopia, then the Fairtrade process is failing.

The mechanisms used by Fairtrade can also have a deleterious effect on those it should be doing the most to help. (I ought to stress again that this is just the specific Fairtrade approach, not trading fairly – a process that is often difficult, both because of trade barriers and because large buying organizations, for example supermarkets, often have a stranglehold on small suppliers.) According to Colleen Berndt, assistant professor of economics at San José State University, California, Fairtrade targets the small landowner but fails to support the poorest part of the agricultural chain, the seasonal workers on that land, whom the Fairtrade mechanism enables the small landowner to employ but not to pay well.

Overall, the Adam Smith report suggests that the biggest philosophical problem with Fairtrade is that it locks individuals into farming in marginal areas – areas where it will never be possible to make a decent living from the land. There is some truth in this argument. It would be better to provide funding directly (so all the aid goes to the recipient, rather than 10 per cent) to help those in such conditions to get out of farming, or to move to a more fertile region. The report is also much more positive about organizations that target developing areas without distorting the market, such as the Rainforest Alliance, and those that give opportunities to buy direct from small producers in developing countries.

The only problem with the Adam Smith argument is that it seems to assume that Fairtrade and helping poor farmers out of their lock-in are incompatible. Yet surely it is better to make some lives marginally better, while helping as many as possible to move out of their situation long term. Fairtrade doesn't have to 'discriminate against success' in the report's terms – as long as it isn't the sole contribution we make to the recipient area.

The low-wage avoidance trap

Many economists would agree that well-run Fairtrade can act as economic first aid if properly applied. Note that this is a quite different approach from avoiding buying from low-wage producers at all – that is a disastrous action. In 2001, New York City Council decided that they would put the world to rights by insisting that council uniforms came from sources that could guarantee what the council considered a decent level of wages and conditions. This sounds like positive action. But think of the actual results. It doesn't mean that workers in a sweatshop are going to get better pay and conditions. It means the jobs will go somewhere that has good pay and conditions, and sweatshop workers will lose their jobs.

Economics is at work in the country where the sweatshop is based. People work in those conditions because the pay is better, or the conditions are better (or both), than in the other options they have. To take away the sweatshop is to reduce their standard of living. Of course, we can encourage (or even insist) that cash-rich multinationals provide a wage that is fair for the location, and that they constantly improve conditions in their factories. But this isn't the same as getting rid of the employment opportunities entirely. That benefits no one.

The difference between such improvement and the New York Council approach is subtle, but devastating. Sweatshops are bad – but they are likely to be better than what was there before (or they wouldn't get employees). They should be part of a chain of continuous improvement in conditions, but they can't be wiped out at a stroke, any more than we can wipe out global warming in an instant. Until we help all developing countries to pull themselves up further, across the board, we can't dispose of badly paid jobs entirely. The big picture is essential.

This isn't just an economic theory; it is a fact that has been played out in practice. After the Second World War, Hong Kong was an extremely underdeveloped colony, lagging behind many African countries in poverty. Protectionists wanted to put up barriers against the flood of 'made in Hong Kong' materials, but so did fair trade enthusiasts, concerned by sweatshop conditions in many Hong Kong companies at the time. Yet by retaining its free trade, Hong Kong has rapidly lifted itself out of that position, in strong contrast to other regions where aid and barriers have been the norm.

Unfair barriers – unfair trade

The tariffs and trade barriers that keep inequalities in place work both ways. Many of the poorest countries have huge restrictions on free trade. At the same time, the US, the G8 nations and the EU also apply trade restrictions to stop themselves being 'flooded with cheap imports'. Often these rich-country barriers seem designed to keep poor countries at the bottom of the economic chain, providing many more restrictions on processed materials than on raw materials. It is notable that whereas 90 per cent of cocoa, the raw material of chocolate, comes from developing countries, only 4 per cent of chocolate is produced there. Barriers to free trade from both sides have hindered poor countries from improving to an extent that Fairtrade can never hope to change.

Even if you wholeheartedly believe in the Fairtrade movement, factoring Fairtrade into your buying decisions, making the best ethical and environmental choice is not necessarily very obvious. A wide range of issues combine to influence what's most effective. A good example is bananas, where the traditional crop is an environmental nightmare. Apart from being shipped halfway around the world, bananas are heavily treated with fungicide, herbicide and insecticide, with several high-risk chemicals in use. The ideal solution might be to go for Fairtrade organic bananas, but failing this, it's a matter of balancing Fairtrade, which will have significant use of pesticide, etc., with organic.

In principle the only truly green choice would seem to be not to buy bananas at all, but leaving aside the health implications – bananas are often among the few fruits that children will happily eat – this is not a straightforward option. Destroy the market for bananas and you will put several states that are absolutely dependent on this crop in danger of collapse, and also risk that whatever eventually replaces banana production will be even worse for the environment. No one said being green was easy.

To ship or not to ship

One final consideration that tends to come into the concept of Fairtrade is shipping. For most of us, the majority of Fairtrade goods are likely to be shipped from somewhere else in the world, apparently contributing unnecessarily to global warming. However, shipping was given a squeaky-clean image in 2008 by Jan Fuglestvedt and colleagues at the Center for International Climate and Environmental Research in Oslo. Their study found that shipping actually reduced global temperatures rather than increased them. It seemed that buying goods from all over the world, provided they were shipped rather than air-freighted, was not only increasing the chances of Fairtrade, but good for the environment too.

This remarkable finding is a result of one of the paradoxes of global warming: some kinds of air pollution have a cooling effect. Small particles in the air – soot, for example – act as a shield, reflecting heat from the sun back into space. These particulates, so common in the dirty output churning from our factories in the mid-twentieth century, have something of a balancing effect on global warming. It is thought that this is why global temperatures fell while CO_2 levels were increasing between the 1940s and 1970s. However, more recent efforts to clean up industry and emissions from private dwellings, though producing cleaner air, have taken away much of this particulate shield.

Shipping is relatively dirty in its output compared with other means of transport, and the Norwegian paper argues that for several centuries to come the particulates will more than balance out the carbon dioxide produced by ships and so make shipping a negative contributor to global warming. Unfortunately, as soon as this research was published, a significant flaw was pointed out.

The study worked by looking at the emissions produced in the year 2000 and seeing how they would affect the world 20, 100 and 500 years later. However, particulates are washed out of the atmosphere in a few days, while CO_2 accumulates unchecked – a distinction that the paper failed to take into account. When the accumulation of carbon dioxide becomes part of the equation, the result cancels out any impact from the particulates: shipping is still a contributor to global warming. Even so, many of us might prefer to support weak economies overseas by buying shipped products, rather than preventing a small contribution to climate change.

Overall, Fairtrade does not seem to be as dangerous as the Adam Smith report portrays it, if only because of its relatively small impact and because it can provide some short-term good – but it is very clearly *not* the long-term solution to the problems of millions of people scratching a near-starvation living from marginal agriculture. Like it or not, all the evidence is that the only way we can do something about this is through free markets, ideally combined with support for those at the bottom of the chain. Like democracy, the free-market approach is riddled with problems – but also like democracy, it appears to be the best of the options we have available to us.

Finding the best option to deal with trade is something that human beings have spent thousands of years evolving. However, our sophisticated modern energy needs, far beyond using simple fires to cook and keep warm, have experienced the sort of exponential growth that makes any planning a nightmare. Dealing with energy is one of the biggest problems facing the logical environmentalist.

7

Perpetual Motion

In July 2007, Irish company Steorn was splashed across the headlines when it promised to demonstrate a machine that would produce 'infinite clean energy'. The Orbo device, boasted the Steorn directors, used magnetic fields to generate power from nowhere. After much hype, the demonstration of the device in London was cancelled due to 'technical difficulties'. As it was supposedly just a matter of the lighting being too hot for the device, causing bearings to fail repeatedly (a pretty unlikely excuse), it would seem reasonable that a new demonstration would be put on a few days later – but the Orbo is yet to be unveiled as this book goes to press.

Steorn's device supposedly uses a combination of fixed magnets and moving magnets that trace strange paths through the magnetic fields to generate power from nowhere. Steorn had joined a long line of failures to build a perpetual-motion machine, one that worked without consuming resources – or, to put it another way, a truly renewable source of energy. In numerical terms, Steorn was trying for a very simple equation: $0 + 0 = 1$. It's odd that the company's founders seemed genuinely bemused when they were mocked.

While scientists realize you can't get usable quantities of energy out of nowhere, science too has had its share of disappointments when it comes to finding an energy source that is cheap, plentiful and safe. When nuclear power was first used to generate electricity it was put about that we would 'enjoy in our homes energy too cheap to meter'. This was a statement made by the then chairman of the US Atomic Energy Commission, Lewis L. Strauss.

Unfortunately, this was one of those hand-waving, future-vision speeches that also included a prediction of an end to famine, much longer lifespans and world peace. No one else working in the nuclear industry or science at the time felt that atomic energy would bring particularly cheap power – it isn't even clear that Strauss was talking about nuclear fission as the source of that power – but the media picked up on this statement and it has become part of the mythology of the nuclear industry that the expectation was that nuclear power stations would make electricity incredibly cheaply.

Since then there has been at least one surge of excitement over a scientific idea that really did seem to have the potential to make cheap safe energy – a concept called cold fusion, of which more later – but the impossibility of perpetual-motion machines like the Orbo depends on what is probably the most fundamental of all physical laws: the conservation of energy. They are called perpetual motion because, if they can get energy from 'nowhere', they can provide the power to keep something moving for ever. However, with one very special exception, it isn't possible to make energy out of nothing. If you use some energy in one place, it has to come from somewhere else.

This means that, technically, renewable energy – that ultimate dream of all of us who would like to see a green planet – is a fantasy. Without a perpetual-motion machine there is no such thing. When we take energy from a source, we take it and it is gone from that source. What we really mean by 'renewable energy' is 'an energy source that's big enough that what we take will make very little impact' – but that's pretty clumsy to say.

Where energy comes from

Realistically, we have five potential sources of energy that have low impact on available resources. The obvious one is the sun, which is a vast nuclear generator, consuming around 5 million tonnes of hydrogen a second, converting the mass of that material into nearly 400 billion billion megawatts of energy output. There's also the Earth, which can, for example, provide heat from geothermal energy, though not all apparent 'Earth' energy is really that – wind power, for instance, comes from the sun's energy. Third, there's local nuclear energy, which is available in two flavours. All existing nuclear power stations use nuclear fission, the energy given out when the nucleus of an atom is split; but there is also the potential to use the same process that powers the sun, generating energy by fusing two smaller elements together to make a heavier one – and that we will examine in more detail later.

Fourth is gravity. The gravitational attraction

between large bodies can provide energy – the obvious application on the Earth is the tidal influence of the moon, giving the potential to generate energy from wave power and tidal motion. Finally, and most mysteriously, there is quantum energy – energy that appears spontaneously in the vacuum of space as a result of the inherent fluctuations that quantum theory predicts. This is unfortunately unlikely to produce a usable source because it appears randomly and in extremely small quantities.

Here comes the sun

Because the sun is so immense it will continue to give out a similar amount of energy – more than we could possibly use – for another few billion years, which makes it the best bet for long-term near-sustainable energy. A tiny fraction of that output goes to warming the Earth and powering our weather systems. There is much more that we could, in principle, use. The maths is stark. Out of the 400 billion billion megawatts produced, a mere 89 billion megawatts are available to us on the Earth – yet that is more than 5,000 times current global energy consumption. So there is plenty of opportunity to get energy from the sun if we could convert solar energy into usable power.

Solar panels have been with us for some time and come in a number of forms. Least glamorous but often most practical in domestic situations (at least until more cost-effective solar cells are developed) is solar heating, where water is warmed by the impact of sunlight as it passes through tubes. But what we tend to think of as solar power comes more often from 'photovoltaic cells' which use the photoelectric effect to generate electricity directly from sunlight. This relies on the fact that in some materials electrical charges are relatively easy for incoming photons – particles of light energy – to smash free, generating an electrical current when light hits the material.

We tend to think of solar electricity generation being intrinsically linked to such photovoltaic cells, but this doesn't have to be the case. At the Solucar Solar Plant near Seville in Spain, there is a scene straight out of a science-fiction movie. A stark white tower stands out 115 metres above the plain, surrounded by a vast array of huge, steerable mirrors (heliostats). On one side these mirrors concentrate sunlight on to a huge solar panel in the tower, but on the other the sunlight is directed on to water pipes. The heat generated boils the water to drive a turbine. (More recent designs heat a molten mixture of nitrate salts, which can achieve temperatures as high as 600°C to make more of the heating capacity.)

One of the benefits of this approach is that the energy does not have to be used immediately, as with photovoltaic cells. The heat can be stored and used to top up the supply when sunlight is not so widely available. A related approach is to use solar troughs – curved mirrors that focus sunlight on to pipes containing fluids and again generate steam to produce electricity.

Current solar technology is both expensive and inefficient, but things won't stay that way. This is an area where economic levers can be used to change attitudes. It's interesting that the country that is home to around half the solar/electric panels in the world is Germany. Clearly this is not because it has lots of deserts in which to site them, or unusually cloud-free skies. Germany has so many panels because the German authorities make it financially acceptable to overcome the high barrier to buying into solar electricity. The government guarantees that the grid will buy any excess power from solar sources at higher than market price.

The huge demand caused by such financial incentives has led not only to a rapid take-up of solar technology, but also to an industry to support it, with some of the biggest manufacturers based in Germany (and the bigger that industry, the cheaper the solar cells can be made, feeding back into the cost equation).

As the price of generating energy with fossil fuel rises, the cost of solar generation falls and the technology improves, there will certainly be an ever-increasing use of solar technology. Already new photovoltaic cells with significantly improved efficiency are being developed. The first cells had an efficiency of around 6 per cent: out of 100 joules of energy hitting the photocell, just 6 were converted to electricity. Current cells work at around 20 per cent efficiency, but designs are in the labs and will soon be commercially available that will provide 40–50 per cent efficiency, and it has been predicted that this could be pushed above 70 per cent.

This is enough to change photovoltaics from a technology worth supporting, after the German model, to one that can stand on its own to make electricity at a viable price, especially as the cost of cells is plummeting. Arguably, reduction in production costs is even more important than improvement in efficiency. As Allen Heeger of the University of California at Santa Barbara, who is working on plastic-film-based cells, has commented: 'The critical comparison is dollars per watt.

Even if our efficiency is lower than silicon, the cost per watt could still be better because this is such a low-cost manufacturing process.' If solar cells could be produced so cheaply that they could practically be given away, they could become a very significant contributor to our power needs.

Power from space

The biggest problem with Earth-bound solar power sources is that they take up a large amount of land or sea – not such a problem in a desert, but certainly an issue in a land-hungry country like the UK. The alternative is to bite off a little of that solar energy that is wasted (as far as the Earth is concerned) – the vast bulk of the sun's output that heads off into space.

In principle, a solar power station in space is very attractive. Before sunlight reaches us on the Earth it has to pass through kilometres of atmosphere, where much of the energy is absorbed and more is scattered. Clouds can make a huge difference to the levels of solar power available. By comparison, in space there is very little to obscure the solar output and a much higher percentage of the sun's power is available for harvesting. A solar panel in the sky can generate twenty times as much electricity as one of the same size on the ground. However, space also has its problems, both financially and practically.

The financial problems centre around the cost of building huge solar panels, getting them into space and assembling them there. While a major space energy programme would require production volumes that should bring down the cost of solar panels, manufacturing cost still remains a significant factor, while getting the components of a huge solar energy collector into space – some plans expect these to be between 5 and 50 square kilometres across – remains a huge and expensive challenge. Then there's the minor matter of getting gigawatts of power back to the Earth, generally assumed to work by aiming a huge laser, or the microwave equivalent, at an Earth station.

The idea of space power stations has been around since the 1960s, when the futuristic dreams of movies like *2001: A Space Odyssey* seemed on the horizon, but up to now the economics has made no sense. However, as energy prices rocket and fuel passes peak availability, cost is liable to be less of an issue, with necessity driving any such project.

NASA has repeatedly shelved space energy projects, although the US military is investigating using space power stations to beam power to battlefields. Japan's equivalent, JAXA, however, is pursuing these ideas with more enthusiasm, in part reflecting Japan's dire lack of natural resources. Japanese plans are well advanced for a system that would produce around 1 gigawatt of power with a build cost of under $1 billion, producing electricity that would be no more than 50 per cent higher in cost than today's coal-fired sources and cheaper than current nuclear power.

There are still issues with space-based solar generation, but as solar panels become more efficient and the cost of launching materials into space drops – both trends that seem set to continue for some while – interest in this possibility will remain. Perhaps the biggest concern is how safe the beam bringing the power to the Earth can be made. What would happen if it drifted off target (or worse, James Bond-style, it was taken over by terrorists), or if a plane flew through the beam? It isn't clear.

Hugging the planet

A more earthbound approach to generating clean power is geothermal energy. This makes use of the natural gradient in temperature between the surface of the Earth and the layers below. Any temperature difference can be used to extract energy and provide power. This is most practical where there is a significant temperature rise over a relatively small distance, so geothermal sources tend to be concentrated in countries like Iceland with high-temperature systems near the surface. The geothermal approach has the advantage over sources like wind or solar power of lacking time variation – it can provide power constantly at any time of day, or in any weather condition.

Fission for solutions

At the time of writing, nuclear energy is back in favour after many years of being considered politically unacceptable, re-badged as a green energy source. This is a move that has torn the green movement in half. Some environmental heroes, like Gaia theory originator James Lovelock, have said that atomic power is a necessary evil, as it provides low carbon emission energy and will see us through until we have better renewable sources. Others have such an automatic negative reaction to nuclear power that they won't even consider it.

It is certainly true that there are big issues with

nuclear fission, the process behind all existing nuclear reactors. In such a reactor an unstable element, such as uranium 235, decays, releasing some energy and neutrons. These neutrons hit other nuclei, causing them to decay, producing a chain reaction that has to be moderated with neutron absorbers to avoid it going out of control. Part of the concern about nuclear power lies in accidents, like the near miss at Three Mile Island and the disaster at Chernobyl. But even if nuclear reactors are run perfectly and without incident – and modern reactors are much safer than the old ones – there is still the issue of what to do with the spent nuclear fuels, which remain dangerously radioactive for thousands of years.

All the evidence is that the uranium needed to fuel nuclear power stations will be in relatively short supply by the end of the century, so nuclear fission isn't a long-term solution. Nor is it a magic bullet. It can't provide all our energy, requires a lead time of about twelve years to get up and running, and will be expensive – but these are all comparatives. At the moment wind, waves and solar are equally unable to provide all our energy and are also expensive. We may need nuclear fission as a stepping stone to future, better power sources.

Fusion confusion

With all the concerns that arise from the waste generated by nuclear fission, the risk of accidents like Chernobyl, the potential for terrorist threat and the doubts about the future availability of fuel, it might seem that nuclear energy is not a realistic long-term prospect. In fact, however, it has one of the best potentials for generating safe, clean energy – provided we look beyond fission to fusion.

This is the mechanism that powers the sun. When smaller atoms are forced together to make bigger ones, energy is given off. The sun generates energy by converting hydrogen to helium. It's a powerful reaction, and it's a clean one. Yet it is difficult to get it to work. In order to initiate fusion, the positively charged nuclei of atoms have to be pushed into extremely close proximity. Being positively charged, they repel each other, just like the same poles of two extremely powerful magnets. Even the temperature and pressure found in the sun aren't sufficient to get them close enough. It's only possible at all because of one of the quirky effects of quantum physics called tunnelling. Because of tunnelling, the particles can jump straight through the barrier of the repulsion, rather like tunnelling through a wall.

In practice, a fusion reactor has to get the raw materials up to around 100 million°C – and that's not easily done. Fusion reactors use 'tokamaks', a term from the Russian, which consist of metal chambers shaped like a ring doughnut in which powerful magnetic fields can be used to confine and control the high-temperature ingredients. The magnetic 'bottle' prevents the intensely hot materials from touching anything else.

Fusion has a lot going for it. It's a tested source (in the sense that the sun gives a pretty good large-scale demonstration that it works), it uses readily available fuel, and it produces little in the way of waste. Admittedly, the deuterium needed to fuel it is limited in availability, but there is enough to see us through several thousand years of use. Similarly, the reactor itself will become radioactive over time, but will not involve anything like the problems associated with decommissioning a fission reactor. It probably is, in principle, one of the most likely ways that we can cope with the energy crisis. Yet despite being worked on since the 1950s, there is not a single working fusion-based power station.

In part this is because of lack of funding. Fusion has never been given the priority it deserves. It is notable that the US, despite having more money to spend than most, has been a small player in the development of practical fusion reactors. It's hard not to see pressure from big oil at work here. But there are also problems from sheer technical difficulty. To get fusion to work requires a small-scale re-creation of the conditions in the sun. Not only does this demand high temperature and pressure, it means that the reacting material has to be kept away from contact with anything physical. Managing the containment of fusion is painfully tricky. It's not a matter of terrible meltdown, like a fission reactor, but simply that the reaction would stop and destroy its containment vessel if there were any contact.

The first working device was the Joint European Torus (JET) at Culham in Oxfordshire. Work commenced on it in 1978, and experiments continue to this day. But JET has always taken more power to run – to keep the fusion process confined and to build the energy of the plasma – than it generates. It has never been self-sustaining. The next generation device, which is expected to get to that self-sustaining state, is ITER, to be based in France and expected to be operational by 2016. (At the time of writing, the US has just, with supreme lack of foresight, cut $160 million from its contribution to ITER, which may well result in the completion date being pushed back.)

Assuming ITER is a success, plans are to have a commercial model available by 2050, though cynics point out that ever since the 1950s it has been said that a commercial fusion reactor was about thirty years away. Other technology is being trailled to produce fusion using lasers to heat the fusing materials, but, again, this is years from being a practical power source.

There is a lot of hope, but the timescales here are such that nuclear fusion could not take up a sizeable part of our power needs until somewhere between 2070 and 2100 – still intensely valuable, but too late to help with our immediate need to cope with climate change and the increasing doubts about the future availability of oil.

Fusion in a test tube

Fusion, then, has great potential, but also great practical difficulties to be overcome. It would be wonderful if it were possible to create fusion without all the unpleasant characteristics of a star – to do it cold. And that is just what was claimed by Martin Fleischmann from the University of Southampton and Stanley Pons from the University of Utah back in 1989. Their experiment involved electrolysis, the simple process where an electrical current is sent through a liquid from one electrode to another. The liquid was 'heavy water' – water which, instead of hydrogen, contains the isotope deuterium, which has a neutron and a proton in the atom's nucleus where ordinary hydrogen has a lone proton.

When electricity is passed through the heavy water, it is broken down (just as ordinary water is in a school demonstration of electrolysis). The negatively charged oxygen ions are attracted to the positive electrode, made of platinum in this experiment, and the positively charged deuterium ions to the negative electrode, made of the rare metal palladium. Palladium is known to store up hydrogen on its surface. What the scientists claimed was that the deuterium became so tightly crammed together that fusion took place at room temperature. They measured an increase in temperature that corresponded to more heat energy being given out than electrical energy was put in.

If this were true, it would be the answer to all our energy problems. No need for vast containment vessels and star-like temperatures – this reaction takes place in a desktop test tube. And it has all the dream-like positives of fusion. The end products would be harmless oxygen and helium. However, right from the start there was controversy. The normal approach to a discovery like this would be to write it up in a peer-reviewed journal and reproduce it in various other laboratories. Instead, Fleischmann and Pons called a press conference and told the world.

This was foolish, but understandable: they did believe they had just solved the world's energy problems. If their experiment were reproducible on a large enough scale, they really could envisage a future of clean energy that was too cheap to meter. But their action immediately brought up the guards of the scientific community. Although at least one other scientist, Steven Jones of Brigham Young University, did measure a tiny effect (much, much less than that claimed by Fleischmann and Pons), others could find nothing. And because of the way the original discovery was announced, the negative results have been produced with something amounting to glee.

For a good number of years the mere mention of cold fusion brought out the same sort of reaction in the scientific community as homeopathy – a combination of amusement and horror that anyone could take it seriously. It was a very brave researcher who dared dip a toe in the cold fusion (heavy) water, but in 2002 a new variant emerged called bubble fusion. This involved a different fluid, acetone – a simple, pungent organic chemical that is best known as the solvent in nail varnish remover. Once again, the hydrogen in the chemical was replaced with deuterium. When sound was sent through the fluid, tiny bubbles were caused to expand and then collapse by the energy of the sound waves. Rusi Taleyarkhan's team at Oak Ridge National Laboratory in Tennessee discovered that the implosion of the bubbles was so powerful that it appeared to be briefly triggering fusion, generating heat.

This time the research was published in one of the world's top journals, *Science*. But again there was difficulty in repeating the results, with a suggestion that the heat was caused by a simple chemical reaction in the bubbles, and in this case it was particularly difficult to see how the supposed cold fusion could be scaled up to be useful. However, bubble fusion has not gone away. When the bubbles collapse, a flash of light is emitted – so-called sonoluminescence – and this may require significant local temperatures. Since the initial experiment there has been a steady stream of results that make it possible that Taleyarkhan was right – but there have also been claims of misconduct by the team. Despite these being dismissed by an investigation, they have left the whole area of bubble fusion under a cloud.

Keeping the idea alive, another claim for desktop fusion was made in 2007 by Pamela Mosier-Boss and Stanislaw Szpak at the US Navy's Space and Naval Warfare Systems Center in San Diego. Mosier-Boss and Szpak were working with a similar set-up to the original electrolytic approach, but rather than looking for heat or using external means to look for nuclear reactions, they used a simple particle detector based on a sheet of polymer inside the chamber that picks up the tracks of particles made in nuclear reactions.

It is a safe bet that desktop fusion (cold fusion would be a misnomer for bubble fusion: although it takes place in a liquid at room temperature, there is still thought to be a very high temperature within the tiny bubbles) will not be replacing power stations any time soon. Yet it can't be entirely ruled out for the future. If ever made to work reliably and scaled up to production levels, it is the nearest thing we have to a truly low impact, extremely cheap and clean means of producing energy.

For the moment, though, fusion is not a practical source of energy (at least on this planet), so we are left with the more indirect ways of tapping into solar-system energy sources, such as wind and waves.

Feel the wind in your hair

Wind power is nothing new. We have used wind to power mills and water pumps for hundreds of years, but modern wind turbines are different in scale and much more energy efficient than a traditional windmill. The UK has plenty of wind. In principle, between five and eight times our total current electricity demand could be provided by wind sources if offshore and land-based wind farms were placed everywhere they could be. However, this is an immense investment, there are practical difficulties offshore, and it carries major environmental negatives. More realistically, we could see around 10 per cent of our electricity coming from wind by 2020 and as much as 20 per cent by 2050 if nothing significant changes.

Wind farms should be an obvious way forward, but they frequently come up against 'not in my backyard' opposition. It is worth seeing just what problems do emerge and whether they are real blockages to this technology making a significant difference to the way we generate energy.

The primary objection to wind farms is often visual. The turbines are large – between 15 and 80 metres high – and don't exactly blend in with the landscape. All too often, the windiest locations are also ones of significant natural beauty. It is possible to site them offshore where they present less of a visual obstacle, though this is considerably more expensive and difficult both in terms of engineering and ensuring that the turbines are not sited too near shipping lanes. And this may not be necessary: it's quite possible that the 'not in my backyard' brigade are more vocal than realistic. We have a wind farm in sight of our house – and though it is fairly obvious, it isn't a scar on the landscape but in fact looks rather graceful.

In a range of surveys, those who live near wind turbines are more enthusiastic about them than those who don't live in sight of one – suggesting that the fear of them is significantly greater than the reality. (It may also reflect a difference in attitude between rural dwellers, who are used to the fact that the countryside is a workplace, and town dwellers who have an idea of an imaginary rural idyll that could be ruined.) No one is saying that every natural view should be littered with turbines, but we could happily place wind farms in many, many locations without spoiling a view that doesn't already have pylons or worse in sight.

Another environmental issue often raised is noise. Although wind turbines look from a distance to be lazily and silently floating around, close up they do make an appreciable sound. In reality, though, the noise issue is more relevant to small personal wind generators attached to houses. Large-scale wind turbines are high above the ground and, except for the occasional 'token' placement like the turbine near junction 11 on the M4 motorway, are not usually sited close to accommodation. It is perfectly possible to hold a conversation standing at the base of a turbine without raising voices. The amount of noise from wind farms is comparable with an average rural background noise level at night – mostly road noise – present, but hardly a major issue.

Perhaps the only other major issue is impact on wildlife. There is no evidence of disturbance to land animals, but a relatively small number of birds will die when a wind turbine is installed, as they can fly into the rotors and be killed. Consideration is given to specialist bird areas and migration routes when a planning appli- cation for a turbine is put in place, but in practice the fears seem overstated. The rotors of a big turbine move slowly and tend to push birds out of the way rather than hit them. In a 2001 study in the USA, the average kill of a wind turbine was 2.19 birds per year, compared with millions of birds wiped out by cars and between 100 million and a billion killed by collision with windows. In the UK alone, cats kill over 50 million birds a year. If people are really worried about bird survival, they should perhaps do something about reducing the cat population before they panic about wind turbines.

It is sometimes pointed out that wind power is inevitably flawed because it isn't windy all the time. Although this problem is evened out to a degree when turbines are scattered around the country, it does mean that a reliable system would always need some alternatives (like waves and tides, discussed below), and possibly some short-term energy-storage facilities like the Dinorwig station in Wales, which pumps water from a low reservoir to a high one when power is plentiful, then lets the water flow back to run generators when extra supply is needed. However, the objections to wind power are largely superficial and it is arguable that we should be going far beyond current targets to enable a sizeable proportion of energy to be generated in this clean, green fashion.

Water, water everywhere

The Dinorwig station is a special case of hydroelectric power – electricity generated by water flowing through turbines. Hydroelectricity was once considered a superb option, with huge dams being built around the world to collect enough water to run the turbines, but all the evidence is that these large-scale hydro plants result in a huge amount of environmental damage, are susceptible to terrorist attack and, surprisingly, can also generate a significant quantity of greenhouse gases in warm climates from algae in their reservoirs. A dam failure, such as the one at Banqiao in southern China that collapsed in 1975, can be just as devastating as a nuclear accident. This single flood caused over 170,000 deaths.

However, traditional hydro power is not the only way to harness water as a clean source: waves and tides are also a potential source of energy. According to the government's independent watchdog, the Sustainable Development Commission, the UK could generate at least 10 per cent of its energy needs from tides alone, while wave power could contribute at least another 10 per cent. (In principle, all the UK's power needs could come from wave and tide, but this would involve an impractically large amount of development.) Five per cent of our needs could come from a single project – the much discussed and often put-off idea of a barrage across the Severn estuary, which would use the large tidal surges to generate power.

As is often the case with a 'renewable' source, there are green arguments both in favour of and against a Severn barrage. Although it will produce a sizeable amount of clean energy, it will have an impact on the ecology of the estuary, with the loss of a significant amount of marine habitat. Having said that, all the evidence from existing barrages in other countries is that there is less impact on marine life than was expected – and in the end it's a matter of weighing up costs and benefits. Tide and wave power are unlikely to provide more than a fraction of our energy needs but, combined with the other options described above, can have a significant and lasting impact on making our energy cleaner.

A stern reminder

Whichever alternative sources are used in the future requires considerable investment now. The Stern Review on the economics of climate change, produced for the UK government by Sir Nicholas Stern, former chief economist of the World Bank, urges a doubling of expenditure on research and development in low-carbon technologies, commenting:

> The development and deployment of a wide range of low-carbon technologies is essential in achieving the deep cuts in emissions that are needed. The private sector plays the major role in R&D and technology diffusion, but closer collaboration between government and industry will further stimulate the development of a broad portfolio of low-carbon technologies and reduce costs.

At the moment there is much more talk than serious money being put forward. It is only when we see hugely expanded investment in fusion technology, a real push for wind energy (including, perhaps, the support of 'free' set-up of micro-generation, as suggested on page 92) and a real financial drive to change the way we deal with energy across the board, that there will be a big enough change to make a difference. As I write, the UK government is toying with investing a lot more in traditional nuclear power. Some such investment may be necessary, but it has to be seen as a short-term measure – and if the choice is available to invest more in other low-carbon options and less in nuclear fission, the government would be shockingly shortsighted to go down that route alone.

Arguably the best way to reduce the impact of energy generation is to avoid using the energy in the first place. An obvious example is re-using products, rather than making new ones, taking the manufacturing consumption of energy and materials out of the loop – or if that's not possible, at least recycling. Our rubbish has a part to play in the overall game of saving the planet.

8

Where There's Muck, There's Brass

Rubbish is a big problem – and a major political issue, as the response to moving from weekly to fortnightly rubbish collection in the UK, supposedly to encourage recycling, has shown. In July 2007, the Communities and Local Government Select Committee branded this move 'an unworkable mess likely to increase fly-tipping, confuse the public and provoke protest riots'. The growing antagonism reflects a total lack of ecological awareness in those trying to solve the problem.

Again and again with rubbish collections, councils fail to appreciate that the carrot is a better incentive than the stick. In essence, the move away from rubbish being bagged in one lump to being sorted by the consumer means that the consumer has become an unpaid worker for the council. In such circumstances, the council should do everything it can to make consumers feel happy with their lot – in the end, the result of heavy-handed behaviour towards involuntary labour can be revolt. Yet councils persist in treating their customers (who are also by implication their bosses) badly.

A simple example makes this clear. Swindon Council

is one of the many that switched in 2007 to collections on alternate weeks, with detailed recycling requirements imposed on their customers. The council stressed that rubbish for landfill would be collected only if placed in a wheelie bin with the lid closed.

At some point, one of the residents in a Swindon street placed a bin bag alongside someone else's wheelie bin. The council's response was fierce. They wrote to everyone in the street saying that 'It has been noted that residents have been placing sacks of waste outside neighbouring properties. **To store waste in such a manner is to expose it unnecessarily to vandalism and animal attacks.**' That's their bold text. This may be true, but this was how the council had been happy for rubbish to be left out week after week for many years beforehand – they didn't seem to think then that it was a problem. The letter continued:

A record has been made of this incident and should it occur again, it is the Council's intention to take further action. In the first instance, a Fixed Penalty Notice (FPN) For [sic] littering, by virtue of section 88, Environmental Protection Act 1990, would seem to be the most appropriate way forward. This will result in a £50 Penalty for the occupier of the household that has caused the waste to be presented in a manner likely to cause litter.

This caused extremely bad feeling in the street concerned. Not only was the council addressing its customers like a schoolteacher with a naughty class, but there is also a logical inconsistency in the threat. If they knew who did it, then they should have addressed the letter to that person, not to everyone in the street. If they didn't know who did it, how could they serve that person with a penalty? All in all, the response was one that seemed designed to irritate rather than to encourage users of council services to recycle.

We want to know why

This deficiency is accepted by some council staff. Richard Fisher, Wastes Data and Resources Manager at Swindon Borough Council, commented that they currently provided nothing in the spectrum between education and enforcement. The council has told council-tax payers what it expects and, if the result is not the intended one, the reaction is to come in with a big stick. What's missing, Fisher observed, is the 'why'.

This is an encouraging recognition from someone in his position. Councils are expecting council-tax payers to separate waste for them without explaining why various restrictions are put in place. A lot more effort needs to be put into getting the message across. To date, much too much communication has been on why it's important to increase recycling and decrease landfill, and hardly any on why particular solutions (for example, fortnightly collections, or recycling only plastic bottles but not other forms of plastic) have been adopted. If councils really want waste management to work, they have a long way to go.

One common problem when explaining environmental issues is a tendency to oversimplify, resulting in anything between mild misinformation and downright lies. There has been plenty of TV advertising telling us, for example, how long you can power electrical goods on the energy saved by recycling just one glass bottle. (Apparently we can run a TV for twenty minutes, or a low-energy light bulb for nearly two hours.) This would be true if the glass you shove in the recycling bin were actually converted into more glass, preventing new glass from being manufactured. In practice, however, it is much more likely to be ground up and used in the construction industry.

Of course there is still an energy-saving, and there's the environmental benefit of not having to dig big holes in the ground to produce the materials (though, as Swindon Council notes, the big holes used in digging out raw materials do make good landfill sites). Even so, the simplistic picture of the glass being re-used in a way that saves electricity is little short of a lie.

It is interesting to set the attitude of most UK councils to waste collection alongside what has been happening in one London borough. As most councils move to fortnightly collections, in 2008 Kensington and Chelsea took the opportunity to *increase* collections from twice to three times weekly. Demonstrating once again that collection rates are all about finances and nothing to do with green policies, Kensington and Chelsea's contractors, SITA, were able to move to more frequent collections without any increase in staffing by replacing hand-drawn rosters with computer-generated alternatives that made use of slack time – a move many organizations took in the 1980s (reflecting, perhaps, the historically low-tech attitude to waste collection).

For most councils, though, the approach taken by Kensington and Chelsea is neither practical nor acceptable. When presented with the facts (and this is where councils so desperately need to improve communication, because we aren't normally presented with these facts), it is easy to be sympathetic to the average council's plight. Let's go back to Swindon as a typical borough.

On the one hand they are under pressure to send less to landfill and to recycle more – but they are not provided with easy mechanisms to make that recycling happen. They can collect material to recycle – but what can they then do with it? The council doesn't have the financial resources to pay for materials to be recycled. If recycling is to be sustainable, it also has to be economically viable. Yet that isn't as easy as it sounds. Swindon, like many other towns in the UK, does not have a recycling plant on its doorstep.

Recycling paths

At the time of writing, Swindon sends its plastic bottles to be recycled in Manchester, over 150 miles away. Paper goes to London, a mere 80 miles, while glass goes to Cheshire, a similar distance to Manchester. This is economically viable, but isn't environmentally desirable. Swindon also finds itself caught in a trap between reality and legislation designed for other parts of the country, particularly London. In Swindon, there is huge landfill capacity because of the amount of gravel extraction in the area, making landfill still a sensible economical approach. Of course there are environmental implications, but the council is being forced to move at a pace that suits the Westminster legislators, not the locality.

A case of considerable local concern is the very selective approach the council takes to recycling plastics. Only plastic bottles (without tops) are allowed. This feels very arbitrary and results in disaffection from the council-tax payers. What they have not been told is that plastic is not a great material to recycle. First, it's bulky. A paper bank that will collect over 8 tonnes of paper for recycling will hold only half a tonne of plastic. This is not good for the council, as their targets are based on tonnes recycled, so plastic is bad for those targets. Second, it's not so easy to find a recycling plant to take any old plastic. By specifying bottles, Swindon has a better chance of finding a recycler that will accept them.

This does make for a deal of arbitrariness and confusion. Swindon's Richard Fisher admits that his girlfriend regularly asks him whether it's okay or not to recycle a borderline container. Most of us just have to throw and hope. In practice, the recyclers are less fussy than the council has suggested. They will, for example, take some bottles with tops, even though the council has specified they must be removed. But if everyone left them on, there would be problems.

Fisher believes that for Swindon the biggest benefit of accepting plastic bottles is not so much the recycling itself, but the positive message it gives to householders. Normally plastics in landfills are considered terrible, as they take hundreds of years to break down. But when you've plenty of landfill space, as Swindon has, it's arguable that low emissions from plastic are better for the environment than the higher volumes of carbon, particularly methane, generated by sending bio-degradable materials like food waste to landfill.

Swindon would prefer to recycle food waste, but it simply isn't practical at the moment. The only good road access from the town is east–west or north, while the only realistic place to ship food waste for recycling is

Bournemouth to the south. Like all the recycling arguments, we shouldn't be entirely sympathetic to the
council's 'there's nothing we can do' stance. If councils
worked together more – they rarely do at the moment –
they could ensure that it was possible to recycle much
closer to home than is currently the case. On the other
hand, they do have a real case that recycling isn't
possible without the industry and infrastructure to
support it.

In practice, the most important contribution from
recycling plastic in Swindon is the favourable message it
generates. By recycling bottles, Swindon reckons that
they get between 10 and 15 per cent more participation
from householders in its other recycling initiatives – and
this is the main impetus for them to do it.

Once a fortnight

Council workers involved in designing rubbish collection
have to be something of the psychologist and the
sociologist, as well as an expert on waste. Perhaps
the best example here is the furore over fortnightly
collections. There has been talk of rodent infestations
and health issues. These are denied by the councils, who
back up their argument with a 2007 study by Cranfield
University and Enviros Consulting which showed that
there is 'no evidence that fortnightly collections of refuse
will cause any significant health impacts for residents or
that any health impacts are likely to be significantly
greater than those associated with weekly collections'.

Clearly there is an economic benefit for the council
from collecting only once a fortnight, and Fisher
admitted this was a significant factor. In moving from

traditional weekly black-bag collections to a combination of fortnightly wheelie bins and recycling collections split between weekly and fortnightly depending on the materials, Swindon has moved from four collections a month to ten. To sustain weekly wheelie-bin collections as well, he argues, would put too much burden on the system. However, according to Fisher, there is a bigger psychological reason. He believes that having fortnightly wheelie-bin collections results in between 15 and 30 per cent more recycling than having weekly wheelie-bin collections with bins half the size. That looming two weeks helps change our attitude to waste – and that, he asserts, is what the whole process is really about.

Perhaps the most telling point that Fisher makes is that local authorities are dabbling in the resource and material supply markets. They aren't experts in selling waste to be recycled and, not surprisingly, are yet to become particularly good at it. They are at a big disadvantage compared with large supermarkets, which can economically recycle borderline items like carrier bags because they have return truck movements. Their trucks take goods out to the supermarket. On the way back they are empty and can be used to move materials for recycling at no charge. Councils don't have this luxury and have to look for other ways to be equally smart in the way resources are used.

Councils are also tied into surprisingly long-term contracts, set up when concerns for the environment were not an important factor. Swindon's twenty-year contract with their landfill contractors doesn't expire until 2016. It's arguable that central government, in imposing particular requirements on councils, should have provided mechanisms to break out of these contracts, some of which have bizarre consequences. Many, for example, penalize councils for *not* sending material to landfill: the councils have to pay for landfill whether they use it or not.

Cash and trash

Perhaps the most controversial suggestion is that councils should charge to take rubbish away. There is nothing wrong with using economic incentives – either the stick or the carrot – to change behaviour, provided it is done in an equitable way that doesn't distort the market. As long as there is no net change in the charges we pay for waste disposal it seems perfectly reasonable to do it by value, both in terms of the cost of waste disposal and the cash raised from recycling.

It has been suggested that rewarding recycling can distort the market, as it encourages us actively to collect materials to recycle – but other than exceptional circumstances, such as failing to stop junk mail (see below) in order to be rewarded for recycling it, this is a fallacy. We pay for practically everything else in a metered way. In fact, it's already true of rubbish to an extent – you can already pay for a skip to go to landfill – and it would make a lot of sense, if it could be done without too much cost, if both our rubbish and our recycling were metered.

The carrot has more benefit in some cases than others. Recycling aluminium cans is one of the more efficient recycling processes, and financially effective too. Recycling companies pay over a penny per can – so there is an opportunity to offer incentives. Imagine a can bank or a roadside collection that paid you for providing cans.

The UK is well behind much of Europe in can recycling. A financial incentive would not only make us more likely to separate cans from landfill, it would encourage the more economically savvy to tidy up their environment. I can remember when young actively looking out for discarded glass bottles because you got a deposit on them from the shop. The same could happen with cans if we gave young collectors a financial reward, rather than relying on the feeling of being a do-gooder.

However, if we spend all our time looking at collection and management, we are ignoring one of the biggest areas of opportunity in dealing with waste. That is not having the item in the first place. If you've got rubbish, then re-use is best, or failing that recycling – but better still is never to have the rubbish so that nothing has to be manufactured, with all the negative impact that is likely to have on the environment. This might seem like a charter for anti-capitalism. Time to join the hair-shirt brigade and stop being a consumer. Yet it doesn't have to be.

Only refuse

I'm inspired by our council-provided wheelie bins, which are labelled 'Refuse Only'. To succeed here, it's more a matter of turning those words around and saying 'Only Refuse'. Only refuse, and you shall be saved – or at least, you can do your best to save the planet. The point is that a fair amount of our consumption has little worth. If we can refuse this consumption – just say no to consuming things we didn't want in the first place – we can have a positive impact without missing out on anything desirable. This may not please those who want us to suffer for our cause, but that isn't the point of this book.

So what do we consume without desiring to do so? Let's make a start with bills. It may seem obvious that we don't want to consume bills, but their very physical existence puts stress on the planet. Each time a bill is produced, paper and ink are wasted, not to mention the fuel burned in carting those tonnes of paper around the country. Each bill that drops through your letterbox has its own carbon footprint.

A simple step many can take is in moving to electronic invoices. Although using a computer has its own complex footprint, the incremental difference in receiving an e-bill if you are already using the computer is almost negligible. Then there are bills that just shouldn't exist. I am the proud possessor of a bill from the mobile phone company Orange for 20p. It simply beggars belief that they bothered to send the bill out in the first place. The postage alone cost them more than 20p, and that's without the two sheets of paper, colour printing, envelope and production costs. There are at least three ways that Orange could have saved the money *and* saved the impact on the planet.

They could simply not send out the bill until the amount reached a sensible value – say £1 or £5. This is slightly unnerving for the consumer, as it's not obvious when the bill will come, but it saves Orange money and footprint. Better still, from the consumer's viewpoint, they could write off any bills under £1. This still saves Orange money (if not quite as much) and footprint, and the consumer benefits too. Even better than this option, Orange could offer a deal where clients who move to online billing could have any monthly bills under £1 written off. This way, Orange gets the extra benefit of not having to send out a paper bill even if my usage does go over £1 a month, yet the customer still gets the same positive benefits too.

Junk the junk mail

Of course, bills aren't the only unwanted bits of paper that arrive on the doormat. There's junk mail too – tonnes and tonnes of it every day being transported around the country, adding to the carbon dioxide churned out by rubbish miles. Short of making junk mail illegal (not a bad idea), most countries have schemes that allow the consumer to mitigate the impact. In the UK there are two – the Mailing Preference Scheme, which allows you to opt out of receiving unsolicited *addressed* mail, and the Post Office's opt-out scheme, which stops the unaddressed junk the postie kindly brings (though if you attempt to use it you get dire warnings that you may miss out on important mailings). If everyone subscribed to these there would be an immediate reduction in CO_2 emissions – and landfill as well, as not all parts of mailings are recyclable.

Companies can do plenty more to reduce our unwanted purchases, even with as indirect a 'purchase' as their signage. Businesses illuminate their signs and buildings for customers' benefit. But what about all the times these illuminations aren't needed? Encourage companies (especially if you work there) to switch them off. Well-known examples are offices that leave their lights and computers on all night, but some examples are even more bizarrely blatant. The Burger King fast-food restaurant in the centre of Swindon closed down in early 2007. As of March 2008, its sign is still illuminated all day and all night.

Stop giving me presents

Other 'purchases' we unwillingly make include packaging and free gifts. There has been a lot said about reducing packaging, and it is important to recognize that there are situations where packaging is there for a good reason, such as food safety, but in many cases it is more for appearance – for example, those impossible-to-open plastic bubbles you buy small electronic items in, where a simple, recyclable cardboard box would do. I'd say about half our household's landfill is now plastic packaging that our local council can't recycle.

Then there are free gifts. As a purchaser of occasional newspapers, rather than a dedicated reader of one title, I have in the past found myself choosing between serious newspapers on the basis of the CD or DVD it came with. Children often choose magazines solely on the gifts attached. And then there are all those little incentives we get in the supermarket – buy two ready meals and get a free toilet brush, or whatever the option may be. Getting something free is a huge incentive, I don't deny it, but it's one that has to be very carefully managed if it isn't just throwing unnecessary and unwanted consumption of energy and production of emissions into the world.

I am now the proud possessor of a Marks and Spencer 'Gastropub' oven glove. I already had an oven glove. I didn't need another one. Yet it is very hard to turn down a free gift when it is offered. Such an incentive would be more acceptable, rather like buying presents for elderly relatives, if all free gifts were consumable. If you want to put a free gift with dishwasher tablets, make it more dishwasher tablets; if it's to go with food, some associated dish. Magazines can always resort to attaching snacks. Or even better, make the free gift that most flexible of all give-aways: cash.

The bag we love to hate

And then there are carrier bags. Plastic bags from supermarkets are something of a bête noir among some campaigners. If you don't have a 'bag for life', preferably made out of organic hemp, then you can't be a friend of the environment. This is fine, as long as those same people aren't buying bin bags and yet more plastic bags to pick up their dogs' poop in the park. It's better to re-use supermarket carrier bags and flimsy fruit and veg bags for these purposes than it is to buy both a bag for life and disposable waste bags.

Recently there have been strong words from the British government on the re-use of bags. In the 2008 budget it was announced that if supermarkets didn't begin charging for bags, the government would have to consider legislation in order to force them to do so. This is greenwash of the worst kind, because most people do already re-use carrier bags, and replacing them with bin liners, which are significantly thicker, results in more plastic going to landfill rather than less. When Ireland introduced compulsory charging for carrier bags, the tonnage of plastic film used went up, as more (single-use) bin liners and dog poo bags were sold.

The whole carrier-bag campaign is one of those issues where image is more important than substance, and with it we can often see that common friend of greenwash – horribly misused statistics. The supermarket Somerfield, in an attempt to demonstrate its environmentally friendly demeanour, has come up with the statement that shoppers in the UK use up to 20 billion plastic bags a year, an average of 323 per household. Unfortunately this statistic doesn't make sense as it suggests there are more households in the UK than there are human beings.

The same statement comments that those 20 billion bags were enough to 'carpet the entire planet every six months'. For 10 billion bags to cover the Earth's surface, each bag would have to stretch across 51,000 square metres. That's over 12 acres. Rather bigger than the carrier bags I use. Another section of the website, describing their bags for life, tells us that British households 'waste almost six billion plastic bags a year (enough to cover the whole of London)'. Leaving aside the inconsistency between 6 billion and 20 billion (perhaps there is a difference between 'waste' and 'use'), someone ought to be able to spot that if 6 billion cover London, 10 billion are not going to cover the world.

There is also a rather worryingly ill-thought-through statement about Somerfield's degradable carrier bags. 'In early 2003,' we are told, 'Somerfield was the first supermarket to nationally launch degradable carrier bags, supported by The Soil Association. They begin to degrade after 18 months – and will completely vanish within three years – leaving carbon dioxide, water and minerals to be absorbed into the soil naturally.' So they are proudly announcing that their bags give off carbon dioxide and contribute to global warming. Hmm. Remind me why that's a good thing.

However, Somerfield weren't the worst misusers of information in the greenwashing rush to shoot down the free carrier bag. The poor old plastic bag is not only accused of being a clogger-up of landfill, but of forming a menace to waterborne life too. Those who have jumped on the bag bandwagon often proclaim that more than 100,000 marine mammals and sea turtles die each year from getting tangled up in plastic bags or eating them. No, they don't. This statistic, nasty though it is, did appear in a Canadian study, but applied to fishing tackle and nets, not plastic bags. Plastic bags may be, as Boris Johnson has suggested, a blight on the landscape, but no one does the environment any good by relying on dodgy statistics and hype.

No more landfill

Of course, ideally, there's no reason for anything to become litter. The gold standard when it comes to rubbish is that everything should be either re-used or recycled. Nothing shoved in a hole in the ground; nothing degrading out of control to give off methane, carbon dioxide and undesirable chemicals a-plenty. It isn't impossible, but right now it would be expensive both in terms of the simple mechanics and the energy used in the process.

The current target of most UK councils is to have 50 per cent of household waste recycled, a goal that is expected to be reached by 2015, but it is already possible to go significantly further. The county of Lancashire is building two specialist recycling plants that will reduce the amount of material going to landfill to just 30 per cent of the waste dumped, with the aim of eventually getting it down to just 15 per cent.

There's a twofold strategy behind these plants. One is to take the onus away from the householder. For most councils, what goes in the recycling boxes goes to recycling, what goes in the wheelie bin or black sacks goes to landfill. The householder is required to do all the work in sorting one from the other. Hard though it may be to believe, occasionally the householder gets it wrong – and they even occasionally say 'I can't be bothered' and dump everything in the wheelie bin. Also, as we have seen, many councils are restrictive on just what they will take in the recycling box, reducing the recycling potential to make it easier for themselves.

In the new Lancashire system, all the landfill rubbish is screened at the plant, extracting metals, glass, paper, recyclable plastic and more. Every piece that comes out is one less item to end up in a hole in the ground. On top of this, the new plants will also extract a fair proportion of the organic waste – the leftover food, bits of wood, paper that's too messed up to recycle normally – and turn it into compost. Not to miss a trick, the methane generated by the bacteria feeding on the waste will be used to power the plants and even to feed the National Grid. Hence the ability to reduce the amount going to landfill to something between 30 and 15 per cent.

This isn't rocket science. It has been obvious all along that there's much that's heading for landfill that could be recycled. The problem is sorting the garbage wheat from the chaff. Until recently it wasn't practical to automate this. Hence the use of an army of unpaid slaves – the householders – to do the sorting for the councils. But this could only ever be a partial solution, which is where the capabilities of these new waste plants come in.

The waste is passed through an array of sorters, using spinning cylinders with slots, air currents and magnets to pull out different types of material. Light sensors probe the types of plastic to extract further solids. Despite all this technology, though, the plants will also have to rely on some manual sorting to ensure that dangerous contaminants aren't left in the material that will be digested to produce compost and methane. An alternative approach currently being researched is to turn the organic waste into a biofuel using an oxygen-free process that results in the production of biochar (a hard charcoal form), which has the advantage of locking in carbon for many years.

Recycle? Refuse and re-use

Recycling is something we could all be better at. As we've seen above, there could be better incentives to handle our rubbish effectively, but there is more that could be done to bring re-use, which is even better than recycling, to the fore.

If I send a jam jar for recycling, I do reduce the amount of natural resources and energy used some-where (though, as we've seen, it's probably more likely to be used in construction than in being remade into another glass container) – but I do even better if I use that jar again, whether to pot up my own jam, as a candleholder, as a vase or however else I might employ it to avoid buying something else. An alternative for many items is to give them to someone else who might want them.

There are many things that we use for a while, then abandon while they still have plenty of life left. It may simply be a matter of what's in style, or of wanting a new toy – as when we upgrade a mobile phone. This is some-thing we really need to think twice about, especially with technology like a phone, which has a high environmental impact. We really don't need to upgrade phones as often as most of us do. I bought mine in 1999 and it is still going strong in 2008. The children laugh at it (even though it was cool at the time – they used them in *The Matrix*), it doesn't have Bluetooth or a camera . . . but it does the job a phone is supposed to do.

Then there's an intermediate category like computers. These do get slower over time, partly as the hard disks accumulate problems, and partly because the load we put on them increases. But when it's time to upgrade, there are bound to be other users who can do something with the computer. (Be careful about erasing any sensitive data.)

Finally, there are re-usables where passing them on is a no-brainer. Children's clothes and bikes, for instance. Even the greenest of 'use it until it falls apart' types would be hard-pushed to argue that a fourteen-year-old could still wear the same clothes or ride the same bike they had at age six.

Whichever the reason, if you have something that can still be used that you are inclined to throw in the landfill, there ought to be an easy way to pass it on to someone who can make better use of it.

To some extent there is – it's called eBay. By auctioning unwanted items this way, everyone benefits. The original owner gets some cash and gets rid of the unwanted item. The new owner gets a bargain and doesn't need to buy something new. But for many items it just isn't practical to sell them, either because the value is so low that they are unlikely to sell, or because it's not practical to send the item through the post.

Junk makes a great gift

There are charity shops and jumble sales for some items, but the alternative for the concerned re-user is free-cycling. The idea, which started in the US but has spread to the UK, is that you let people in the neighbourhood know what you have that you don't want and they are free to pick it up and take it away. No money changes hands, so there's no financial benefit for the original owner, but there's the warm glow of knowing that it's not going to help fill a hole in the ground.

The best way to work freecycling, if possible, is through a personal network, whether it's friends in the office or a postcard at the local post office. There are also online networks in many towns and cities, bringing together people who wish to get rid of or acquire items. This does work, though in my experience these groups can feel officious to the outsider.

Dumping nappies

Rubbish, like many others, is an area where studies commissioned by interested parties have muddied the waters. Nowhere is this more obvious than in the confusion many people now feel over whether to buy re-usable or disposable nappies.

In the good old days, when most parents switched from washing terry-towel nappies to buying disposables, there wasn't much of an argument. Towelling nappies were disgusting to handle and the sterilizing fluid played havoc with the seal on your washing machine. Disposables were quick and easy. My, how things changed. Once we all became environmentally aware, disposables were frowned upon. They used up lots of resources and they expanded landfill horrendously. Billions are thrown away every year, making them the biggest single filler of landfill space.

The strong-willed switched back to terry – the rest of us winced and went on using disposables. However, a study published in 1990 appeared to show that all that angst was unnecessary. Disposables, it claimed, were no worse environmentally than re-usables. The catch here is that that study was undertaken for Proctor & Gamble, the maker of Pampers disposable nappies. As with many such reports, it was all too easy to prove whatever the sponsor wanted.

The reason for this unscientific flexibility is that such studies rely on the input of assumed values for attributes of the system they are measuring. These values are not known for certain, so they can be set in a way that best gets the message across. 'Lifecycle analyses' are infamous for their ability to prove almost anything. In a recent one, CNW, a company that specializes in marketing for the car industry, decided that monster 4×4s like Hummers are greener than a hybrid like Toyota's Prius.

This outrageous claim required them to assume that the environmental impact of manufacturing the car was about ten times the size of the impact of the fuel it burns in a lifetime (the opposite of what everyone else has assumed). They also decided that people will keep the big gas-guzzlers twice as long as they keep a Prius, and that gas-guzzler drivers will travel twice as far in a year. Add to that the bizarre accuracy they give their guess-work figures (apparently a Hummer will last 34.96 years) and you start to see why these studies are not worth the paper they are printed on.

In the nappy studies, two crucial measures were how many cloth nappies were used and how long they lasted. Both studies recognized that the tendency among many parents to use two cloth nappies rather than one meant there would be more than one nappy to wash per baby change. But the pro-disposables study assumed an average of 1.9 nappies were used per change, while the pro-re-usable study assumed the figure was 1.72.

Similarly, pro-disposable studies assumed that a re-usable nappy could be used 90 and 92.5 times respectively. The study for the cloth manufacturers assumed 167 uses before the nappy had to be retired. These figures were picked out of the air.

Other assumptions made for the Proctor & Gamble study lacked credibility. They allowed for the composting of some disposable nappies, while in practice this was hardly happening. Even more doubtfully, they included a cost for the work involved in washing the nappies. While there is no doubt that nappies add incrementally to the effort of washing, it is very difficult to separate out the extra cost of adding a few nappies to the washload. Other factors the study included were the depreciation of the washing machine, and the water and pesticides required for growing the cotton. With so many variables, the result was an uncontrollable mess. (Or rather one that could easily be slanted towards a desired outcome without it being obvious.)

Such a study really proves very little. For that reason it is depressing that the UK Environment Agency did exactly the same thing in 2001. Its lifecycle analysis makes a big thing about all the measures taken: 'The environmental impact categories assessed were those agreed by the project board: resource depletion; climate change; ozone depletion; human toxicity; acidification; fresh-water aquatic toxicity; terrestrial toxicity; photochemical oxidant formation (low level smog) and nutrification of fresh water (eutrophication).' That's fine – but it doesn't mean that it's any more able to give accurate values for these variables, or to assess the relative impact of, say, a disposable being in landfill or a cotton nappy being washed.

The conclusion of the study was that there was no significant difference between disposables and reusables in their environmental impact. That's not to say that neither has any impact; the report suggests that, for one child over two and a half years, the most significant impacts (resource depletion, acidification and global warming) were the equivalent of driving a car between 1,300 and 2,200 miles. There are no green babies.

Despite being unbiased in a way that couldn't be assumed for the Proctor & Gamble research, this study was also controversial. It was, for instance, based on a relatively small number of cotton-nappy users. And life-cycle analysis is fraught with dangers. Two assumptions that were made, for example, were that '32 per cent of cotton nappy users wash at 90 degrees' and that 'some tumble-dry their nappies'.

These assumptions seem quite plausible, if lacking good evidence to prove them, but a Channel 4 report on the study called them 'surprising assumptions'. Why surprising? In the real world, some nappies *will* be tumble-dried, especially in winter. And though nappy manufacturers recommend washing them at 50 or 60 degrees, I would be very surprised if there aren't still mothers who think the only safe wash for a nappy is a 'boil wash'. Like many of the assumptions, the detailed figures are probably wrong, but in this particular case they don't seem to be surprising.

Making the decision between disposables and cloth nappies on environmental grounds is impossible to undertake sensibly. In the end, we might have the sneaking suspicion that disposables don't make the grade, but the only real guide we can use in this case is personal preference, not scientific determination.

Water waste

The whole recycling business overflows into an environmental topic that most of us don't associate with rubbish: water. Water is, at first sight, a strange rare resource. The whole concept of running low on water seems an insane one. Looked at from space, the defining feature of the Earth, when compared with the other planets in our solar system, is water. Our world is blue with the stuff. In round figures there are 1.4 billion cubic kilometres of water in the world.

Divide the amount of water by the number of people on Earth and we end up with 0.2 cubic kilometres of water each. More precisely, 212,100,000,000 litres for everyone. If you stack that up in litre containers, the pile would be around 10 million kilometres high. With a reasonable consumption of 5 litres per person per day, the water in the world would last for 116,219,178 years. And that assumes that we totally use up the water. In practice, much of the water we 'consume' soon becomes available again for future use. So where's the water shortage?

Things are, of course more complicated than this. In

practice, we don't just get through our 5 litres a day. The typical Western consumer uses between 5,000 and 10,000 litres. In part this happens directly. Some is used in taking a bath, watering the lawn, flushing the toilet – but by far the biggest part of our consumption, vastly outweighing personal use, is the water taken up by manufacturing the goods and food that we consume. Just producing the meat for one hamburger can use 3,000 litres, while amazingly a 1kg jar of coffee will eat up 20,000 litres in its production.

However, even at 10,000 litres a day, we still should have enough to last us over 57,000 years without even adding re-usable water back in. So where is the crisis coming from? Although there is plenty of water, most of it is not so easy to access. Some is locked up in ice or underground, but by far the greatest quantity – around 97 per cent of the water on the planet – is in the oceans. It's not particularly difficult to get to, certainly for any country with a coastline, but it is costly to make use of. The fact that an island nation like Britain is prepared to spend huge amounts of money on reservoirs to collect a relatively tiny amount of fresh water, rather than using the vast quantities of sea that surround it, emphasizes just how expensive is the desalination required to turn sea water into drinkable fresh water.

There are some decisions about using water where the maths works out very simply. An obvious one is washing up. Although a dishwasher will consume a considerable amount of energy in its construction, once in use it beats the environmental hell out of washing up by hand. The amount of water used is tiny by comparison – up to a tenth the amount used in doing the same job in the sink – and uses a quarter of the energy to heat that water.

Other water decisions are less easy to make because there is no clear standard measure for numerical comparisons. We are often told that showers are better for the planet than baths – and this is true if you have a normal shower, using the same water-heating process as the bath. However, if you compare a power shower (which pumps the water through so fast that you would have to have a very deep bath to use a comparable amount of water), things are much less obvious.

Similarly, an instant electric heating shower, using cold water, will be less efficient than a bath. There's also the matter of what 'a shower' consists of. If it's a three-minute, get-it-done-as-quickly-as-possible splash, it will be better than most options. But if you have to leave the water running for a few minutes to get up to temperature, and then take a leisurely ten minutes over it, the shower doesn't look so good.

In practice, some of us are better at keeping water use down, and re-using and recycling our waste, than others – and it should come as no surprise that there is a strong correlation between the tendency to recycle and to conserve water and the purchase of organic food. It's all about caring for the planet. Isn't it?

9

The Organic Bounty

It's easy to see organic food as the ultimate in environmentally friendly eating. Thanks to sterling work by the Soil Association in the UK and other bodies around the world, organics have a shiny green image that is second to none. Yet, just as it's important that we don't believe the greenwash from energy companies and other big businesses, it's equally essential that we don't let the PR from the organic lobby pass us by without passing it by the bullshit-checker of ecologic. Bear in mind, however committed they may be, organic producers are still trying to *sell* you something. As always, this means the truth may come second best to a well-crafted press release.

In a way, the problem starts with the name. As ex-MP and now peer Dick Taverne points out, the word 'organic' is itself an unfortunate one. All that being organic means is having a chemical nature (yes, organics are chemicals) and containing complex carbon compounds. There could never be such a thing, for instance, as organic salt (if you see it, despise it), because salt is sodium chloride, an inorganic compound.

However, though Taverne's assertion is correct and the use is unfortunate, it's too late to moan about it. We might as well look back to the days when 'gay' meant joyful in a light kind of way. The word has a new usage, and it's too late to change things. Even so, the way that 'organic' has been used should tell us something about the PR-led nature of the beast.

The birth of organics

This usage of 'organic' was coined by Walter James, Lord Northbourne, from his conception of the farm as a living organism in its own right, put forward in his 1940 book *Look to the Land*. Northbourne's idea was a miniature precursor to the Gaia concept, which uses the metaphor of the whole Earth as a single living organism. (There is, however, some argument over the origin of the term 'organic' – the Soil Association attributes it to the American J. I. Rodale when he started the magazine *Organic Gardening* in 1942.) But the roots of the organic movement stretch back further in time. Northbourne was strongly influenced by the eccentric Austro-Hungarian philosopher Rudolf Steiner.

Steiner and the twentieth-century English triumvirate who would take forward the organic message were in a strange political juxtaposition to the modern movement. Now it has a left-of-centre, liberal feel, but the original champions were driven by a strongly right-wing concept of a mystical association between a people and their land. At the same time, there was an increasing distaste for the adulteration of food that had become common during the earlier part of the Industrial Revolution, and a concern that mass migration away from the land and into the cities had had the effect of turning food into a commodity.

Rudolf Steiner, born in 1861 in what is now Croatia, was without doubt a striking figure. A philosopher, he was influenced by the Theosophical spiritualist movement and developed his own equivalent, Anthroposophy, as well as devising a holistic approach to education still practised in the Waldorf schools. Throw in designing a number of buildings and the development of eurhythmy, a unique (some would say bizarre) form of performing art, in which gestures and movement correspond directly to sounds, and there is no doubt that Steiner was versatile.

His contribution to the origins of organics was his concept of biodynamic agriculture. Steiner was a devotee of Goethe, whose own ventures into science always mingled the human and the objective, and Steiner's ideas had a similar heady mix of science (or pseudo-science), philosophy and spirituality. In 1924 he developed the concepts that would inspire the organic movement in response to concerns from the farming community about the intensive methods then beginning to emerge.

Steiner felt that the ideal was to have a farm that was, as much as possible, self-sustaining, not dependent on outside products. He was wary of artificial fertilizers and pesticides, believing that natural living materials had a different spiritual essence to synthetic, never living, substances. Steiner saw the farm itself as a living entity that had to be respected and treated well in order to thrive. Respect for the land and the idea of sustainability had distinct potential value, but some of the other ideas incorporated in biodynamics stray well away from any scientific realism.

Mysticism and muck

Perhaps most worrying for those who now look back at Steiner's ideas are those closely associated with astrology. Steiner believed that the position of the moon and planets had a significant influence on the way that plants grew, and so required planting and other agricultural decision points to be tied to heavenly movements. He also suggested that the farmer take into consideration the impact of airy concepts like 'elemental forces', which Steiner believed entered cows through their horns (he insisted that horns should not be removed for this reason).

It is perfectly possible for a reasoned, sensible approach to emerge from what was once superstition and romance. Astronomy emerged from astrology and chemistry from alchemy, for example. A strong potential parallel with the organic movement is the way that modern medicine has developed from a practice that took on a wide range of spiritual aspects, requiring healing herbs, for instance, to be picked at the right phase of the moon. The concern here is that modern organics hasn't managed to shake off the arbitrary ideas on which it was based to produce good science. (It's interesting that, when lecturing on biodynamics, Steiner apparently asked his audiences to test out his theories scientifically, as he had not done so – but this never seemed to happen.)

There is still something of a tendency, for example, for organic bodies to stray in mystical directions. In evidence given to the House of Lords Select Committee on Organic Farming and the European Union, Patrick Holden, then director of the Soil Association, dismissed the idea that the benefits of organic farming should be tested – he even doubted that they could be, using a typical argument of those who have no evidence on which to base their claims, that 'current tools of understanding that are available to the scientific community are not sufficiently well developed to measure what is going on'. Also typical of such an approach is the tendency to pick up on any positive scientific research – suddenly science can come up with the answers – and dismiss the research that doesn't support the claim.

Steiner's beginnings alone would probably never have sparked an international movement. But it wasn't only in Austria that doubts about the new intensive farming methods were growing, and soon an approach that tipped the balance more in favour of the scientific, while still keeping the philosophical ideals, would emerge in the UK.

British groundbreakers

The earliest of three distinctive British characters predates Steiner in his first awakenings to the need for an organic approach, though he came to real prominence later. This was the botanist Sir Albert Howard, who spent nearly twenty years in India up to the mid-1920s. He had travelled there to help spread modern Western agricultural methods, but began to realize there was much to be learned from the inherently organic Indian approach.

The second of the triumvirate was Walter James, Lord Northbourne, who, as we have seen, introduced the term 'organic farming'. Influenced by Steiner, it was he who encouraged the third of the British founders of organics, Lady Eve Balfour, who put their ideas to the test in the Haughley Experiment, begun in 1939 – the first (and still one of the only) full-scale, side-by-side comparison of organic and conventional methods in a full working farming environment.

Although Howard, Northbourne and Balfour moved in circles far removed from the everyday food-shopper or farmer, and though the early interest in organic farming was largely limited to wealthy enthusiasts, their work had a huge impact on the spread of the movement. Lady Balfour's experiment gave birth to the Soil Association, the biggest influence on organic standards in the UK. The writings of Howard and Northbourne, and Balfour's work, would encourage others around the world to develop the organic message.

Organic means profits

For a long time, organic methods and concepts were considered fringe, but in the last decade they have become much more mainstream, in part as consumers have become more aware of how their food is produced, and in part as supermarkets and other large companies have realized the financial advantages that come with an organic label. As we saw on page 134, the organic label is a great way to identify customers who are prepared to pay extra for a product – often significantly more than the extra cost of organic production. According to one source, organic fruit and vegetables can be up to 73 per cent more expensive in supermarkets than they are from an organic box scheme, where the produce is likely to be fresher and to have racked up significantly fewer food miles.

When we dig beneath the rosy glow of organic claims to be more 'natural', what do we find? There seem to be four principal arguments in favour of organics: that organic food is better for you, that it's better for the environment, that the food tastes better and that it involves better animal welfare. We need to examine each of these in some detail.

The idea that organic food is better for you is a complex one, but broadly divides into two strands. Conventionally farmed products may be subject to more pesticides, herbicides and other potentially toxic treatments that could remain in the food. And there may be aspects of the organic production method that result in a better nutritional content in the food. The pesticide is a potential bogeyman, the improved nutrition a consideration that may have some merit.

Residual regrets

Many people cite a reduction in chemical residues as one of the reasons they prefer organic food. We know that some pesticides are dangerous, and many conventionally farmed products do retain some residues. Bananas are often cited as a particular risk because, as we have seen, they are sprayed more than any other food crop. Paul Waddington, in his book *Shades of Green*, points out that 'of samples of bananas delivered to UK schools in 2005, all contained pesticide levels at or below the maximum allowable level'.

Of itself, this statement isn't necessarily worrying, as it could mean that none of the bananas had any pesticide on them at all, but this presumably isn't what Waddington meant. Similarly, Joanna Blythman from the Soil Association has made a strong case for the dangers of residues in our food. Blythman pointed out that everything from fruit and vegetables to wholemeal bread contain pesticide residues, with as many as 72 per cent of apples having some contamination, while at least 40 per cent of all fresh fruit and vegetables retain some agrochemicals.

This is scary stuff. Blythman doesn't pull any punches. 'You can switch to organic . . .' she says. 'Or you could just accept that every third mouthful of food you eat contains poison. Are you up for that?' This is not just scaremongering, it's wrong. Practically *every* mouthful of food we eat contains traces of poisons, some natural, some synthetic. It certainly makes sense to wash fruit and vegetables before consuming them. This applies equally to conventional and organic produce. The delicious carrots from my organic veg box may not have any pesticide residues on them, but they are certainly covered in soil containing a wide range of microorganisms, probably including those responsible for tetanus and MRSA.

However, I'm not panicking about my carrots – and the chances are that those pesticides aren't quite as worrying as they sound either. Ecologic is often about balancing different types of information, but here it's a matter of understanding the significance of quantity. Practically every substance is poisonous in large quantities. No one is arguing that pesticides aren't bad for us, in large quantities. The difficulty is in establishing just what a large quantity is.

Water, for instance, is poisonous if several litres are drunk in a short time; it has killed some athletes, who have overdosed as they attempted to rehydrate. Even deadly poisons can be consumed in very small quantities without negative effect. In fact, many of the trace minerals we require are poisonous. Although it has no scientific basis, homeopathy operates on the assumption that a very small quantity of a poison can be beneficial. It's rather ironic that organic farming, which encourages the use of homeopathy, also uses traces of pesticide residues as a scare tactic.

It's not enough, then, to say that produce contains poisonous residues, or that a product has pesticide traces 'at or below acceptable levels'. We need to know just how much residue is present and what that implies. Would you eat, for example, produce that significantly increased your exposure to radiation? Probably not consciously, but that is exactly what happens when you eat shellfish. A regular shellfish-eater can add a risk of contracting a fatal cancer of around 1 in 100,000. The dosage of a heavy eater is around 0.5 mSv (milliSieverts) a year – about the same as received during 100 hours of flying, or by having seven chest X-rays.

However, that danger has to be put in context. The natural background level of radiation in the UK to which we are all exposed is 2.5 mSv, while by moving to Cornwall you increase this to over 7.5 mSv, adding ten times the radiation received by a heavy shellfish-eater. There *is* a risk – shellfish are naturally contaminated with radioactive materials – but the levels are not high enough to turn down the occasional dish of mussels. (Shellfish also tend to accumulate other contaminants like heavy metals from the way they filter water, so consumption is definitely best kept relatively low.)

The same caution about the numbers has to be applied to those residues on fruit and vegetables. The levels are generally very low – much lower than the natural contamination levels in shellfish. Everything we eat, drink and breathe contains tiny amounts of contaminants that aren't in big enough supply to make any difference. Lord Krebs, a leading zoologist and past chairman of the UK's Food Standards Agency, makes two devastating points to help establish the significance of the quantities of poisonous residues on foods.

The first concerns deaths. There is no doubt that eating the wrong things can kill us. According to Krebs, more than 100,000 deaths a year in Britain can probably be ascribed to bad diet, resulting in heart disease and cancer. Another 50–300 are down to food poisoning. (He points out that these numbers are similar to those for deaths from choking on food, or accidents getting in and out of bed.) But there has not been one example where pesticide in food was the killer.

Coffee concerns

It's possible to be suspicious of the numbers in this case, as it might be difficult to ascribe death to pesticide residues, though if they do accumulate sufficiently to cause death or serious illness they should be easily detectable in the body. However, Krebs' other point is even more striking. This is derived from the work of Bruce Ames, professor of Biochemistry and Molecular Biology at the University of California, Berkeley, who says that a single cup of coffee contains the same quantity of cancer-causing chemicals (carcinogens) as a whole year's consumption of agrochemical residues in our diet.

Worse than that – our knowledge of just how many dangerous chemicals coffee contains is very limited. Coffee contains around 1,000 chemicals of which thirty have so far been given the same sort of massive-dose testing in rats that is used with pesticides. Of these, twenty-one proved carcinogenic. Yet on the whole, most of us survive drinking coffee. This is not an anti-coffee campaign, but rather emphasizes just how relatively small the impact of residues really is.

The only difference between the chemicals in coffee and those in pesticide residues is that the chemicals in coffee were already there – they are 'natural' – but they are no less dangerous. Similarly, Ames points out that if we screened food for natural poisons in the same way that we look for residues, then potatoes, grilled food and peanuts (for example) would all be considered unfit for consumption: their natural toxins would all be too carcinogenic. Every single organic potato or chargrilled pepper is much more dangerous than the traces of residue on our conventional food.

If you want to worry specifically about pesticides, Ames points out that many plants contain natural pesticides – chemicals that are just as dangerous as those we use to kill pests. Rachel Carson in *Silent Spring* warned that, 'For the first time in the history of the world, every human being is now subject to contact with dangerous chemicals, from the moment of conception to death.' She was wrong. We have always been in contact with dangerous chemicals. Evolutionary defence mechanisms can be deadly, as many toadstools demonstrate all too well. We typically consume 10,000 times more of the deadly natural pesticides than we do of equally deadly synthetic pesticides. Luckily, even that volume – around 1.5 grams a day – is not high risk, but it puts the levels of residue we consume on food into stark perspective.

It's fascinating to look at the cancer risk from a typical diet. Presented as a graph, it paints a surprising picture. The figures show the relative cancer risk from the different items in a normal US diet, stacked in order of scale. By far the largest is alcohol, amounting to more than 90 per cent of the risk. The first synthetic carcinogen doesn't come into the picture until well over 99 per cent of the risk has been totalled. In fact, the entire synthetic component is less than the risk from the typical consumption of celery.

It seems, then, that the residues on conventional fruit and vegetables (which we ought to wash like any other produce) are not too much of a concern.

Eat organic, get healthy?

What, then, about the positive nutritional benefits of organics? Here the picture is less clear. Early studies tended to show no clear benefits for organic food. The Food Standards Agency regularly put out information concluding that there were no significant nutritional benefits, and in 2000 the Advertising Standards Agency forced the Soil Association to withdraw advertising that said organic food was healthier than conventional produce as a misleading statement.

However, more recent research has highlighted

Cancer Risk from Diet

OTHER (see opposite) 4.3%

COFFEE 2.6%

ALCOHOL 93.1%

100

80

60

40

20

0

RELATIVE CANCER RISK VALUES — PERCENTAGE RISK

Alcohol	93.13295744
Coffee*	2.58702660
OTHER	
Lettuce	1.03481064
Orange juice	0.77610798
Black pepper	0.77610798
Mushroom	0.51740532
Apple	0.51740532
Cinnamon	0.18109186
Carrot	0.12935133
Potato	0.10348106
Celery	0.10348106
ETU	0.05174053
Plum	0.02587027
Pear	0.02587027
UDMH**	0.02587027
Toxaphene	0.00517405
DDE/DDT***	0.00206962
Parsnip	0.00181092
Toast	0.00181092
Dicofol	0.00051741
Lindane	0.00002587
PCNB	0.00001035
Chlorobenzilate	0.00000259
Folpet	0.00000021
Captan	0.00000016

* Only 30 of the 1,000 chemicals in coffee have been tested.

** Quantity prior to the banning of Alar, the main source.

*** Note 1990 levels which will have fallen due to the ban.

a number of potential benefits for organic food. A four-year study funded by the European Union found that organic fruit and vegetables had higher levels of antioxidants – as much as 40 per cent more – and higher levels of trace minerals such as iron and zinc than conventionally grown equivalents. Antioxidant levels were also higher in organic milk compared with that from conventional herds. (This research had not been peer-reviewed at the time of writing – these are preliminary results.)

What was particularly significant about this study was that it was a direct comparison between organic and non-organic produce on adjacent sites, so there was no variation in freshness. Often the benefits of organic food seem to come from the fact that it is more likely to be local and fresh than from any inherent nutritional content, because if vegetables are stored for any length of time, nutrient levels are influenced.

It seems, then that there are real differences in nutritional content from the way organics are farmed. What is less clear is whether or not these differences are hugely beneficial. Antioxidants attack chemicals in the body called free radicals which can cause damage to DNA and so need to be 'swept up'. There is good evidence that the antioxidants naturally produced in our bodies are essential in helping to keep us healthy. What is less clear is whether or not *consuming* antioxidants has any benefit. Just because something internal to our body's system is good or bad for us does not mean that consuming it will have the same effect.

Tests have shown that people given antioxidants received no benefits over others who were taking a placebo. If anything they made things worse. This is not to say that fruit and vegetables are suddenly bad for you. There is good evidence that a diet rich in fruit and vegetables is excellent. However, it does seem that there isn't a simple link between the antioxidant content of food and nutritional benefits, so the distinction discovered between the organic produce and the conventional in the EU trial does not of itself show that organic food is better.

It's even harder to spot the nutritional pluses of organic meat. Red meat in any significant quantity, for example, is going to be bad for you whether it's organic or not and processed meats, like bacon and sausages, are even worse. Organic farmer Helen Browning comments, 'Bacon is not a health product. Our nutritional statement is that our bacon is better for you than a bag of doughnuts.' Here it's more likely that other considerations will make the difference. There is some concern about the use of antibiotics in non-organic animals, but organic farmers are allowed to use antibiotics, just not routinely. This isn't hugely different from many modern conventional farmers, especially those with free-range animals, who are much less likely than has been suggested to use routine antibiotics, which come at a cost to them.

Sometimes the restrictions placed on organic farmers seem at best arbitrary. Lowland cattle farmers in the UK need to immunize their herds against lungworm, an unpleasant infection that causes the cows much distress and can be fatal. Non-organic farmers typically use a routine live vaccine to build immunity, just as we immunize our children against dangerous diseases. However, the organic stance is that the herd should not be immunized. The Soil Association will give a derogation – special permission – but the plan has to be to manage without immunization.

One lowland organic farmer I spoke to tried going without immunization as required and three of his cattle died of lungworm in a single year. Such immunization in relatively damp conditions is essential and shows the cracks in the sense of the organic rules. To make matters worse in this case, the vet treating the cattle asked what the Soil Association would allow for treatment of lungworm and got no reply. Eventually the Soil Association demanded tests which would have taken so long that the cattle would have died before the results were available. In the end the farmer had to treat before being given the go-ahead and so risk losing his expensive organic certification, getting the derogation retrospectively.

Environmental pros and cons

The nutritional benefit of organic versus conventional might not be an easy one to call, but it's much simpler than the 'better for the environment' argument. Here we not only have to deal with the environmental impact of the farm and its methods, but to be clear about what environmental benefits we are looking to get out of a farming method. Once more, the immediate reaction is the knee-jerk one that organic has to be better for the environment because it's natural. Not necessarily. Wildfires, volcanoes and tsunamis are natural, yet they have a devastating impact on the environment.

The extent to which this organic-equals-natural-equals-better image can take hold is shown in a story told in the village where I live. We are surrounded by farms, and in a nearby village are two adjacent farms, one conventional, the other organic. A TV company was in the village making a documentary about the organic farm. Some owls were discovered nesting in a barn, so of course they appeared in the documentary as evidence of the more 'natural' appeal of the organic farm. Unfortunately, the owls were actually nesting on the conventional farm.

However, there is little doubt that the organic movement, particularly in the UK and the US, encourages methods that help improve biodiversity and wildlife habitats. This is not inherent to the organic processes themselves, except in the reduction in use of pesticides and the resultant increase in insect population and the birds that feed on them, but rather is down to the ethos that accompanies an organic approach.

It is equally possible, for example, to maintain hedgerows without being organic, and increasingly non-organic farmers do so. There is a system of farming called integrated farm management (IFM) which is non-organic but has better results in maintaining biodiversity than organics, at significantly lower cost. IFM combines traditional farming methods like crop rotation with modern technology, using only the minimum of fertilizers and pesticide when necessary.

Low cost is not something you will see the proponents of organics putting forward as one of its benefits. As we have seen, supermarkets may use the organic label to squeeze more profit out of their customers, but even bought locally and direct, organic food-growing tends to cost more because the yields are relatively low and the land requires more working. Despite not having the costs of pesticides and artificial fertilizers, this makes it relatively expensive. It is easy for middle-class consumers with plenty of disposable income to put cost aside as an irrelevant factor, but for many it is an issue when buying food and needs to be part of the equation.

More organics, more climate change

Biodiversity is an asset, and it's the pretty face of environmental impact. But there is another aspect, and a worrying one, where organics don't fare quite as well. This is in the impact on climate change. Although the production of those pesticides and herbicides used by the conventional farmers does have an environmental impact, it has to be weighed against the inefficiencies of organic methods. Not only do organic farms have a much lower yield, requiring more land to be maintained, but they have a higher CO_2 emission in the process.

Because of the lack of pesticides and herbicides, organic plants have to be mechanically weeded much more frequently. That's more use of tractors, pumping out carbon dioxide, and more tilling of the land. And each time those ploughs cut through the soil, carbon dioxide is churned from the soil itself into the atmosphere. To make matters worse, because of the almost anti-scientific approach taken by the organic movement, some chemicals have been used on organic farms that are not at all good for the environment.

A good example was the use of the blue-green chemical copper sulphate, familiar from many an old chemistry set. This was traditionally used as a fungicide and, simply because it wasn't new and scientific, it was accepted on organic farms. Unfortunately there is sound evidence that copper-based products are not only less effective than modern fungicides, but they are also more toxic to insect life and more damaging to the environment. When the EU wanted to ban copper-based products in 2002, the ban was held off because of lobbying from the organic movement. This is simply bizarre, demonstrating how the worst aspects of organics are an obsession with the traditional rather than the sensible. At root, organics is a romantic movement, not a scientific one.

Another example of total lack of logic in organic standards is the approach taken to the addition of potassium in the form of potassium chloride. This is the harmless chemical used in 'low-salt' preparations to reduce the amount of sodium for those in danger of high blood pressure. It seems that, in the early days of setting organic standards, someone didn't know their chemistry and, because chlorine is a dangerous, poisonous gas, also thought that a chloride was dangerous – so organic farmers are not allowed to use potassium chloride on their land. But they are allowed to use sylvinite, which is a mix of potassium chloride and sodium chloride (salt). Potassium chloride is a natural mineral, dug up out of the ground like salt, and it often forms layers with salt – sylvinite is just the pair of layers dug up together. Now the really bizarre thing is that in this attempt to avoid the chloride in potassium chloride, the organic specifications require the farmer to put on *twice* as much chloride. To get the right amount of potassium, you need twice as much sylvinite as pure potassium chloride.

We will come in a moment to animal welfare, but putting that aside, organics also shares some environmental issues with free-range farming. The unpleasant fact is that factory farming of chicken is better for the environment than free range. Yes, they use chicken specially bred to mature in ridiculously short timespans and cram them into sheds with hardly room to move. But this approach is very energy efficient. A 'standard bird' as they are known, uses 32 per cent less energy in its production than an organic chicken. Personally, I'm inclined to release a little more CO_2 and have better welfare, but it is a good example of how weighing up the environmental impact of our actions is more complex than it first appears.

It must taste better, it's more natural

The penultimate deciding factor on organic food is taste – what the product itself tastes like. It would have been very useful if the EU study that found the differences in nutrients between organic and non-organic products had done double-blind trials on taste, but this seems not to have happened. All the evidence is that the taste difference mostly reflects the fact that locally grown, fresh food tastes better than long-term refrigerated food shipped halfway across the world. There is no doubt that good, fresh, local organic produce tastes great – but so does good, fresh, local non-organic produce.

It's also true that many organic farms specialize in the better-tasting crops. I would always prefer a non-organic Cox's Pippin apple to a Golden Delicious, no matter what its organic pedigree. But more often than not the organic produce will be from a good-tasting stock because, with organic food, taste is usually put ahead of appearance, while supermarkets often stress to their suppliers the appearance of their fruit and vegetables over and above the taste.

Looking after our furry friends

Last, but not least, comes animal welfare – and here we have to be particularly careful to separate the decision of whether or not to buy organic from the emotional knee-jerk. Most human cultures keep pets, and the UK and US are particularly enthusiastic about animal welfare. It's no real surprise that in the UK the Royal Society for the Prevention of Cruelty to Animals significantly pre-dates the National Society for the Prevention of Cruelty to Children. What's more, unlike the children, the animals get a royal charter.

Until relatively recently we lived in a certain amount of ignorant bliss when it came to the welfare of farm animals. With a rosy but inaccurate picture of the bucolic life on the farm, we like to think of chickens scratching around in a farmyard or pigs roaming free across the fields and wallowing in mud to their hearts' content. The reality has, for many years, been very different.

Before looking at what the different farming systems offer in terms of animal welfare, I ought to stress that it's not a level playing field across the world. UK farm animals have better welfare than those in many other countries. Sow stalls – tight-crammed metal stalls or close-tied tethers, in which female pigs used to be kept through most of their pregnancies – are now banned in the UK but still used in the rest of Europe, including Denmark from where we import a lot of bacon. Sheep are often kept permanently indoors in the US and Australia, a practice that is unheard of in the UK, where it's also much rarer for beef cattle to be kept indoors all year round, though they tend to be sheltered for the winter.

Farrowing crates, used in pig breeding to confine a sow in a tiny space for several weeks from just before the birth of her piglets until they are several weeks old, are still used in the UK, though they are likely to be dropped here sooner than in other countries. The government department responsible, DEFRA, is funding research into alternative systems, but warns that many alternatives lead to unacceptably high piglet mortality when the sow, weighing a hundred times more than the piglets, accidentally crushes them.

Perhaps the best-known example of difference in welfare between the UK and elsewhere is that of veal calves. These always suffer a little from the 'aww' factor because they are immature animals, but veal calves in the UK are usually kept in vastly better conditions than those on the continent, which are sometimes kept in darkness to make their meat whiter, and packed into sheds with slatted floors and no straw bedding. Unfortunately, veal has become unpopular in the UK, in part because of animal welfare concerns, and that reduction in popularity has resulted in more animals suffering. Unlike poultry, where unwanted male birds are gassed as chicks, unwanted male dairy calves are regularly shipped abroad as live exports, raising concerns about welfare both en route and once established on continental veal-production farms.

Who is really to blame?

However, this doesn't mean that all UK animal welfare is of the highest standard. Some of it is still appalling, though it is entirely possible to avoid the worst examples. Oddly, the blame for the extremes of factory farming is almost always put in the wrong place. Supermarkets blame the consumer: 'We only sell intensively reared chickens because the customers demand cheap meat.' Protest groups demonize the farmer – yet all the farmers I spoke to in researching this book genuinely cared for their animals and would prefer not to indulge in intensive practices.

Dodging the flack in the middle were the supermarkets. It is they who really should shoulder the blame. Customers don't rush in saying, 'I want a £2.50 chicken.' Of course ask any customer if they would like to pay less and they will say yes. They will also say they would like food for free, but even the biggest supermarkets don't seem to be doing this 'because the customer demands it'. It is a null argument. Customers buy cheap meat because it's available. Some, when they know about the welfare standards that accompany factory farming, prefer to pay more and get better welfare. Others are on such a tight budget that they have to go for a bargain. It is availability that drives demand.

As for the farmers, they are caught in a trap. Supermarkets give them little choice, specifying what they want with ridiculous exactitude. Farmers don't set out to be nasty to animals, and although the farm is their business and they can't be sentimental about the livestock, most are as enthusiastic as anyone else about avoiding animal suffering.

The good news is that animal welfare is a real plus for organics. There is no doubt that an organic animal will be up towards the top of the animal-welfare hierarchy. But there are alternatives that deliver similar benefits, so it is worth making a comparison.

Checking chickens

In the chicken world there are two streams: eggs and chickens for meat. The egg argument is largely won in the UK. Even McDonald's uses free-range eggs. The proportion of free-range eggs on the supermarket shelves has grown significantly and, because of this, the price differential is not huge. Given the difference between being cooped up in a small cage that's effectively part of a production line, never experiencing the outside world, and being allowed to roam outside and undertake natural chicken behaviour, free-range eggs are worth pursuing, and the laying chickens will have very similar welfare standards to organic layers.

With meat chickens the same benefits apply, but there are currently far fewer free-range meat birds than intensively reared birds, so free-range has a higher cost differential. It also means there is likely to be much less choice. When I complained to my local Sainsbury's that they never had large free-range chickens, they claimed there wasn't enough demand for them. How they know this when they never have any, I'm not sure.

Free-range meat birds also tend to have a second cost factor. The factory – 'standard' – birds have been selectively bred to put on weight at an astounding rate. They typically come to maturity in about thirty-nine days – less than six weeks from egg to slaughter. Putting on weight this fast appears to produce flabby, less tasty meat. So free-range birds tend to be the slower-growing varieties – and the longer a bird takes to be ready for eating, the more it's going to cost.

Standard chickens live in appalling conditions, crammed together for their whole life in a shed where, living in a bed of their droppings, they often develop burns on their hocks from the ammonia in their urine. I find this unacceptable and suggest that the bare minimum standard to be considered is the intermediate 'freedom food' standard, while free-range or organic are probably well worth going for if available.

The poor pig

Some argue a chicken is just a bird, and not exactly an intelligent one at that. But this argument can't be applied to pigs, which are also kept in cramped conditions indoors in the UK.

Pigs are the most intelligent of the meat animals, and arguably the ones to whose welfare we should give most consideration. Although dogs beat pigs on some intelligence tests (in fact, dogs outdo our closest relative the chimpanzee in some aspects of comprehension), there are others where pigs come out on top. By nature they enjoy rooting around in the ground, and probably like wallowing in mud and generally making a superb mess – something that can't be duplicated in a shed.

That 'probably' should be noted. We can't apply human ideas of the good life to animals. Pigs are also very clean animals, so just because in nature they resort to mud baths to cool off doesn't mean they wouldn't prefer to be both cool *and* clean. However, it's certainly true that, of all the meats, free-range pork – or organic with its similar welfare standards – is the most essential to look out for in welfare terms. British sheep are all free range, as are cows in summer, but pigs get a poor lookout at the cheap end of the market.

Oddly, there is one aspect of pig life where free range

or organic isn't necessarily humane. Traditionally animals were bred in an environment that suited them. Sheep, for instance, were hill animals, whereas pigs were animals of the plain. After the Second World War, when food was in short supply, the traditional way of doing things was thrown out and the methods of farming adapted to push animals into whatever environment was available. This has led to more foot disease in sheep bred on wetter lowland fields, while pigs bred on the high downlands can be susceptible to the cold, as they don't have much in the way of fur to protect them from wind. Though free-range pigs are provided with arcs – those semi-circular corrugated-iron sties (sometimes spelled ark, but the name seems to refer to the shape rather than to Noah) – they don't get the degree of shelter that is ideal for them.

With this proviso, buying British organic meat is one way to ensure best possible welfare standards. As Helen Browning explained to me, organic farming puts the animal at the centre of the system. Instead of 'How should we feed a pig?' Browning suggests the organic farmer asks, 'How does a pig like to be fed?' She admits that sometimes the approach taken by organic farmers *increases* the risk to the pig – as already mentioned, not using farrowing crates means more piglets will be killed by their mothers. However, Browning suggests that it is a fair balance, adding a little risk in exchange for a better quality of life. We all do this every time we eat something that's bad for us, or allow our children to take a walk outside rather than keeping them indoors just in case they are exposed to any danger.

If animal welfare is of importance, her argument is persuasive. Organic certification also ensures that the animal is humanely slaughtered. This means that there is no organic halal meat without stunning. Browning believes that the practice of killing an animal with a single cut to the throat and allowing it to bleed to death is unacceptable. She also points out that while conventional farms use matter-of-course mutilation, such as docking the tails of pigs, it isn't necessary on organic (or free-range) farms. Docking may not be a huge problem in itself – the pig's suffering is brief – but the reason they have to be docked – because otherwise they tend to eat each other's tails – suggests they are under significant stress in the conventional system.

This again sounds an impressive argument, though the picture isn't as clear as it is in the slaughter case. Although cannibalization *sounds* unnatural, forced on the animals by stressful conditions, the unpleasant fact is that a degree of cannibalization is quite common in the natural environment. Interestingly, free-range chickens are more likely to suffer cannibal attacks than conventionally farmed ones.

So is organic meat better as far as welfare goes? Browning is refreshingly unpartisan. Most British beef and lamb from non-organic farms, she says, is absolutely fine and she would happily eat it. But for pork and poultry, the organic standard – or an equivalent truly free-range non-organic farm – is well worth hunting out as it really does make a difference.

Not all organics are equal

Perhaps the biggest problem with organic produce is that it is whatever the opposite is of a bogeyman (a namyegob?). As we've already seen, organic is a word that immediately creates a set of assumptions and mental patterns that are hard to break. We hear 'organic' and think healthy and green, nutritious (assuming we're talking food, as you can now buy some decidedly non-edible items in organic form) and safe. Yet from what we have seen above, the differential between organic and conventional food is often slight – and even within the organic world not everything is created equal.

One problem is the variation in organic standards around the world. The UK's Soil Association is about the most stringent regulating body in the world – some other countries are significantly more lax about what they will allow to receive an 'organic' stamp of approval. This can lead not only to confusion over what you are buying (and let's face it, if you are thinking of food miles, organic produce shipped across the world doesn't stack up well), but also to downright deception. The organic standards in some other countries are so different that some non-organic stock from the UK could be shipped overseas, given organic certification and returned to this country as apparently organic produce.

Another problem is whether all the benefits of organic farming can be gained when buying organic produce from a supermarket, or from an industrial food company. The organic ideal is that you grow or rear the food in your garden. Failing that, a local (no more than a few miles away) producer that you know and can visit is best. Next is the sort of intermediate organic producer, like Riverford Organics in the UK, which supplies vegetable boxes to around one-third of the country. Admittedly they don't all come from the same farm in Devon – they use other, more local farms – but even so, you can expect a few more food miles to be added on. I use Riverford, and the supplying farm for us is about 37 miles away.

Then there are supermarkets dealing with 'traditional' organic suppliers. A good example would be the supply of organic meat by Helen Browning, coming from her farm in a Wiltshire village but feeding into the supermarket supply chain with its extra food miles and storage energy costs. And last, and probably least appealing, are organic products from industrial food concerns, where the ingredients have been organically sourced (from somewhere) but you can still be dealing with significantly processed foods.

Perhaps the only area of industrialized food where organic ought to make a significant difference is in meat. If you buy conventional ready meals, the meat could have been raised anywhere in any conditions. At least with an organic ready meal you can expect a good level of animal welfare.

It's easy to understand why supermarkets and industrial food processors have jumped on the organic bandwagon: it's an easy way to get people to spend more money. In the early days of organics, supermarkets often kept their organic products separate from traditionally produced equivalents. From the economic viewpoint this made sense, as it meant customers couldn't easily make a straight comparison of the difference in price and so realize just how much more they were paying. Now, with organic sales at healthy levels, the differential can be brought down sufficiently that it is no longer necessary to keep the two separate and you are more likely to see similar products near each other, effectively as the 'normal' and 'premium' versions.

If normal economic processes continue – and there is no reason to think of organics as anything other than a business product, despite the nice green glow they give us – eventually we will see 'normal' produce labelled as 'cheap and nasty produce' while organic is closer to the norm. Although supermarkets don't literally have ranges called 'cheap and nasty', they do all have 'basics' or 'everyday' ranges, which are intentionally packaged in an unappealing way (usually in very basic colours plus white) to emphasize that these are really only for the desperate. It doesn't mean there's anything particularly different about the product, just that this sets the base price on top of which some are prepared to pay a premium.

Principles are more important than certification

Organic produce, then, like many premium products, has a few good things going for it because the organic movement also tends to link into the local, fresh-food movement and gives more consideration to animal welfare and the environment than some systems of conventional farming – though it has to be stressed that there can be equally good welfare on free-range non-organic farms.

It was interesting to note that Helen Browning, a leading light in the Soil Association, said she was less worried about 'proper' organic certification than about getting organic methods into wider use in conventional farms. Perhaps the biggest problem with organics is that it is used more as a marketing tool than as an educational approach to help every farmer make better use of the land. There is much to learn from organics – it is just a pity that the certification process is so rigid and sometimes seems based more on philosophy and even magic than it is on science.

Browning claims this rigidity is partly imposed by the media and the outside world. If they make exceptions, she says, 'the world beats us up for it'. It is possible the public perception of what is 'natural' and good for us, whipped up by the media, does make it hard for the organic certifiers to be more flexible – but they have hardly helped by aggressively putting down conventional farming.

I don't want this to seem like an attack on organics. Some organic products are excellent. There are plenty of lessons conventional farmers can learn from the organic side, whether in animal welfare or reduction in the use of fertilizer. In fact, much good science is about learning from nature, whether it's in the use of stem cells or in agriculture.

Take one simple example. The organic Sheepdrove Farm was losing a lot of its chickens to foxes. A wily stockman who really knew nature started hanging chicken corpses on the outer fence. Certainly not a pretty 'organic farm'-type solution – but it worked. Foxes are very territorial (and lazy). Before long, a dominant local vixen decided the 'offering' on the fence was for her and set about making sure that no other foxes attacked the chickens. By working with nature – understanding the psychology of the predator – the stockman reduced chicken losses to practically nothing.

The problem with organics is in the way it is regulated. In the end, although much of the organic method is useful and the products excellent, the philosophical and spiritual foundations of organics appear to be flawed and based on unproven, knee-jerk feelings. And nowhere is this more obvious than in the organic take on sustainability.

10

Sustainability's Balance Sheet

Sustainability is an appealing concept. It implies that we are being proper stewards of the planet, passing an undamaged world on to our children. Sustainable development means leaving a light footprint on the Earth, rather than ripping it apart for short-term gain – surely a desirable goal. Yet no green concept needs more careful application of the tools of ecologic than the idea of being sustainable.

The amazing vanishing nutrients

Sustainability is at the very heart of organic farming. The ideal is that nothing need be brought in from outside. If something is brought in, that too should be organic and natural. This is certainly the picture the organizations that benefit from sales of organics portray, but is it possible? Ecologic says no. The maths here is the simplest of equations: $1-1 = 0$. Take something out without replacing it, and you end up with collapse.

When organic produce leaves the farm, it takes with it the essential components of growing things – water, carbon, nitrogen and key nutrients, all tied up in the food. Some of these can be replaced naturally. Water from rain (climate change permitting) and carbon from carbon dioxide in the air, but what about the rest? There needs to be a mechanism for getting nitrogen, minerals and other nutrients back into the system.

Take a single organic cabbage from my vegetable box. Where do those nutrients go? The tatty outer leaves and stalk are likely to end up on my compost heap – organically useful, but not to the farm. The rest will be eaten. And unless human sewage is returned to the land as fertilizer – something that currently isn't widely acceptable – that will always present a problem for sustainability.

In fact, even if every bit of both human and animal manure were returned to the land, it still wouldn't be enough. First of all, only about one-third of the essential nutrients that go into an animal are excreted. Others are retained, so we would need to use all human dead bodies and all animal corpses as fertilizer too. And then there's the problem of composting.

Composting is essential to break down some natural materials so that they provide nutrients to the land – but for other materials it's highly detrimental, because it cooks the materials, destroying essential nutrients just as over-cooking removes nutrients from vegetables. Organic standards require farmers to compost animal manure, but this process removes a high percentage of its nutrient benefits – and results in potentially dangerous liquids leaching out of the composting area.

It's much better to spread manure direct – but this isn't allowed by the organic standards bodies. Of course there is composting and composting, and it has been said that the difference between a successful organic farmer and an unsuccessful one is that the successful farmer's idea of composting manure is to stick a fork in it, then get it straight back on the land as quickly as possible.

Playing the three-card trick with nitrogen

Organic farmers make heavy use of manure because of nitrogen, an essential for growing plants. But manure doesn't reduce the need to add nitrogen into the system. It just moves that need back from applying it directly to the land, to needing the nitrogen to grow the animal's foodstuff. Worse still, this dependence on animal manure means that organic farms pretty well have to be mixed, at a time when (see page 242) sources like the Centre for Alternative Technology are telling us we need to take meat virtually out of the diet, because animals are both bad polluters and a very inefficient use of energy.

Conveniently, there is a way to get nitrogen out of thin air (which has more nitrogen in it than anything else). Some plant species, particularly legumes like peas and beans, 'fix' nitrogen, taking it in as they grow and passing it on to the soil. By growing such crops on a field for two to three years it is possible to make enough nitrogen to use that field for other plants. Clovers, too, are also increasingly used by livestock farmers to fix nitrogen. However, many farms are not able to get all their nitrogen this way. The obvious way to replenish it is to use a simple nitrogen-based fertilizer, but these are banned by the organic regulators. So the nitrogen has to come from elsewhere.

Canny organic farmers play a game of hide the lady.

They buy in nitrogen-rich materials like manure from other organic farms, simply shifting the problem to someone else. At some point, though, the buck stops. A typical solution is to buy straw from a conventional farm. This is allowed to rot down to provide a 'natural' nitrogen source. Yet the nitrogen got into that straw from a chemical fertilizer. Alternatively, the straw can be used as bedding – and of course if the animal eats it, it's not the farmer's fault. It's the three-card trick of the farmyard, an unnecessary manipulation of the truth, all to avoid admitting the reality that nitrogen-based fertilizers are required to keep organics going.

Things are even worse with some of the other nutrients. Potassium, for example, can't be obtained from the air. There is no way to replace this essential element without bringing it in from outside the organic system. Again, farmers will get potassium sources from other organic farms – dried blood is a good example – as much as they can, but some will eventually run short. Here the organic regulators have been forced to fudge the issue. If potassium runs very low, it is allowable to use a chemical replacement. Yet an inherent requirement for the system to function has been dressed up as a rare emergency measure.

Does this mean that the organic movement is doomed? Not at all. But ecologic enables us to uncover the deceptions that are practised and give us a way to define a much more honest approach to organics which accepts the need to make use of some chemical fertilizers, rather than shying away from the word 'chemical' because it is scary.

We need chemicals

The scientifically illiterate attitude that puts 'chemical' on a par with 'unacceptable' is, sadly, not uncommon in the organic standards published by the Soil Association. Remember our attitude to salt (see page 33). Chemically produced sodium chloride is much purer and potentially safer than 'natural' mined or sea salt. Yet it's easy to fall for the natural allure. Take two of the essential chemicals required for plant growth – phosphates and potassium.

The Soil Association's principles state that organic farms should 'sustain or build soil fertility'. This requires chemical nutrients like phosphates and potassium. For each 1,000 tonnes of grain sold from a farm, the equivalent of 25 tonnes of phosphorus, potassium and a third chemical, magnesium, are required in fertilizer form. Although it's possible to slow the impact of crops on the soil by rotation, those nutrients are still disappearing and it is practically impossible to replace them all with the low content in composted animal manure. Many organic farms are living on borrowed time: once nutrient reserves are depleted, it will prove very expensive to build fertility levels back to those originally present.

With permission from the Soil Association, a landowner can top up phosphates – but only using 'natural rock phosphate' or 'calcined aluminium phosphate rock'. In both cases, these are guaranteed to bring in more contaminants than a pure chemical phosphate. This is even recognized in the standards, which point out that rock phosphates can be contaminated with the heavy metal cadmium – yet still they stubbornly stick to that 'natural' source, putting appearances above safety.

It's even more complex with the potassium mentioned above. The first line of defence is wood ash, and plant extracts which, yes, will have contaminants. (In fact, the wood ash may well contain a good sprinkling of those nanoparticles the Soil Association is so worried about; see page 34.) Failing organic sources, as a last line of defence natural rock potassium sources (inevitably contaminated, of course) or even pure chemicals can be used to treat 'severe deficiencies', but as we have seen, to suggest that this is an emergency measure is a delusion.

Another example of the lack of logic is the assertion made in the Soil Association standards that in the treatment of sick animals you must use complementary therapies and trace elements, and may only use conventional veterinary treatments if these fail. Even Prince Charles, with all his enthusiasm for complementary medicine, is unlikely to say this. The clue is in the name. It is supposed to be complementary, not a replacement for the real thing.

Unless a complementary treatment has a good scientific basis, it has no place in standards that are applied either to animal welfare or to the production of food. This is simply putting animal and human health at risk.

Organics sustain poverty

On a wider scale, the prospects for sustainable organic farming become even more worrying. Farming is effectively organic already in many parts of the world where farmers can't afford to buy chemicals, and the inefficiency of the approach means that there are problems providing enough food in all but the most fertile of regions. Although much is made of the devastation of the rainforest when it is cut down to clear farm land, what is less well publicized is that part of the reason for the devastation of the rainforest is that the organic farming practised by the poor farmers is so inefficient that they constantly need to destroy virgin forest to cope with population growth.

Doctor C. S. Prakash, professor in plant molecular genetics at Tuskegee University, Alabama, comments darkly: 'The only thing sustainable about organic farming in the developing world is that it sustains poverty and malnutrition.' Organic farming is not sustainable if it kills the farmer.

Lessons from nature

One of the buzzwords that is often seen alongside sustainability is 'permaculture'. This concept, which originated in the 1970s, is founded on a simple and reasonable principle. Nature is inherently sustainable. So if we want to have sustainable agriculture and sustainable communities, we ought to model them on the processes of nature. A sustainable human habitat should be like a natural one.

There is no doubt that we can learn many lessons from nature, whether it is in the use of natural-based technology – such as the dirt-resistant glass produced by Pilkington that makes use of a mechanism found on a water lily – or observing what works and doesn't work agriculturally, but there is a danger of resorting to sympathetic magic in this approach. Sympathetic magic is based on the fallacy that if something looks like something else, or behaves in a similar way to it, then it will have a similar effect. Permaculture's attempts to learn from nature can also suffer from this simplistic non-sequitur.

Just because a solution occurs in nature, it doesn't mean that the same approach can be effectively applied to human beings. In nature, many animals die of diseases that we treat medically. The natural way of dying rather than living is not better, it is just what happens to have evolved. Evolution is how nature has come by its way of doing things. This process is very effective over a long time, but we always need to remember it is not efficient – it takes a lot of trial and error; and it's not guided – evolution is blind.

The evolutionary process certainly develops those traits that are better for a species and rejects others, but that does not mean the same traits will be best for a different species, or even that they are the best option for the species where they are developed. They are merely the most effective of the random mutations available. The result can be for nature to produce dead-ends and to miss out on options. Nature can certainly provide useful guidance, but it always needs to be tempered with human intelligence and creativity.

From this viewpoint, permaculture inevitably has some weaknesses. It can seem a little like the agricultural equivalent of the New Age movement, pulling together a set of not always well-integrated ideas that are driven more by spiritual conviction than by logic or a good understanding of the natural world. Most of the ways that permaculture draws lessons from nature are yet to be subjected to any rigorous form of testing and can't be regarded as an acceptable approach for sustainability just because proponents of the movement say they are – which to date is really all that its claims are based on.

Sustainable plantations

With ecologic we can turn the concept of sustainability on its head, finding sustainable solutions in unexpected places. It has been accepted green wisdom for many years that one of the biggest threats to the rainforest, and hence to the planet, were farmers who slashed and burned the forests to plant crops. Yet things are not always so straightforward. If we move the focus on devastated forest from the rainforest pin-up of the Amazon to West Africa, the picture is nowhere near as bad as it might have been, thanks to the right crop selection.

Plantations of cocoa trees for making chocolate can provide a forest environment that has many of the benefits of the natural rainforest itself, yet is more sustainable than pure rainforest as it enables the local inhabitants to make a living. Even where this does involve some damage to virgin forest, a cocoa plantation is much better than the traditional maize and palm-oil plantations that were responsible for such negative slash-and-burn activity. Increasingly, new cocoa plantations are being made where the forest was already cleared for maize but then the land proved incapable of supporting that crop. Cocoa plantations in these circumstances are having a positive effect on the environment, bringing employment and enabling the world to enjoy chocolate with a morsel less guilt.

A useful attitude to sustainability is that it has to include our need to sustain human life as well as the planet. It's very easy when focusing purely on carbon emissions, for instance, to overlook the wider picture. Virgin rainforest is an ideal, but where it has already been cut down, cocoa plantations are a plus. Similarly, sustainability means it's probably worth being a little less fussy about air miles when it comes to lightweight products that may mean the difference between survival and starvation in some parts of the world.

There has been quite a fuss made about the shipping of items like green beans and baby corn to the UK from countries such as Kenya. Recently the Soil Association has been expressing concern about the CO_2 emissions from flying food from abroad. Cynics have suggested this is a form of protectionism for UK farmers, but that is probably unfair. However, the amount of energy required to bring vegetables by air from Kenya is only around 15 per cent more than to grow those same vegetables in the UK in heated greenhouses. Although the Soil Association points out that 11 per cent of carbon emissions from food distribution are down to air freight, the amount produced in shipping a pack of beans to the UK is still small compared to the typical drive to the supermarket. There are plenty of other ways to save on emissions without hurting trade with poor countries and swapping the starvation of thousands of people for a tiny fraction of a degree's impact on CO_2.

Returning to our roots

Another huge lesson for sustainability can be learned in the cottage garden. Beds planted with annual flowers are very pretty, but anything but sustainable. The plants have to be replaced every year, at significant expense to both gardener and environment. A cottage garden full of perennials that last year after year is much more sustainable.

Now compare this with agriculture. At the moment about 80 per cent of agricultural land, the land that grows all our staples, is planted with annual crops, re-seeded each year and requiring expensive cultivation techniques to achieve suitable yields. Ecologic turns sustainability on its head and exposes the roots. If it were possible to change to crop plants that live many years, it would not only increase sustainability, but the long-lived plants' well-established root systems would preserve the soil and enable more cultivation of marginal areas.

In the end, grain crops are all derivatives of grasses. We are all familiar with perennial grasses with well-established root systems that can survive pretty well anything we throw at them and come back green year after year – we've got them in our lawns. Similarly, perennial plants are very common in nature. More than 85 per cent of North American native plant species are perennial. In the UK, anyone who walks the countryside will be familiar with many perennials, from trees down to the smallest wayside plants. Perennials thrive because their pervasive root structures lock in nutrients, rather than letting them flow away to have to be replaced (along with the seed) year after year, as is the case with shallow-rooted annuals.

When humans first began to cultivate crops, it doesn't seem likely that they would intentionally have picked out the fussier, harder-to-grow annuals. So how have we reached a position where annuals provide the staple food crops? It was probably Darwinian evolution. The plants with the biggest grains would be selected for re-use. Annuals have the advantage in evolutionary terms of being re-planted every year. So that selection process would go ahead much quicker, year after year, sifting out bigger and bigger grains. The annual plants would change more rapidly, meaning that over time they got further and further ahead of the perennials. In time no one would give the poor old perennials, hardly changed from their wild ancestors, a second look.

Now, with the long view in mind, everything seems to benefit from the switch to perennials. They allow much less soil erosion, hang on to water and nitrates better and need less care. With no need to plough every year and less fertilizer, pesticides and herbicides, they are cheaper to grow and have much less impact on the environment. Because the perennial crops lock away a lot more carbon in their root systems, they reduce carbon in the atmosphere, whereas annuals, by the time they have been tilled and fertilized and sprayed, add CO_2. There is a bigger diversity of wildlife in a perennial field. And perennials are less fussy about the quality of the soil, enabling land that was unusable for annuals to be brought into productive use. Perennials even cope better with the raised temperatures that global warming is liable to bring.

Perennials are miracle crops – and this isn't a new observation. The idea that we would benefit from perennial grain crops has been around for years, but there are significant technical difficulties in obtaining suitable stock for agricultural use. Current predictions suggest it could take between twenty and fifty years to bring perennial grains up to the level of annuals. Even though modern plant-breeding techniques are much more effective than used to be the case, it is still necessary to go through many generations, and perennials are inherently slower to propagate than their annual cousins.

Perennial food crops will begin to be viable relatively soon, but it's arguable that those who bang on about sustainability should be doing much more to ensure that the development required to move to perennials takes place as quickly as possible. Sadly, all too often those who speak in favour of sustainability are really con-servatives with a small 'c', more interested in keeping things the way they were in grandfather's day than in looking for opportunities for true sustainability that require more creative thinking.

The sustainable home

In the debates over food, we need to remember that sustainability is not just about agriculture. Arguably the ideal is 'sustainable living' – the concrete side of the wishy-washy concept of permaculture – where a human being's impact on the planet is controlled and balanced so that they don't leave a long-term deficit. One essential when using this wider view of sustainability is to take a look at our homes.

This can mean examining how they are built, but for the moment let's just consider one aspect – the environ-mental running costs of our housing. The UK government has a target that all new housing will be 'zero carbon' by 2016, and it has recently been announced that they hope to have a zero-carbon target for all new building of any sort – perhaps by 2020. At the moment buildings contribute about half of the carbon emissions from the UK (around 27 per cent of the total comes from homes alone), so the potential for each new house is high – though of course the country would retain millions of less efficient buildings as well as the newcomers.

We can't ignore that existing housing stock. A remarkable 50 per cent of UK homes have totally inadequate insulation – something that could be acted on much more quickly than savings requiring new build – but there is an attractive air of sustainability about the concept of a building that emits no CO_2. In principle, zero-carbon homes already make good financial sense – the government has removed stamp duty, saving thousands of pounds on buying one – but the current definition is so tight that only a handful of homes are so far classified as being stamp-duty exempt. For example, getting energy from a green supplier isn't allowed – it has to be self-generated.

If current government plans continue, the intention is to build 250,000 new homes a year from 2016 so, though the new build is a small percentage of the overall stock, it would in principle have a noticeable impact from an early stage. Yet the zero-carbon target is frighteningly difficult to achieve. This isn't just a matter of being carbon neutral (see page 56) but of having no overall emissions from the house, or activities in the house including washing, heating, TV, lighting, computers – all those ways we manage to use and waste power.

Although current tax regulations don't recognize it, a zero-carbon house needs to share some of the ways that it copes with energy use – for example, by having a shared wind turbine across a community. Being zero carbon is a desirable goal, and one that will increasingly be seen as a benefit when buying a house. As is often the case with the energy-saving aspects of green actions, once the initial cost is out of the way a zero-carbon house is great for the inhabitants because they should have to pay much less to keep it running, with negligible heating bills and other outgoings. Cutting out stamp duty is a good start, but it would make a lot of sense for governments to give more incentives to help people over the initial financial hurdle.

Zero-carbon Britain

The desire of the government to see all new housing zero carbon by 2016 pales into insignificance when set alongside the proposal of 'zero-carbon Britain'. This is an initiative by the Centre for Alternative Technology (CAT) in Wales, which posits a near future in which the whole country reaches zero-carbon status. To quote CAT's development director, Paul Allen: 'We are confident that if Britain treated this as the serious emergency the climate science is saying it is, we could eliminate the need for fossil fuels within 20 years.' Mind-boggling stuff. There is no doubt that such a move would be stunningly effective in terms of our impact on the planet, but how do they propose doing it, and is it even marginally feasible?

The zero-carbon Britain (ZCB) proposal suggests using a personal cap and trade system (see page 67) to bring energy usage down over twenty years to half current levels, while at the same time building up renewable energy sources sufficiently quickly that this amount of energy can be completely supplied from non-emitting sources. Outcome – zero-carbon Britain. I put it to Paul Allen that many green groups oppose cap and trade because it feels in some way immoral to sell the right to pollute. He responded that these quotas (referred to as TEQs) 'would be given as a right to individuals, thus ensuring energy equity in an unsure world. TEQs would be auctioned to industry and government, around a year in advance of their surrender.'

The ZCB scenario is, as its authors admit, challenging. It envisages domestic flights practically done away with and international flights 'severely reduced'. Meat-eating also 'would have to be reduced', not because of any hippy tendencies of the CAT (real though these are), but because meat production is not a carbon-efficient way to produce food, requiring significantly more land and energy input per kilocalorie of food value output.

As a regular meat-eater I was a little sceptical about this. Paul Allen said, 'The introduction of [personal cap and trade] would send a price signal which would return meat eating to a weekly "Sunday roast". This would actually be beneficial to our diets in comparison to today's excess.' Well, yes it would – but since when have we done what's good for us without coercion? ZCB suggests that the land freed up from animal use should be used for growing 'renewable wood fuels' – most likely coppiced trees to produce wood for burning.

Petrolheads would be gnawing their own hands off, as we would be required to see a 'wholesale switch to electric transport'. Electricity would largely come from wind, supplemented by other renewables, while domestic heating (a small requirement with superbly insulated new homes) would be left to heat pumps extracting heat from the ground and solar panels, plus boilers running on wood chips from those renewable plantations.

The authors emphasize that their scenario is just one possibility for achieving a goal they feel is essential. But is it practical? There are three requirements. That the technology will do what is expected of it, that we can get from here to there, and that the picture reflects the real world. Few of the technology proposals are extreme, although there are some concerns about the idea of running domestic heating off wood chips. These may be from a renewable source, but wood burning produces a much higher pollution level from particulates than other fuels, which would need to be addressed – and there is also the matter of distribution. You can't get wood chips down a pipe like gas. (There is also some doubt about classing wood burning as zero carbon. Although the wood takes carbon from the atmosphere, the process of growing, harvesting, processing and distributing wood chips is not carbon neutral.)

Do androids dream of electric cars?

Perhaps the biggest fantasy element in this proposal is the suggestion that electric vehicles could replace petrol and diesel in twenty years. At the moment there are no serious electric cars on the market. Not just a few – none. (Anyone who would like to propose the G-Wiz for this accolade has a very strange idea of 'serious'.)

At the time of writing, GM's Volt electric/petrol car, with a 40-mile radius on electricity alone, is admittedly relatively close to being on the road, but it isn't a pure electric vehicle, and this is a very first model – hardly likely to displace the whole of the petrol market. The Volt has an onboard petrol engine with the job of charging up the batteries as and when required, and is claimed to give around 150 miles per US gallon with this set-up. But such cars will initially be priced at the luxury end of the market.

Although there are those who would have us believe that the slowness in developing electric vehicles is a petrolhead conspiracy against electric cars (and it's certainly true that Jeremy Clarkson doesn't like them), car manufacturers really don't care what powers their product. If they could make viable electric cars (by which I mean both economically and technically viable), they would do so like a shot, because they would sell like hot cakes. In reality, the battery technology is fiendishly difficult to achieve – and then we've a whole new car infrastructure to build from scratch. The ZCB's statement that 'electric vehicles have been feasible for nearly 20 years' is a fantasy, unless you regard a Sinclair C5 as a viable vehicle. This is more likely to be a fifty-year than a twenty-year journey.

All this is a shame, as one of the nicer little twists of the ZCB report is the idea of using vehicles to support the electricity grid. Fossil fuels are, in effect, energy stores. Without them we need some other way to hold energy until we have to use it, dealing with surges in demand. If we are largely dependent on wind energy, there is a distinct problem that the wind input will not match demand – we won't want more energy on windy days and less on still ones – and even with wind turbines distributed around the country there will be days when there just isn't enough wind.

If we do all switch to electric cars, at any one time a

percentage of those will be plugged in for recharging. The idea of 'vehicle to grid' is that at times of high demand the grid can borrow power from the car batteries. This would have to be carefully metered, and there may be issues if, for example, you wanted to do a long journey the day after a seriously wind-free day, but it's an intriguing concept.

Hydrogen-fuelled cars, often trumpeted as the saviour of the environment, are just a different way of transferring energy from one place to another. Hydrogen has to be produced using a lot of electricity – and it's only if that electricity is already green that a hydrogen car comes into its own. Given the fact that hydrogen is also an extremely dangerous fuel, and would need a new national distribution system, whereas we already have one for electricity, hydrogen vehicles are highly inferior to electric cars, provided the battery technology *can* be developed.

Forcing us to change

Getting from where we are now to the ZCB ideal also raises issues. It's all very well to say 'domestic flights will have to be practically eliminated' or 'we will need to reduce meat consumption' – but how is that to be achieved, particularly within a relatively short time? Legislation against meat-eating is not going to get anywhere, and it's very hard for a regular meat-eater, when faced with a nice steak, to think of the environment and choose a nut cutlet instead. Similarly, if the government regulated against domestic flights there would be an outcry. It is only by massive investment in trains and other alternatives that we would find pricing and convenience to equal flying, and there is little sign that any flavour of government would be bold enough to sanction that.

It may be possible to imagine the UK getting to zero carbon on energy generation and food, but what about the rest? I am typing this on a computer assembled by a US company in the Republic of Ireland from components largely made in China (except for the monitor, which is Japanese). On my Swedish-made desk are pieces of equipment from China, Japan and the US (and the UK). Each of these required significant carbon emissions in their production. By halving the UK's energy requirement and generating that from renewables we do nothing to reduce the carbon emissions from our imports. ZCB depends on the whole world buying into this scheme, and that remains its biggest weakness.

To be fair, ZCB doesn't imagine Britain acting in isolation, pointing out that you can't stop climate change on your own. Its proponents suggest the only viable way forward is 'contraction and convergence'. This applies the same approach of setting limits for the whole world and gradually reducing them (contraction), while moving gradually from the current 'unfair' situation where per capita CO_2 outputs vary wildly to one where there is an equal entitlement for each individual (with trading to make this manageable). Given all we have seen from Kyoto, Bali and other international fiascos, the chances of getting a worldwide agreement, especially one with such a dramatic goal in mind, seem very slim.

When I put this to CAT development director Paul Allen he said, 'The report is based around the acceptance of the urgency of the situation. Is it feasible to continue with business, and more importantly politics, as usual?

The Bali Routemap leads to the UN Climate Change Conference in Copenhagen in December 2009. We aim to be there presenting a zero carbon EU27 strategy.' In other words, it ought to be possible in principle, and we will be asking the politicians to do it – but realists might argue that it ain't going to happen. Like it or not, we *do* have politics as usual.

It's arguable that we could aim for ZCB in a 'unilateral disarmament' mode, where we go ahead whatever, but without the wider world context it is hard to imagine it being practical. Apart from anything else, business is too global to stand for such an approach in a single location. The UK would become a backwater. However, we shouldn't be too hard on ZCB. It is a demonstration of the sort of serious goal we should be aiming for, rather than the wishy-washy attempts that we see at the moment.

Long-term environmentalist Sir Jonathon Porritt, who now tends to work from inside the establishment, has attacked the UK government for making 'soaring speeches' without backing them with action. He told the BBC's *Today* programme, 'What we are seeing at the moment is such a woeful falling short of what could be done that we are really nowhere near the pain barrier.' The approach taken he describes as crabby incrementalism: 'Just a little bit here, a little bit there, without actually sending a signal to citizens in the UK that this is indeed now the most serious problem that we have to deal with and we have to use the tax and expenditure systems in this country to address it.'

The ZCB scheme might not be 100 per cent practical, but neither is any other suggestion for dealing with climate change and sustainability. It is, however, a well-thought-out and stimulating picture that we could and should use as a starting point for devising a way forward that is more than posturing and incremental change on a road to nowhere, but really accepts the sort of action we need to face up to if we believe that climate change is indeed the threat that most climate scientists tell us it is.

For all the arguments about the sustainability of different agricultural methods (or even houses and the country as a whole), however, there's one thing no one can argue about. There's nothing sustainable about aviation.

11

Economy Class

Nothing better sums up our ambiguous relationship
with green issues than our attitude to travel. We all
know that flying has a terrible impact on our carbon
footprint, and that cars and the road network continue
to be disastrous for the environment, but it doesn't stop
us jetting off on holiday or dropping the kids off at school
in the 4×4. Yet taking an ecologic look at travel reveals
some surprising facts.

Is flying so bad?

We first need to address the initial assumption I made in
saying everyone knows that flying damages the environment. Surely it's not that bad? Unfortunately (and I say
this wincingly as a former employee of British Airways)
it really is. A typical mid-range long-haul return flight
can churn out 2.5 tonnes of CO_2 per passenger (one and
a half times this figure if you fly business class and
double if you go first). That's the equivalent of driving
over 15,000 kilometres in a typical car. Take a few long-
haul flights a year and with no other emissions

whatsoever you are already above average as a polluter.

Remarkably, given the widespread use of flight in the US, this isn't as much of a problem there as it is in the UK. Average US flight emissions are under one tonne a year, where the UK average is around 1.6 tonnes. Our enthusiasm for cheap flights has made flying a commonplace here. There is a sufficient number of Americans who never venture out of their neighbourhood to counterbalance heavy usage elsewhere. Here in the UK flying is considered an inevitable part of going on holiday, to the extent that surveys will often assume the two are the same thing, and my children, aged fourteen, are considered strange by their fellows because they have never flown for a holiday.

Lean, green, budget machines

Cheap airlines are, consequently, particularly wary of being made a scapegoat for environmental damage. They are, they point out, only serving a demand. The consumers *want* cheap flights, and the airlines are simply responding. When pressed, the most outspoken of budget-airline spokesmen, Ryanair chief executive Michael O'Leary, commented: 'The best thing we can do with environmentalists is shoot them.' He might have been a little prickly, but you can understand his feeling of persecution.

Some budget airlines go even further. Andy Harrison, chief executive of Ryanair's rival easyJet, made this startling statement on BBC Radio 4's *Today* programme: 'If you care about the environment you should fly easyJet. We fly new aircraft, [and have] high passenger load factors which means we emit 27 per cent fewer emissions per passenger kilometre than a traditional airline.'

There is some truth in easyJet's assertion. Using new planes does mean they are more fuel efficient, though their advantage here may be relatively shortlived. Airlines replace aircraft fleets in waves. While at the moment easyJet's fleet is one of the newest in Europe, in five years' time that balance may have significantly shifted. It is also true that they get more bodies on a flight than a 'traditional' carrier. That means fewer emissions per passenger. You can quibble with their figures, which are based on the standard capacity of an aircraft specified by the manufacturer, rather than the number of seats an airline has on board – and the load factors (percentage of seats occupied) vary for all airlines from year to year – but flying easyJet will result in less emissions than from a traditional airline, *provided there is competition on the route.*

That's a significant proviso. Some cheap airline seats are in direct competition with seats on less efficient carriers, but the budget airlines boast how they have opened up many new destinations, so many of their flights are to totally new airports. If the traveller would not have flown at all, but is now flying with easyJet or Ryanair – which must often be the case – the outcome is not a saving but a disastrous increase in emissions of the entire amount required for the flight. The easyJet claim might not be entirely greenwash, but it has more than a hint of it.

The green Virgin

It's not just the budget brigade who can resort to attempts to paint a thin green veneer on an otherwise environmentally damaging activity. Unsurprisingly, Richard Branson, king of the publicity stunt, has resorted to more than one 'green' initiative that's all show and no real effect. Virgin claimed to be 'the first airline in the world to fly on renewable fuel'. This sounds very impressive. But the truth is less so. They use 5 per cent of biofuel – which, as we have seen (page 93), is of highly dubious green merits – and the rest is good old-fashioned kerosene.

Then there's the idea of providing business customers with a Heathrow Express train ticket instead of a limousine ride to the airport. Not exactly surprisingly, only one per cent took up the offer. But best of all was Virgin's much-vaunted scheme to tow aircraft off the stand on to 'starting grids' at the ends of runways, saving on the inefficient practice of taxiing the aircraft on its jet engines. Virgin claimed this would save up to 2 tonnes of CO_2 per flight. Not a trivial amount (though it is less than one person's worth of emissions on a long-haul round trip). The saving comes from switching on the engines up to ten minutes later than usual. Claims of reduced noise levels and 'dramatically cleaner air' near airports were also made.

In practice, this happened only six times before the concept was shelved. Not only were airports unable or unwilling to provide the 'starting-grid' locations, but Virgin were warned by aircraft manufacturer Boeing that excessive towing would put too much strain on the undercarriage, meaning it would have to be replaced more frequently.

When the starting-grid proposal was put forward in 2006, Virgin was quick to jump into the limelight, even bringing in Governor Schwarzenegger of California to endorse it. Strangely, they have not been quite so noisy about the fact that the starting grids were non-starters.

Fantasies of growth

The future of the airline industry is where the inter-section between politics and the environment becomes most unsavoury. Governments protest their green credentials while all the time supporting airlines and airports in their assertion that growth is essential. This is a dubious strategy at best.

Take the much disputed third runway at Heathrow. Those in favour of the runway often provide the same sort of illogical two-way choice as supporters of Creationism give when thinking of the origins of life. Creationists argue that either evolution is true, or if it isn't then the Creationist view of a world created 10,000 years ago holds. So if they can find anything wrong with evolutionary theory, they hold it up as a positive argument for their own ideas. But it's not an either/or situation. It is quite possible for some aspect of evolution to be wrong without the alternative being Creationism.

The same applies to airports like Heathrow. Its supporters say that either Heathrow grows or it will collapse as a trade gateway, with dire consequences for the UK economy. Yet why should this be an either/or situation? It's arguable that the expansion of cheap flights damages the UK economy rather than helping it but, leaving that aside, Heathrow could be frozen in size without any damage to the economy – it doesn't operate in isolation. We are a small country, and Heathrow is not particularly well situated for most of the population or for most business.

The whole idea of vast airport growth, fixed long before we had any idea of the impact of flying on the environment, seems still to be on the minds of some parts of government, while others struggle to reduce our emissions. It's time someone pointed out the dire inconsistencies. There has also been a certain amount of misleading information about expansion. BA, for example, claimed that building a third runway at Heathrow would reduce CO_2 emissions from aircraft using the airport. The twisted logic required to come up with this statement says that, without the new runway, aircraft have to queue longer to get off the ground. During that queuing time their engines are running, churning out CO_2 – so less CO_2 will be emitted if there's an extra runway. The same goes for all the emissions from the planes stacked up waiting to land. Unfortunately, this argument (blocked by the Advertising Standards Agency in January 2008) bears no relation to what the government says will happen with a third runway.

BA's rosy picture applies only if there are no extra flights out of Heathrow – but, of course, the third runway is not planned with this in mind, but rather with an expansion of around 200,000 extra flights a year, and that means millions of extra tonnes of carbon. Interestingly, according to the government's own plans, Heathrow is not currently full at all, but operating at about 70 per cent of its current capacity with the existing runways, provided large aircraft are used. It could take up to 30 per cent more passengers with appropriate aircraft. Logic seems to go out of the window where flying is involved.

This lack of logical consistency in government

thinking goes far beyond airport expansion – it is also apparent in the difference in taxation between road fuel and air fuel. Perhaps the time has come to look beyond fuel tax when dealing with aircraft emissions. After all, we are not dealing with a sale to individuals, but to large corporations. If auctioned permits work well elsewhere (see page 286) and are economically efficient, perhaps we should be auctioning aircraft permits that are costly enough to have an impact, rather than attempting fuel taxation. What's certainly true is that not enough effort has been put into designing efficient economic means to reduce airline emissions.

Moving away from planes

If cleaning up the airlines' act isn't all that practical, we need to look at the choices we make in deciding to fly at all. Like many others with a green conscience, I try to keep my flying down to a minimum, but the alternatives aren't always as obvious as they seem. Our mental travel hit-list tends to be 'trains good, cars bad, planes awful', yet like most green decisions, it's more complicated than this.

Let's start with trains and cars. If you are driving alone – and like it or not, on business particularly, a lot of us do drive alone – there is no contest. Although the train has a lot of weight to shift, it works out significantly more carbon efficient than the solo car. But if you've a family of four in your car and it isn't an absolute gas-guzzler, it will release *less* carbon per passenger than a train would for the equivalent passengers. Does this mean that, given the choice, an ethically minded family of four should always drive? Strangely, no.

The reason is the relative incremental change. If your family decides to travel by car, the incremental change to the CO_2 emitted is a whole car's worth. However, should you decide to travel by train, they won't put on a new train. You will be occupying space in a train that was doing the journey anyway, so most of the train's CO_2 emissions for your seats would have happened anyway. There will be a slight extra emission because the train has a heavier load, but that won't compare with your car's output.

Now if everyone decided to travel by train, they *would* have to put on more trains, but the fact is that this isn't going to happen, so incrementally you are still better off by train. Except. Yes, there's another exception. Cars are more flexible in their routing than trains. I always take a train for a business trip if I can, rather than use a single-occupancy car, but there are some journeys where it simply isn't practical. Admittedly some of the journey time is spent sitting around on stations, but even so I can travel up to twice the number of miles on the train as I would if making the same journey by car. To make matters worse, trains tend to use hub and spoke arrangements, which we will see in a moment have their own problems.

Take a concrete example. I recently travelled from my home in Wiltshire to give a talk at a school at Kimbolton in Cambridgeshire. I confess that I drove. The driving distance was 95 miles. If I had gone by train I would have had to drive (no suitably timed buses) to my nearest station – 5 miles – get a train to London Paddington, a tube or bus to London St Pancras, another train to Bedford and a taxi for 15 miles to Kimbolton. The total distance would have been 160 miles. Part of the journey wasn't by train. And trains through London end up having the same congestion problems as cars, adding to emissions, whereas my car journey was cross-country. Overall it's hard to say which mode of transport was better for the environment.

Between trains and planes, the distinction is usually clear on a relatively short journey – at least for conventional trains. But before I feel smug about taking the train to Switzerland recently, I need to check just where the power for that train has come from. At the moment, a high-speed electric train in the UK would be responsible for a significant emission total from the power stations driving it: in France, though, with a high percentage of nuclear power, the impact is much lower. Eurostar reckons a passenger from London to Paris or Brussels is responsible for 'ten times less CO_2 than [if] flying'. Much of this greenness is thanks to that nuclear power input. And as we move to more green electricity production, those high-speed trains will become less and less emitting.

For existing trains in the UK, the balance varies considerably. Virgin claims its new electric Pendolino London to Glasgow trains use '78 per cent less carbon dioxide than domestic flights'. However, these trains tend to have lower passenger numbers than Eurostar – and they are the clean extreme. Many more Virgin services are operated using diesel-powered Voyager trains. These emit three times as much CO_2 as the equivalent required to power the Pendolinos, an amount that means load factors will have a huge impact on whether the plane (or the car) or the train is more effective.

Green roads

What we have to grit our teeth and face up to is that the best way to travel from the green viewpoint is by bus or coach (assuming the journey is too far to walk or go by bike). Here you have all the benefits of scale without the sheer weight of a train or fuel-guzzling capabilities of a plane. Coaches are being made more sophisticated, but there are still problems with timetabling and flexibility. To make that same journey from Wiltshire to Cambridgeshire by bus and coach, a journey that would take ninety minutes in the car and five hours by train would take a horrendous nine hours using bus and coach.

If you do decide to travel by car yet want to be green, it might seem a no-brainer (until the Volt is available) that the thing to do is to jump into a hybrid like a Toyota Prius. The Prius is by no means the only hybrid car that combines a petrol engine with an electric drive motor – Honda and Lexus also have well-publicized models, for example – but the Prius has become the icon of the visibly green movie star and as such tends to be held up as the shining example, or as the dubious token to be knocked down.

As we have seen, for an average UK driver to switch from a petrol car to a hybrid electric/petrol car like a Prius would save around 0.8 tonnes of CO_2, while gas-guzzling vehicle owners could save around 2.5 tonnes a year by switching to a hybrid. Yet hybrids aren't just a good way to irritate Jeremy Clarkson; they are also not always as green as they seem.

A hybrid is more expensive to build in carbon terms than an ordinary car, as there is more technology to offset (especially those carbon-heavy batteries), so it needs to be clearly out in front before it gets the green seal of approval. The good news for Prius lovers is that it is one of the lowest carbon emitters on the road at just 104 grams of carbon dioxide per kilometre. The bad news is that an efficient, modern, small diesel car has very similar emissions. In fact, at the time of writing the Prius was beaten by both Volkswagen's Polo Blue Motion diesel and Seat's equivalent Ibiza Ecomotion which only put out 99 grams per kilometre.

There is something in the Prius's favour, however. Diesels may be low carbon because of their high miles per gallon, but they do put out more particulates and oxides of nitrogen. Even so, modern diesels are getting cleaner and cleaner, and the distinction verges on the marginal. Toyota itself has a clean diesel system known as D-CAT. This not only removes particulates, but cleans up other exhaust pollutants too.

Things get even worse for the Prius when in country use. The stop/start life of an urban car is particularly effective for the electric motor, but those of us who spend most of our time on motorways or country roads will find the Prius similar to a petrol car, and significantly worse than a good diesel. In out-of-town tests, the Prius is beaten by a BMW 318d saloon, and would be absolutely slaughtered by a more fuel-efficient car.

It might be wondered why the Prius is a petrol car, rather than a diesel, combining the best of both aspects. Toyota says this is because diesel engines are more expensive than petrol – a spurious argument, as people who buy a Prius aren't hugely price sensitive. The more significant point Toyota makes is that 'diesel is not a popular fuel in all parts of the world (especially [the]

USA)' – and there's the real reason why we don't have a more efficient hybrid. The average US driver doesn't understand diesel, so we get second best.

The hybrid car's limitations are often concealed, and not only by the manufacturers. The UK government has a website, promoted through TV advertising, where you can compare different new cars and see which is the best on CO_2 emissions. There is a problem with the way this website is arranged, however: you have to select a type of car, so can't compare the Volkswagen above with the Prius (the VW is classed as a supermini, where the Prius is a 'small family' car). But more problematic is that the site shows only the combined urban/motorway figures that result in the Prius getting 104 grams per kilometre. It doesn't show figures for rural or mostly motorway driving, and it doesn't even indicate that the ranking shown will be highly misleading if you don't live in a city.

The Department of Transport responded to this concern by saying that 'those data, rightly, cannot take into account the driving styles of individual motorists'. This may be true, but it doesn't make the website any less misleading. They ought to make it clear that their ranking is useless except for urban drivers. It would be perfectly possible to have three types of typical user – mostly urban, mostly motorway and mostly rural, and to be able to offer the best emission suggestions for all three. The top of the charts would differ hugely, given the poor performance of hybrids out of the city.

I travel to London on a regular basis, but would never consider driving there – I always use public transport. That a government site assumes city driving is part of your typical cycle is arguably not only misleading, but downright irresponsible. (The site also fails to point out that it's better for the environment not to get a new car if your current one isn't a terrible emitter – see page 54.)

The benefits of driving a Prius are fairly marginal, but we haven't seen the end of cars that are more economical on fuel and stingy on their emissions. Car manufacturers in the past have tended to concentrate more on 0–60 acceleration, top speed, horsepower – even number of cup-holders – rather than emissions and fuel economy (a conspiracy theorist might think they were in the pay of the petrol companies). Now there is much more consumer pressure – even in the traditionally mpg-insensitive US – to have greater fuel efficiency. The X Prize, that was awarded to the first private manned space vehicle by the independently funded X Prize Foundation, has now been followed up by the Automotive X Prize, a $10 million fund to encourage the production of cars that can give at least 100 miles to the US gallon (that's 120 miles per gallon in the more familiar units) with carbon emissions of no more than 60 grams per kilometre.

Some of this can be achieved incrementally. For example, technology that turns the engine off when the car is stopped, restarting it transparently when the accelerator is touched, is already in use in the diesel version of the Mini Cooper and reduces emissions by around 10 per cent. More savings can be made by making a car lighter. Even so, it's proving a hard task. In principle the solution is easy: an electric car. But as we have seen, in reality this isn't a simple proposition.

For the moment, however we travel, unless we are walking we will be responsible for some degree of atmospheric pollution and carbon emissions. Even bike riders don't escape – unfortunately there's plenty of carbon pumped out in the production of that fancy racing frame, and we won't even consider (thankfully) what goes into the Lycra shorts. Yet atmospheric pollution is a problem that has been subject to some surprisingly successful solutions already.

12

Pollution Versus eBay

Everyone agrees on the need to control pollution, but it's not so easy to implement controls in practice, nor is it always obvious how to balance the impact of different pollutants. We are so constantly bombarded with the impact of carbon dioxide on the environment that it is entirely possible to forget how dangerous other pollutants can be. We are sometimes encouraged, for instance, to cook on wood stoves rather than use a heat source like gas. Unfortunately, burning wood churns out some really nasty pollutants – both particulates and carcinogenic volatile organic compounds. The knee-jerk reaction is that carbon dioxide has to be the *really* bad thing – because . . . it's carbon, isn't it? – while these other pollutants are okay really. This is not a safe assumption.

Even if you can get a good view of the relative impact of different pollutants, it's not easy to bring them under control. Businesses are driven by a desire for profit, and pollution control can be costly. Individuals do not see their own small contribution to global pollution, whether it is landfill or CO_2, as significant. It's not enough to have good intentions, or for that matter to take token green actions. To make significant change requires mechanisms that will support, encourage and where necessary police changes to improve the environment. Surprisingly, one of the most powerful ways of doing this involves an auction, a sort of environmental eBay.

Taking auction against pollution

The traditional way of controlling pollution and other negative environmental impacts is to impose statutory levels – to fix standards and say that everyone should stick to them. There are, unfortunately, real problems with this approach. When it is applied at country level – for example, when the European Union sets standards for its member states – many countries feel able to ignore the standards. Although there are usually sanctions for those that stray too far outside the standards, they are rarely enforced and, even when they are, can take years before they have any impact.

Worse still, that impact is hardly ever at a level that could be considered punitive by as big an economy as a country. A million-pound fine may be horrendously large for an individual, but to a country it's hardly noticeable. To pay a million pounds a year, the UK would only have to raise around 0.03 pence a week from each person in the country.

When standards are imposed at a company level they are more likely to be followed, but they are still a very blunt instrument – certainly not an efficient way to get to the desired results. The problem with this approach is that the negative impact of the regime – and control of pollution often does have a negative impact – is not divided fairly among businesses. Companies that have relatively low impacts on the environment still have to jump through the hoops to show they come up to the standards, with the associated cost. This leads to the classic problem of focusing on meeting the targets rather than attempting to solve the problem with which the targets are supposed to help.

Hailing green taxes

A better approach, in terms of strict economic logic, is the imposition of green taxes, which are increasingly being employed, particularly in Europe. But tax is a complex tool, and one that politicians almost always mess with until it ceases to have the desired result. This is because effective taxes are often unpopular taxes.

To see this meddling in action, take the relatively self-contained green taxation issue of road use. Originally taxes on drivers, whether a fixed annual sum like the UK Road Fund Licence or taxes on fuels, were intended as a way to fund the infrastructure costs of driving. Road building and maintenance were expensive – and why should everyone pay at a time when relatively few had cars?

However, governments don't like ring-fenced cash, so the income from car taxes was subsumed into the general Exchequer. And governments (of all colours) *do* like what the Tory party has referred to as Stealth Taxes – taxes that the taxpayer doesn't really notice paying. So over time, the taxes from car use have increased well beyond any road-building costs.

Now, though, we aren't just worried about road building. There is the need to have green controls, and taxes seem a natural route. This is particularly the case with individual pollution like that emitted by cars, which isn't easy to reduce directly by legislation or by more complex measures like permit-trading. (There is legislation on the output levels from cars, but this doesn't influence how an individual uses the car.)

Once the intention of taxation changed from supporting infrastructure to reducing pollution, it became necessary to re-examine the tax structure. The Road Fund Licence is a fixed amount paid once a year, however much the car is used. It varies from car to car on carbon emissions, and there are proposals to make it vary more dramatically in the future, but its main function is to set an entry level for car-ownership. Once it is paid, the more you drive, the cheaper per mile this particular tax is – it's a tax that *encourages* pollution.

The first logical move for a government that wants to make car taxes more environmentally effective is to scrap the Road Fund Licence. This would have a double effect. The licence is unpopular, so getting rid of it would go down well, and it has entirely the opposite effect to that desired. On its own, though, getting rid of the Road Fund Licence isn't enough, and that's where things get tough for the government. You almost feel for sorry for them.

As well as scrapping an ineffective tax, it is also necessary to apply an effective one. The only simple way to do this is by using fuel duty. This is nothing new. At the time of writing around 67p in each pound spent on petrol is tax, leaving only 33p in the pound for the fuel itself. Technically the tax is only partly fuel duty, as petrol also carries VAT (on both the petrol cost *and* on the fuel duty), but this is really only a matter of labels – it all goes the same way.

A simple transfer of the Road Fund Licence to fuel duty would mean putting between 5p and 10p a litre on fuel (arguably a rise that would seem less painful than doing without the large annual lump sum). But if the aim is to discourage emissions, then it will be necessary to go beyond current levels of duty – a dangerous route, as the government discovered in 2000.

Lessons from a fuel crisis

Oil prices were rising, with crude oil passing $35 a barrel. (Pretty reasonable compared with $109 per barrel as I write, but expensive at the time.) Although Chancellor Gordon Brown had scrapped the 'fuel duty escalator' in 1999 – a mechanism introduced by the Conservatives in 1993 to ensure that duty would rise above the rate of inflation (a genuine green tax) – petrol duties were still steadily rising. The most recent increase in the 2000 budget had been around 2p a litre – and the higher the cost of oil, the larger the amount the government received from VAT. On 7 September 2000, a grassroots blockade by road hauliers under the banner 'Fair play on fuel' closed the giant Stanlow oil refinery in Cheshire.

Other protests followed, with refineries blockaded and slow-moving lorry convoys causing chaos on motorways. It was a risky strategy by the road hauliers. It could have caused the general public to take against them in a big way. If you wanted to get somewhere in a hurry, their convoys held you up. And as supplies to petrol stations dried up, getting fuel at all became an issue. However, everyone was feeling the pinch – there was strong public support for the action.

By 11 September just four days after the action began, there were already severe shortages and the government was given emergency powers to bring fuel supplies under its control. In the end, three days later, with public support beginning to turn against them, the protestors caved in, giving the government sixty days to respond. While stressing that they weren't giving way to pressure, the Chancellor announced a 3p cut in tax on some fuels in the November pre-budget statement.

By now the once-united protestors were split into factions and public support had reached an all-time low. For the moment the unrest caused by fuel taxation was over, though concerns rumbled on, and at the time of writing, with petrol costs well above £1 a litre, they are starting to resurface.

Interestingly, the view of what happened in 2000 has become rose-tinted for those who support the cause of the protestors. Although technically it was the protestors rather than the government who caved in, the protest is often represented as a victory. There is also some confusion over what triggered it. One of the better websites on the subject, petrolprices.com recognizes on one page that this occurred 'despite the fuel escalator being abandoned in 1999', yet elsewhere comments that 'The protests of 2000 achieved some success in that the fuel duty escalator was frozen.'

There remains a strong swell of suspicion that fuel duty is being used more to fill the government's coffers than to benefit the environment. Typical comments from petrolprices.com see it as a way to suppress the poor, to run down those who rely on cars for their work, and to rip off motorists. If there is any recognition of the green issues, it is to say, 'I know we have to save the planet, but . . .' In the end it is given second place to 'I need my car for my job' or just 'Motorists have the right to drive.'

Raising fuel duty causes widespread protest about being hit in the pocket – something that one way or another is going to have to be faced as resources run short and if we are to take climate change seriously. But it also produces one legitimate complaint that is often lost in the howling over extra expenditure: although apparently a fair, evenly distributed tax, fuel duty is in fact a selective tax, hitting those who live in rural areas harder than those who live in cities.

This is an example of what economists call 'externality' – having to bring into the economic equation not just the straight cost and benefit of buying and using the fuel, but also the impact of the surrounding environment. In this case, the big difference between rural and city environments is the availability of effective alternative transport. This is easily seen when comparing a 5-mile journey across the centre of London with the same journey from a rural village to the nearest shop.

In the case of the village, the only alternative may well be to walk, to go by bike or to ring for a minicab. There may be a bus service, but if there is it will probably operate only a couple of times a day. By comparison, the Londoner can take the tube or a frequent bus service, or hail a taxi, as well as having the options available to the villager. Many Londoners don't bother with cars because the public-transport options are often quicker than driving. A simple tax on fuel hits both the villager and the Londoner the same for their 5 miles. (In practice it does hit the Londoner a little more, as they will probably make the journey more slowly with many more stops and starts, thus using more fuel, but it is in principle a flat-rate tax.)

Taxing by route

For this reason, it makes sense to charge more tax for mileage on routes with good public transport than on those with limited transport. This also tends to apply to motorway journeys, where the routes parallel rail and air options. As it happens, the city-centre and motorway routes also tend to be the most heavily congested – so finding some way to increase the tax burden there and to decrease it on country roads is both fairer and liable to help reduce the serious congestion problem faced by a small, highly populated island like Great Britain.

A crude but simple approach is the sort of congestion charge used in London. At the moment this is a per day charge, though it could be made more effective by making it per trip. But the best impact would come from variable charging based on distance travelled and which roads are being used. This would be effective only if combined with the removal of both the Road Fund Licence and fuel duty.

In 2007 the UK government came out with such a road-pricing suggestion, based on monitors in each car. This scheme has been almost universally described as an anti-congestion measure, though in practice it is also a fairer form of green taxation. It is a very expensive and complex scheme to install and administer, but it would have the desired effect. Unfortunately, even more so than simple fuel duty, it has caused panic among motorists. Inevitably in such a scheme there will be winners and losers, and those who are likely to lose most heavily – the people who do a lot of motorway and city driving – are those who will shout loudest.

Because of the way the scheme was presented in the media, with headlines screaming about paying 'up to £1.30 a mile' – admittedly speculative, because no one really knew how the rates would be applied – it seemed that practically everyone would lose out. The result was a huge negative response from the general public, including an e-petition with over 1.8 million respondents and a heavy-duty campaign from one leading newspaper (the *Daily Telegraph*).

The public showed an interesting conflict of opinion, however. The majority believed that there should be a fairer way of paying for what's used, but most were unhappy with the road-pricing approach. Combined with an impossibly complex system to monitor and administer payments, this resulted in a quiet pushing aside of the scheme in late 2007. A fairer approach to fuel duty may still be produced, but the lessons of the last few years are that doing so will require extreme delicacy and transparency, plus the simplest systems possible to achieve the desired effect – something governments are rarely good at devising.

When suggesting a pay-to-drive scheme, legislators face cries of 'It's unfair on the poor' – but observed logically, this is an odd argument. We don't say that having to pay for practically anything else is 'unfair on the poor' – if necessary we subsidize the poor, but we don't suddenly make all other purchases from food to electricity free. Why should access to another limited resource – the roads – be free? Anyway, combined with the removal of the Road Fund Licence and fuel tax, a pay-to-drive system is advantageous for those who make less use of a car.

Like it or not, a pay-per-trip system based on the pollution produced, likely congestion and other impacts on the environment is the *fairest* possible solution, and the most effective one to counter pollution. If governments are to adopt such a scheme, they will need to do a huge selling and education campaign; to be very clear that they are scrapping other taxes on road users; and to simplify the implementation so that it doesn't depend on each car having a supercomputer calculating its moment-by-moment impact and relaying it to a central database.

Pollution counts

Explicit green taxation seems a very modern concept, but it goes back a long way. Well before we were aware of the larger-scale impact of carbon dioxide and other emissions, it was obvious that the sulphurous gases from impurities in coal could have a drastic impact on health. London was famous for its choking smogs, a very visible form of pollution. Such pollution is a classic case of an externality.

Economics is a great way to make decisions, but the trouble is that our actions often have impacts that aren't taken into account in a simple financial equation. These are the externalities. When I take my car out for a drive, I can weigh up the cost of running it against the benefit of getting from A to B quickly, secure from the elements, and relatively safely. But I don't factor into that equation my impact on climate change or, for that matter, what my exhaust fumes do for the air quality of the passers-by.

In the nineteenth century, as heavy industry grew and great cities like London became burdened with ever more chimneys, a vast amount of pollution was pumped out into the air. By the turn of the century smog was common. Just like me in my car, the individual polluters were weighing the cost of the fuel against the benefits it brought them, whether it was heating their houses or powering their machines. They ignored the externality of the impact on the atmosphere of the waste gases from burning those fuels. The economist Arthur Pigou came up with the concept of green taxation in 1920 in an attempt to overcome this problem.

What economists try to do when faced with externalities is to bring them into the equation. This involves finding the impact of an extra use (whether it's an extra journey or an extra piece of coal on the fire) and imposing a cost that fills up the gap between the benefit the user gets from that piece of coal and the disadvantage it causes to the external world. Pigou suggested taxing to allow for this negative impact and identified two key ingredients to such a tax: it should be uniform, and it should be based on the emissions produced rather than on (say) the amount of coal used.

Getting the tax right

Making the tax uniform is essential if a measure like this is to be effective. It should cost anyone, whoever or whatever they are, the same to pollute by the same amount. If you think about this, it's pretty obvious. Let's take it to a ridiculous extreme. Imagine it cost my neighbour £1 to dump a sack of rubbish in landfill, and it cost me £100. Then instead of dumping one bag for that £100

I could happily dump fifty sacks by slipping my neighbour £2 for each one he took off me. Despite having to pay (in theory) a punitive tax, I have no real incentive to cut my levels of pollution.

It is also important, as Pigou pointed out, that any taxation should be based on the amount of pollution produced. This is so obvious that it's hard to see initially why anyone would go for anything else. The more you pollute, the more you pay. The problem with this approach is that it isn't always easy to measure the amount of pollution produced. In such circumstances it's tempting to forget measuring what's right, and go instead for what's easy.

Imagine you had a brick-making company and, as part of the process, your bricks were left out to dry in the sun. During this process, let's say they gave off a pollutant. (This is an imaginary example – I have no idea if drying bricks pollute.) It would be quite difficult to measure how much pollution you were giving off, so some bright spark would almost certainly come up with a scheme where you paid a certain amount of tax per brick. Easy to measure, easy to tick the box and move on.

The trouble is, it's unfair. I might have developed special low-polluting bricks, or use a drying process that lasts half the time of those used by my competitors, or dry the bricks in a special room with extractors that absorbed the pollutant. It wouldn't matter. I would still pay the same. So I wouldn't have any incentive to develop these cleaner processes – and if I had done so, I would feel hard done by.

In practice it is relatively easy to monitor the pollution produced by many industrial processes, but there are plenty of exceptions. In agriculture, for instance, it can be very difficult to measure the impact of a farmer's use of pesticides on the local water quality, and so it is necessary to resort to measuring (and potentially taxing) the input – in this case the quantity of pesticide used – rather than the true impact on the environment.

So economists strongly argue that we should have green taxes, and it should apply uniformly and on outputs. And what do governments do? Nod their heads sagely, agree that green taxes are the only way forward, and go ahead and apply them anything but uniformly. In practice, domestic consumers are taxed much higher on the environment than are businesses. Uniform green taxes are rare indeed.

To make matters worse, green taxes are rarely set high enough to change behaviour. It is hard not to conclude that many green taxes to date have been less about reducing pollution and more about getting cash into government coffers and ticking the green box in the manifesto. Many of the early adopters of taxation on CO_2 emissions have seen *increases* in output of carbon dioxide over the first few years the taxation has been in place.

Tax in the real world

In principle, then, there is a clear way to control pollution with taxation, but the real world is not as simple as an economic model and political forces are a major factor in the effectiveness of any control. Increasing taxes and regulations makes governments unpopular, and though governments may be driven by personal conviction, they are certainly strongly influenced by pressure groups. Many of the problems of pollution are caused by a relatively small group – often big businesses – while the impact is felt by a large group – private individuals.

It might seem that this gives the natural benefit to the large group, but the numbers don't work like that. If a swingeing pollution-control policy is applied, it will result in large costs for each of the small group of polluters. So it's worth them spending a lot of money to lobby politicians to reduce the impact on business. 'Jobs will be lost,' they cry. 'We won't be competitive with the rest of Europe/America/Asia [delete to taste], who won't have the same burden.'

On the other side of the balance, most individual citizens who benefit from the imposition of pollution control will get only a relatively small improvement. Because the value is low, they are less likely than big business to lobby politicians. To undertake a full-scale, expensive political lobby, an individual would have to pay much more than the benefit they would gain. The diluted nature of the benefits across so many individuals mean that they are less likely to influence government policy.

Of course, it isn't all down to individuals. There are environmental pressure groups like Greenpeace and Friends of the Earth who will inevitably weigh in to support pollution-control policies. Such groups do have lobbying power, but there is a negative to their contribution too. That word 'inevitably'. Fighting for this sort of thing is their *raison d'être*. While business is lobbying to keep pollution controls weak to save jobs and competitiveness, the environmental groups are just doing what they always do. We've heard it all before and can hardly expect otherwise. So green lobbyists can find it hard to take on the arguments of industry.

The result is not only insufficiently high taxes to change behaviour, but also taxes which are not uniform, stacked in favour of industry. In a survey in 1997 of five European countries with an explicit CO_2 tax, all but one (the Netherlands) had a lower tax rate for business than individuals, with the most extreme, Denmark, taxing individuals around nine times the rate of tax on business. (In practice the differential was more extreme, as overall company tax rates are different from those for individuals, driving the effective differential in Denmark up to fourteen times. Even the Netherlands made individuals pay twice as much when this is taken into account.)

What seems to have been the case in these countries is that the environmental lobby groups were ruled more by appearance than by content, while the industry lobby groups focused on the content and won the day. Environmental lobbyists forced the need for a green tax, but then seemed to feel that the job was done. Industry lobbyists pushed repeatedly for a favourable *design* of the tax scheme and made the scheme unfit for purpose.

It seems (and by now it shouldn't come as a surprise) that the environmentalists are ruled too much by the heart than the head. It's not enough to get the token aspect of taxation; it's essential to go the whole hog and get an effective form of taxation. This means being in it for the long haul, rather than jumping on to the next bandwagon that lumbers into the public eye – something environmental groups have an unfortunate tendency to do.

With some European countries, the initial suggestion was for a uniform scheme, but industry then lobbied very strongly against this. The environmental lobbyists, presumably thinking they didn't need to argue for what was already on the table, took a back seat until it was too late. The industry faction had already swung things hugely in their own direction.

So effective was the lobbying in Denmark that the initial scheme provided businesses with a refund mechanism on the tax: the more pollution a company emitted, the bigger the refund. This was supposed to make things easier for companies that had the most to clean up, but in practice it meant that they were being subsidized to pollute. The Danish industry lobby actively encouraged its members to pollute more so that they could get a bigger refund. When this system was later revamped, the environmental lobbyists were very active in initial consultations about the changes needed, but had much less input than industry to the detailed decision-making process. The result was a tax system that was still highly favourable towards business.

Politics and green policy

There seems to be something of an assumption in what I've said so far that governments are empty-headed pragmatists, buoyed along by whatever lobby groups pound against them the most. It's certainly true that both New Labour and David Cameron's Conservative Party have shown a tendency to worship the focus group and to be easily swayed by lobbying. But traditionally there has been a reasonably clear political split between left-wing support for the workers, centrist governments focusing on the people as a whole and right-wing governments fighting for business. It would be surprising if this split had no effect on governmental approaches to pollution control.

In Europe, traditionally left-of-centre governments (Social Democratic and Labour) have tended to favour hitting businesses and giving stronger support to environmental lobbyists, though there is always the dichotomy that anything that hits business is also likely to damage the opportunities of the workers.

To the right of centre there tends to be more enthusiasm for voluntary schemes, or for taxation that is riddled with exemptions and refunds so that it gives the appearance of providing green measures on the surface while not presenting any real difficulties for business. Strangely, although market-based mechanisms ought to appeal to the right wing, they are rarely found acceptable. For example, in 1990 Margaret Thatcher's environment secretary Chris Patten suggested a permit-based system, where businesses would have to buy and trade permits to pollute, but this was squashed by the Thatcher government. Although the market-based mechanism should have been ideologically acceptable, its use was not deemed appropriate.

Taking with one hand, giving with the other

One way that governments can make taxes more acceptable to business (and individuals) is by giving some of the money back. This may seem a strange thing to do – taking money away with one hand and giving it back with the other – but it is a primary role of government and it can be done in such a way that it doesn't reduce the impact of the tax on cutting pollution.

One essential is that, while the tax is linked to the pollution levels, the money given back isn't. The refund makes the impact of the tax system less burdensome, but there is still an incentive to reduce pollution. If any refund is proportional to the original level of taxation (and hence pollution), all you have done is weaken the tax. One approach to reimbursement that is particularly effective from a green standpoint is to earmark the refunds for environmental projects.

In such a scheme, rather than simply paying back some of the money raised in green taxation, companies are given money to engage in agreed environmental projects that will either reduce their environmental impact or have some other offsetting approach. For example, it could be to develop a new, lower-emission manufacturing process, or to put in a wind turbine to reduce reliance on carbon fuels.

Where money is given back without earmarking, it needs to be done in a way that will counter arguments against green taxation. It is often argued, for instance, that green taxation makes businesses less economic, so results in lost jobs. In such a case, a government might give the money raised in green taxes back by reducing the overheads on employing people – income tax and National Insurance, for instance. The net income to the Treasury is the same, polluters pay more, yet it's more financially attractive to employ people.

Some companies won't be happy. This kind of re-imbursement gives more benefits to labour-intensive industries and penalizes businesses that have high energy use but small labour forces. An alternative approach could, for example, base reimbursement on the level of corporation tax paid. But this favours the more profitable firms. *Any* form of redistribution will leave some companies unhappy, but by appropriate uses of reimbursement governments can introduce green taxes that fairly apply the same rate to businesses as individuals, while offsetting some of the impact on the economy.

If the whole business of taxing and then giving the money back still seems crazy, it becomes clearer when seen at a personal level. Imagine the government put a huge carbon tax on domestic electricity and gas – say doubling the price. They then give *all* the tax revenue back to the taxpayers in the form of a tax credit that is evenly distributed among households, however much or little fuel you consume. The Exchequer does not benefit at all. Use the average amount of energy and you are no better off. Go over the top with your energy use and you will suffer. Cut back on energy use and you will make money.

As with businesses, there will be domestic winners and losers. People with large families might argue that the credit should be on a per capita basis, rather than per household. But the principle is that if a swingeing tax is combined with giving the money back, then it is possible to avoid crippling the taxpayer but still to make it attractive to reduce energy use and pollution. You could then gradually increase the tax, always offsetting it with a credit, encouraging more and more efficient use of energy.

If normal taxes don't have enough impact, some will suggest a negative tax – a subsidy, a positive incentive to reduce pollution. After all, the carrot is often better than the stick. Subsidies can be useful to kick-start an economic change, provided they are widely and easily available. For example, subsidizing installation of low-impact energy generation like solar power. But from an economics viewpoint, it is essential that such a subsidy is short term.

Imagine we decided to subsidize companies to reduce their pollution levels. Then from an economic viewpoint we have an industry that is unfairly supported. It isn't operating under proper market forces, so it will be operating in an inefficient way. There will be more companies in the particular line of business than there needs to be, because there are financial incentives to operate. There is also a constant temptation to cheat. If you are paid for cutting pollution levels, it is only a small step away from managing unnecessarily high initial pollution levels so that you can be paid extra for a big reduction. Subsidy can become money that encourages pollution.

Buying our way out

However we apply taxes there seem to be inequities, but is there an alternative? In the late 1960s economists devised a mechanism that is just as efficient, but feels fairer and sits more comfortably with a capitalist system that prefers markets to regulation imposed from on high. This is the approach we've already met of using permits to pollute. These can control a market without the difficulties of standards or subsidies, provided (and it's a non-trivial proviso) that the permits can be traded and that there is transparent information available to support the trading.

Permits to pollute are very attractive to business. A knee-jerk reaction might be 'of course they are, it means they can get away with pollution just by spending money', but that's not the point. Compared with straightforward green taxation, permits can provide the same level in pollution cuts at a much lower cost to the producer. To take an example from the Kyoto Protocol, to provide the 5 per cent reduction in CO_2 levels required between 1990 and 2012 would cost business thirty-nine times more under a taxation scheme than under a permit scheme.

This assumes taxation without reimbursement, which is not attractive to business – but while giving tax money back is much better for those suffering the tax, it is something governments are reluctant to do, because they lose cash they would otherwise control. Permit-trading is attractive because the costs of reducing emissions are not the same for every business, nor in every country. Permit-trading allows the market to find a more cost-effective way to produce the desired reduction in emissions. If this seems underhand or even immoral, think of it in terms of two power stations.

For an old, inefficient coal-fired power station it is relatively easy to reduce global emissions. All sorts of changes can be made to pull down the pollution level. For a wind-power station it is very difficult to reduce global emissions, because it doesn't contribute much in the first place. It's obvious in this case that it would be sensible to find a way to encourage improvement or replacement of the coal-fired station. Yet this is really all that permit-trading does, except it's on a global scale and makes use of tools like auctions to facilitate the movement of improvements to the places they can be done most cost-effectively.

What's more, by trading permits the benefits can be

shared. If a country with relatively efficient power plants buys permits from a country with less efficient plants, both can benefit. It costs more to reduce emissions on an efficient power station than it does on an inefficient one. The country buying permits saves money compared with the high cost of reducing emissions further on their efficient plants. The selling country gains the price of the permits *and* can reduce emissions on their inefficient plants relatively cheaply – a double benefit. It really is one of those rare win-win situations, provided the permits are traded in an effective manner.

That proviso is important. It is essential that at least two aspects of the trade are dealt with correctly – the initial allocation of permits and the mechanism for doing the trade. If the initial allocation is wrong, then a huge amount of unfairness can creep into the system. And if permits are not sold on an open, transparent auction it's also possible to get things very wrong. It's important, though, that moral indignation ('They ought not to be able to buy the right to pollute') doesn't cloud the issue.

Losing our fear of touts

Let's step away from pollution for a moment to a parallel issue with a similar tendency to raise hackles – reselling event tickets. I'm sure you've seen the kind of thing. Tickets are sold for a very attractive event, say at £100 a time. They sell out in minutes. And soon after, the tickets are being resold for hugely inflated sums. Then the media and attention-seeking politicians break out in outrage that such a thing should happen, particularly if it's a charity event.

The arguments are of two kinds. One says, particularly if the event is raising money for a charity, that a third party shouldn't benefit. The other suggests that touts will buy up blocks of tickets and resell them at huge profit. Both are genuine concerns, yet it's important not to get tangled up in all this and jump to the conclusion that it's not fair for someone to resell a ticket. That is a simple market operation. If I buy a ticket and someone else wants it so much they are prepared to pay more, I should be able to sell it. They're happy – they've got the ticket at a price they were prepared to pay. I'm happy – I've made a profit. The organizers are happy – they've got their ticket price. Who has lost out? No one.

To get over the negative concerns, those same two measures described above are required: correct initial allocation and transparent auction-based reselling. It's first important to allocate the tickets safely, so that touts can't buy up blocks. This can be done by limiting the numbers that can be purchased by an individual, or by using a lottery to allocate them. However, making tickets non-transferable is entirely the wrong approach. If I decide I don't want to go to the event, I ought to be able to resell the ticket at whatever I can get for it.

The second concern is that extra money doesn't go to the organizers (especially if it is a charity). This is also possible to overcome – by supporting those who want to resell, rather than criminalizing them. If the box office offered a service whereby anyone who wanted to resell their tickets could put them into an auction, and they would then be sold to the highest bidder, the buyer could be refunded the purchase price and any profit could be split between the buyer and the organizer. Here absolutely everyone wins. Of course, the organizer could just auction all tickets in the first place, but this would mean they would go only to the highest bidders. A sense of fairness might incline them to sell some or all initially at a flat price, but then allow reselling through the auction.

The auction microscope

The reason auctions are great (as long as they are 'open' auctions rather than sealed bids) is that they provide those involved with information to help them make sensible decisions. One of the hardest decisions when selling tickets for an event is what to charge. Set the price too high and you won't sell any. Set it too low and you could sell the tickets many times over, losing profits. An auction gives everyone the chance to see just what those tickets are worth to people.

Moving back to pollution, the use of auctions has been tried and tested to great effect in the case of the US pollution permits for power generators. If the Environmental Protection Agency (EPA) had just asked power companies how much it would cost to clean up emissions, the companies would have looked very serious, sucked in breath and declared it would be very expensive. However, by auctioning off permits to pollute it quickly became clear just how much power companies thought they were worth – and hence how much they thought it would cost to clean up their act. This then makes it easy to tweak the scheme gradually to make it less worthwhile to buy permits and more worthwhile to reduce emissions.

The US case is a good demonstration of how wrong you

can get it without using a mechanism like an auction to open up information. Based on what they were told by the power companies, the EPA reckoned the cost of cleaning sulphur dioxide from emissions was between $250 and $700 a ton. But just three years after auctions commenced, permits were selling at $70 a ton – and not selling very well even at that, because the companies found it cheaper to clean up their outputs. By setting sensible initial levels of permission, using the auction system to monitor the value regularly and gradually reducing the availability of permits, it is possible to regulate in a way that keeps costs for industry to a minimum – after all, the agenda should not be to cripple business – and maximizes the benefits everyone is looking for in reduction of pollution.

Part of the reason for the success of the scheme is the combination of effective monitoring and a single controlling body. To be part of the scheme, power stations have to have remote sensing monitors, sending information on pollution levels back to the EPA. Should a station exceed limits, the penalty is drastic – a fine of $2,000 per tonne, between ten and fifteen times higher than the price of buying a permit. It just isn't worth cheating. Such a scheme is easier to monitor and control at the national level than with the concept of international carbon trading – though this doesn't mean that trading carbon permits is a bad thing.

It is interesting that initially American environmental groups fought the concept of permit-trading. In sheer knee-jerk reaction terms it sounds like a licence to pollute, which must be bad. Yet that initial reaction was the classic green problem of responding to appearance rather than substance. Now environmental groups in the US support permit-trading because they have discovered that it results in bigger cuts in emission targets than other forms of regulation.

The lesson from the US is clear. There need to be clear mechanisms and rules of trading, a well-designed auction system to redistribute permits on a regular basis, good monitoring and stringent enforceable punishments for those who cheat. These are all harder to impose at an international level, but not impossible. Without these requirements being met a permit scheme is at best fudged and potentially worse than useless.

A load of hot air

Even with a well-designed scheme there can be points of detail that will be argued. Where permits are traded in carbon emissions, for instance, there is considerable debate over whether or not to allow the sale of 'hot air'. This is where an incentive is given to an organization or country by setting their initial cap higher than their actual current emissions. That way they can sell permits and raise cash without any reduction in pollution. Environmental groups reject hot-air trading, as it has no benefit in reducing pollution, but it can be a necessary start-up cost to get some disadvantaged organizations or countries to join a scheme – a pragmatic hit taken to gain the long-term benefit of everyone being involved.

Many still argue against cap and trade as a viable solution to carbon issues because of problems with early attempts like the European Carbon Trading scheme. However, the problems arise not from the concept itself but from weakened initial settings for levels of caps and cost of permits that have emerged from industry lobbying and national interests, or from poorly organized reselling mechanisms, not from an inherent problem with trading. Politics, as ever, makes for bad science and bad economics.

A real pollution eBay

To go even further, we could all benefit from having a personal pollution trading scheme, just as charities would benefit from setting up a post-sale auction site for redistributing event tickets. Until eBay showed just what was possible on the internet, there was no possible mechanism for handling permits at the individual level, but in principle a country or economic union (or even the world) could set up an online auction house where we could all bid for grey (I was looking for the opposite to green, but grey will have to do) permits. Permits to allow us to dump waste, or emit CO_2 or any other individual pollution we want to undertake.

As Zero Carbon Britain, which advocates a form of individual tradable quotas, points out, such a scheme could be made practical. Their idea is to take the current split of 40/60 between individuals and businesses. The individuals are given their 40 per cent free. Businesses would have to bid for their parts of the quota. Individuals can trade quotas, which will be needed for purchases of fuel, whether electricity, gas or petrol. There is no need, as some have suggested, for such a scheme to cover every purchase. Ordinary goods would reflect the business quotas in their pricing.

A more dramatic idea, which I haven't seen suggested but would certainly make pollution control democratic, is to give *all* the permits to individuals. Everyone, from schoolchild to corporate chief executive, would get the same allowance. It would then be up to industry to buy the appropriate permits via a transparent auction from individuals. Only companies that had public support would function. That really would be fascinating.

Such a scheme is unlikely to happen, because it would be difficult to sell as a concept – but if it were undertaken properly it would result in a much better control of pollution at the individual level than any alternative. It's interesting that this approach is being championed in the Zero Carbon Britain initiative by the Centre for Alternative Technology, as traditionally green activists have been against any form of trading or market, but the CAT has recognized that it would make a real difference on the ground.

If we could overcome our puritanical reaction to markets, the concern over people making profits, variable pricing and auctions, there's no doubt that this scheme would be a success. While politicians and environmentalists probably wouldn't buy into it, they could probably understand the logic. However, in our final chapter, there's a suggestion that would have any environmentalist baying for blood.

13
Going McGreen

Let's put McDonald's in charge of the environment.

I'm finishing the book by using this provocative suggestion, doubly surprising given the uncomfortable relationship that McDonald's has had with the environment in the past – an unease made clear by the McLibel trial.

In the 1990s the global fast-food giant brought libel charges against five activists from the London Greenpeace organization (not connected to the better-known Greenpeace), accusing them of distributing a pamphlet that charged McDonald's with unethical marketing that targeted children, cruelty to animals and environmental damage. Three of those accused apologized, but the remaining two, David Morris and Helen Steel, decided to fight.

With no experience and no legal team, Morris and Steel took on the McDonald's machine, attempting to prove their allegations in court. The trial, one of the longest in British history with 313 days in court, resulted in a pyrrhic victory for McDonald's that was much more costly than defeat. Not only had they spent an estimated £10 million on the case (McDonald's did not apply for costs), but the judge held that Morris and Steel had proved a significant number of points in the pamphlet – McDonald's had shot itself in the foot.

So how can McDonald's be part of the answer, rather than part of the problem?

Thinking differently

Before you throw the book down in disgust, wait a moment. This suggestion is based on a technique I use in creativity workshops. To provoke an organization into thinking differently, I ask them to consider how they would deal with a problem if they were taken over by a company with a totally different culture. A company like McDonald's. The result is to look at the problem in a startlingly different way.

Let's assume that McDonald's were asked to take on the project of improving the environment for the world, not by making tiny environmental gestures in their own business to appease customers, but by applying their undoubtedly powerful business expertise to green issues. If they ran the world, what would McDonald's do to counter global warming, make trade fairer, deal with our rubbish and give us a more sustainable environment? Putting McDonald's in charge (purely as a thought experiment) has to be the ultimate exercise in ecologic.

Before looking at the outcomes of the exercise, I need to say just a little more about creativity in this context. Creativity is something we are all capable of, but we naturally tend to suppress our ideas. In practice, this is partially due to socialization. We are brought up to reduce creativity, because being creative can be harmful in a physically dangerous environment. Anyone who has small children is aware of how perilously creative they can be, for instance when attempting to play with live coals or in traffic.

Over the last fifty years, psychologists and business experts have developed techniques to facilitate problem-solving and idea generation, which is what I mean by creativity in this context. These techniques force us out of our normal way of thinking, overcoming assumptions and enabling us to devise a much broader range of good ideas than is possible if we just sit down and think. Many of these ideas will initially be impractical – but it's much easier to take an appealing but impractical idea and make it workable than to come up with a great, practical idea from scratch.

The McDonald's provocation

That is the context in which this technique is used. The idea is not actually to put McDonald's in charge of the environment, but to see what we think of, provoked by this technique. In doing so, there are two ways to look at McDonald's. One is what I'd call the caricature. This says that, in their solutions, McDonald's will make us all wear paper caps, badges with stars to measure our achievements and have the equivalent of eco-drive-thrus and green Happy Meals.

The other, more useful, way to look at McDonald's is to say that this is a very successful organization that has managed to make a huge change to the way we eat worldwide. We might not all approve of their food, but it's impossible to avoid acknowledging how effective they have been in changing the way we eat. McDonald's has managed to move into countries with such different cultures as the UK and Russia by combining marketing, in-store presentation and products that were different from anything available at the time. So also try to think how they could use those same management and business skills to change the way we look after the environment.

I'm going to give you the ideas I've come up with in a quick session using this technique – but consider trying it yourself. Be as outrageous as you like – an extreme approach generates more original concepts. If you produce some ideas, why not share them with the rest of us? I've set up a Facebook group http://www.facebook.com/group.php?gid=11196441242 to discuss this issue – log on and add your thoughts.

My ideas included:

- *McDonald's use badges with stars on to identify staff training, and make wide use of branding on their products to reinforce the experience of eating in their restaurants.* We could put badges (or labels) on all products from food to cars, from CDs to clothes. These will indicate three things. First, a footprint that's red, yellow or green. This shows if the carbon footprint for manufacture plus half a typical life of use is in the worst 20 per cent, the middle 60 per cent or the best 20 per cent. Then the year of manufacture, so you can see how long it has been used. Then the typical half-life in years (not needed for single-use consumables like food). This will be green, indicating the product will still have the same footprint after this time, orange (its footprint rating will be worse relative to the products of the time) and red (probably needs replacing by then).

- *McDonald's use Happy Meals, which include a free toy and cost less than they should to entice parents in.* This suggested the idea (mentioned on page 92) that the government should give away free micro-generation (solar/wind) to anyone with a suitable location for deploying it. The home-owner receives only 10 per cent of the financial benefit until the investment is paid off, then receives all of it.

- *McDonald's advertising often appeals to the emotions, showing happy families, etc., but they also have very clear, listed menus detailing what each product costs.* We can learn from this in dealing with the bogeyman, where emotion tends to overwhelm logic. Separating emotion and facts and figures into different channels would ensure that the facts aren't covered in a sea of feelings.

- *McDonald's doesn't just sell individual products, but offers meal deals, combining high-profit items like drinks with lower-profit items like sandwiches.* We should look for the equivalent of a meal deal for fair trade – an issue with Fairtrade is that it takes only one very specific aspect of the problem and ignores the rest. If we can produce a balanced 'meal' that doesn't just give better payment to subsistence farmers and others in a similar state, but also helps them move to a more sustainable future with perhaps different employment, we can do a lot more than by propping up a poverty trap.

- *McDonald's aim to make the experience of having a quick family meal out more fun than the other options available when they arrive in a country.* We need to consider how to make cap and trade fun – at the moment carbon trading is big business and dull for the ordinary person. Make it more personal, give us all the chance to get active at an individual level. Change it from dull utilitarian consumption to something bright and colourful that makes it enjoyable to save. Too many environmental campaigners are all hair shirt and no fun.

- *Let's have McOrganic – McDonald's don't sell chicken nuggets, they sell McNuggets. They set their own, very specific standards from how a burger is cooked to how their raw ingredients should be sourced, rather than accepting someone else's standards.* If the current organic certification bodies with their ties to the mystical past of the organic movement are a problem, let's have a new organic body (we don't need to call it organic) that concentrates purely on the measurable benefits and gives us good, healthy, low-carbon-footprint food with excellent welfare standards, yet without all the unscientific baggage.

- *Remember the (root) beer fiasco – even McDonald's have had failures. When they first came to the UK they tried a one-size-fits-all policy, giving pretty well exactly the same menu as in the US. This included root beer – something hardly anyone in the UK likes. It soon vanished. Similarly, in France McDonald's had to learn the hard way that it was necessary to serve beer in their restaurants.* We can learn from this. Almost every attempt at dealing with environmental issues, from carbon offsets to wheelie-bin collections every other week, are one-size-fits-all. We need more variation by location (let Swindon, for instance, make more use of its plentiful landfill) and more by individual.

- *Follow the pennies – McDonald's is notorious for keeping an eye on every penny, spending logically rather than emotionally.* All too often, cash for environmental issues is spent where the next unhappy polar bear picture emerges, not where there's most potential leverage. Let's see more money going into carbon capture, nuclear fusion and perennial food crops, for instance, and less into gloss and spin.

I really believe that your ideas will be even better. One tip – don't try to take on the whole of the environment at once. Use the McDonald's approach to reducing carbon emissions, or making agriculture more sustainable, or whatever appeals, then move on to the next topic.

There is hope

I wanted to finish the book with this exercise because I believe that it is important to show that there is hope. Ecologic demonstrates how all too often what is being done in the name of the environment doesn't make sense. We put up bogeymen that don't really exist. We indulge in greenwash, or are influenced by ideas of natural bounty that are at best romantic and at worst a dangerous lie. We cheat to achieve what we want, despite its influence on the environment.

Yet in all the areas I have looked at, ecologic shows that we can get around our natural inclinations to misread the situation. We can bring some logic into our ecological actions to ensure that we make use of science and economics to do our best for the environment, rather than just concentrating on appearances and paying lip service to saving the planet.

There is still plenty we can do, and plenty of new ideas we can use to improve our world. It starts here.

Notes

Chapter 1

p. 12   The science-free articles referred to in the *Ecologist* magazine were from the December 2007/January 2008 issue.

p. 13   The Ultimatum game is described in Marc D. Hauser, *Moral Minds*, London: Little, Brown, 2007.

Chapter 2

p. 17   Andrew Marr calls journalism 'industrialized gossip' in Andrew Marr, *My Trade: A Short History of British Journalism*, London: Macmillan, 2004.

p. 18   Jonathon Porritt's remark about politics getting softer as science gets harder was made at the Converging World/RSA 2050 Now event in Bath on 30 October 2007.

p. 23   The article on Wi-Fi in the *Ecologist* was by Mark Anslow, 'The Gathering Brainstorm', *Ecologist*, December 2007.

p. 25   The questionnaire-based study on the impact of mobile phone masts was Santini et al., 'Investigation on the health of people living near mobile telephone relay stations' (original in French), *Pathol. Biol.* 50 (6): 369–73, Paris: 2002.

p. 26   Ben Goldacre's analysis of the BBC *Panorama* Wi-Fi programme is from his blog Bad Science (www.badscience.net)

and appeared in part in his *Guardian* column, 6 May 2007.

p. 28   The interviewee described as using 'vague, deceptive and suggestive language' is Professor Olle Johansson at http://www.vof.se/visa-forvillare2004eng

p. 31   Comparative risk of flying and car journeys is taken from Brian Clegg, *The Complete Flier's Handbook*, London: Pan, 2002.

p. 34   The Soil Association's assumption that nanoparticles are safe if they are 'natural' is reported in the editorial, 'Natural does not mean harmless', *New Scientist*, 26 January 2008.

p. 34   The Soil Association's defence of their stance on nanoparticles is from an email from Soil Association representative Gundula Azeez, dated 8 April 2008.

p. 36   The daminozide story is from Cynthia Crossen, *Tainted Truth*, New York: Touchstone, 1996.

p. 40   The assertion that seven kilograms of Golden Rice needs to be consumed each day is a quote from Greenpeace in the Action Aid report *GM Crops – Going Against the Grain*, May 2003.

Chapter 3

p. 46   Methane being twenty-three times as powerful a greenhouse gas as carbon dioxide is cited by Dave Reay in 'Climate Change Begins at Home' on the Popular Science website www.popularscience.co.uk/features/feat22.htm

p. 46   The article on bogs that ignores methane is Trevor Critchley, 'The rainforests on our doorstep', *Ecologist*, February 2008.

p. 49   Arcadia Biosciences' attempt to develop GM crops that require less fertilizer is described in Peter Aldhous, 'Genes for Greens', *New Scientist,* 5 January 2008.

p. 50   Some of the information on Roundup from Briefing Note: 'Herbicide use and GM Crops', Friends of the Earth, February 2004.

p. 50   The paper suggesting that environmental benefits of no-till are marginal is J. Lankoski, M. Ollikainen and P. Uusitalo, 'No-till technology: benefits to farmers and the environment?', *European Review of Agricultural Economics*, 33:2: 193–221 (2006).

p. 54   Figures on carbon emissions from different types of car and car construction from Fred Pearce, 'Why bother going green?', *New Scientist*, 17 November 2007.

p. 55   Tips on reducing fuel consumption in cars from Brian Clegg, *The Global Warming Survival Kit*, London: Doubleday, 2007.

p. 56   Comparison of amount of CO_2 from Spanish and British tomato production is from Paul Waddington, *Shades of Green*, London: Eden Project Books, 2008.

p. 57   Tim Harford's attempt to subvert being carbon neutral is described in Tim Harford, *The Undercover Economist*, London: Little, Brown, 2006.

p. 59   Information on carbon offsetting at the 2006 World Cup from Quirin Shiermeier, 'Climate credits', *Nature* 444: 976–7 (2006).

p. 62   Details of Future Forest's Orbost carbon offset from Fred Pearce, *Confessions of an Eco-Sinner*, London: Eden Project Books, 2008.

p. 63   Carbon emissions for a journey from London to San Francisco from Atmosfair, The CarbonNeutral Company, Climate Care/Rough Guides and MyClimate websites.

p. 65   Information on the Converging World's offsetting programme from their website www.theconvergingworld.org and their publication: John Pontin and Ian Roderick, *Converging World*, Totnes: Green Books, 2007.

p. 65   The figure of twice the reduction of CO_2 emission from a wind turbine in India compared with the UK is from the RSA's Converging World/RSA 2050 Now event in Bath, 2007.

p. 69   The estimate of between 50 and 80 per cent increase in the price of a passenger flight for inclusion in the European emission trading scheme is by Ottmar Edenhofer of the Potsdam Institute for Climate Impact Research, quoted in Quirin Shiermeier, 'Climate credits', *Nature*, 444: 976–7 (2006).

p. 69   Information on Carbon Rationing Action Groups is from the website www.carbonrationing.org.uk

p. 70   Number of participants in Crags in the UK in 2007 taken from CarbonLimited, 'Who Has the Best Policies on Climate Change?', *RSA Journal*, December 2007.

p. 72   Details on the International Passenger Survey from Michael Blastland and Andrew Dilnot, *The Tiger That Isn't*, London: Profile Books, 2007.

p. 73   The implications of raised CO_2 levels on plant growth are from Ned Stafford, 'The other greenhouse effect', *Nature*, 448: 526–8 (2007).

p. 75   Technology to recycle CO_2 from the air to produce hydrocarbon fuels is described in Duncan Graham-Rowe, 'Let's hear it for CO_2', *New Scientist*, 1 March 2008.

p. 77   John Hutton's prediction of up to a third of British energy using carbon capture and storage is quoted in Fred Pearce, 'Cleaning Up Coal', *New Scientist*, 29 March 2008.

p. 78   Zeolitic imidazolate frameworks to capture CO_2 are described in Andy Coghlan, 'Crystal sponges capture carbon emissions', *New Scientist*, 23 February 2008.

Chapter 4

p. 81   Media coverage of Heather Mills' suggestion to drink rats' milk instead of cows' milk is from the *Metro* (London) newspaper, 20 November 2007.

p. 83   Rachel Carson, *Silent Spring*, London: Penguin, 2000.

p. 84   The survey was 'FOOTSIE 100 – Green Washers and Green Winners Survey', Chatsworth Communications, 23 September 2007.

p. 85   Information on BP's approach to green issues in an email from BP press officer Robert Wine, dated 9 January 2008.

p. 87   George Monbiot's assertions that oil companies are being sneaky in trying to adopt a green image come from George Monbiot, 'Environmental Smoke and Mirrors', *New Scientist*, 27 December 2006.

p. 88   Information on Aviva's green activities from an email from Aviva's Media Relations dated 6 May 2008.

p. 89   Consumer concern about energy companies' motives is discussed in the TSEC Trust (Role of Trust in the Transition to Sustainable Energy) Theme 4 – see http://www.psi.org.uk/tsec/resources.htm

p. 90   Allan Asher of energywatch's comments on breaking the link between energy sales and consumption is from *The Times*, 25 February 2008.

p. 94   Jean Ziegler's report on the impact of biofuels is Jean Ziegler, 'The Right to Food', UN General Assembly, 22 August 2007, available at http://www.righttofood.org/A62289.pdf

p. 95   Fidel Castro's concerns about biofuels are from Fidel Castro Ruiz, *Gramma*, 27 March 2007.

p. 96   Eric Holt-Gimenez is quoted on biofuels, and information provided on energy efficiency in Kurt Kleiner, 'The Backlash against Biofuels', *Nature Reports Climate Change* (http://www.nature.com/climate/index.html)

p. 98   The observation that three-quarters of photosynthesis takes place in algae is from Brian Clegg, *Light Years*, London: Macmillan Science, 2007.

p. 98   Use of algae for biofuels is described in Rachel Nowak, 'Algae hold the key to the biofuel conundrum', *New Scientist*, 2 February 2008.

p. 100   George Monbiot's political action and shopping comment is from George Monbiot, 'Green consumerism will not save the biosphere', *Guardian*, 24 July 2007.

Chapter 5

p. 106   Senator Barbara Boxer's discovery of an organization paying large sums for articles countering the 2007 IPCC report and Tim Worth's comparison with the tobacco industry are from Sharon Begley, 'The Truth About Denial', *Newsweek*, 13 August 2007.

p. 107   Information on the meeting at the American Petroleum Institute and amounts paid to global-warming-denying groups by ExxonMobil from Sharon Begley, 'The Truth About Denial', *Newsweek*, 13 August 2007.

p. 108   Peter Hitchens' enthusiastic support for *The Great Global Warming Swindle* was from Peter Hitchens, 'Drugs? Those fools should just stick to shorthand', *Daily Mail*, 11 March 2007.

p. 108   Carl Wunsch's statement that he was misled is from Geoffrey Lean, 'Climate change: An inconvenient truth . . . for C4', *Independent*, 11 March 2007.

p. 109   Carl Wunsch's refutation of the content of *The Great Global Warming Swindle*, 11 March 2007, is from his website http://ocean.mit.edu/~cwunsch/papersonline/channel4response

p. 110   Martin Durkin's statement that the scientists are the bad guys is from an interview published by National News in *Lifestyle Extra*: 'Global Warming is Lies, Claims Documentary', 4 March 2007, http://www.lifestyleextra.com/ShowStory.asp?story=CZ434669U&news_headline=global_warming_is_lies_claims_documentary

p. 112   The possible mechanisms for the collapse of the Greenland ice sheet are from Brian Clegg, *The Global Warming Survival Kit*, London: Doubleday, 2007.

p. 114   The assertion that the atmosphere rather than the sun warms the ocean is from Christopher Monckton, '35 Inconvenient Truths', Science & Public Policy Institute, 18 October 2007, http://scienceandpublicpolicy.org/monckton/goreerrors.html

p. 114   Information on Svensmark's cosmic ray theory of

climate change is from Henrik Svensmark and Nigel Calder, *The Chilling Stars*, Cambridge: Icon Books, 2007.

p. 115   Lomborg's ideas from Bjørn Lomborg, *The Skeptical Environmentalist*, Cambridge: Cambridge University Press, 2001.

p. 116   The 2008 oil prices are from the BBC News website, news.bbc.co.uk – note that Lomborg's prices are adjusted for inflation, while the current prices aren't, but the effect over the few years involved is relatively small.

p. 119   David Bellamy's list of educational credentials is from an email to the author dated 26 January 2008.

p. 119   David Bellamy's 'Poppycock!' headline is from David Bellamy, 'Global Warming? What a load of Poppycock!', *Daily Mail*, 9 July 2004.

p. 119   David Bellamy's argument against computer-generated scenarios is from an email to the author, dated 26 January 2008.

p. 123   David Bellamy's peer-reviewed paper on the impact of carbon dioxide on global warming is D. Bellamy and J. Barrett, 'Climate Stability: an inconvenient proof', *Proceedings of the Institute of Civil Engineering*, 160: 66–72, (2007).

p. 124   David Bellamy's letter on glaciers appeared in *New Scientist*, 16 April 2005.

p. 124   George Monbiot's checks on Bellamy's glacier letter are from George Monbiot, *Heat*, London: Penguin Allen Lane, 2006.

Chapter 6

p. 128   The description of biasing polls is from Jonathan Lynn and Antony Jay, *The Complete Yes Prime Minister*, London: BBC Books, 1989.

p. 130   The poll question with the request to take out the statement as it conflicts with the brand appeared in an online poll entitled 'Dreaming of a Green Christmas', which closed on 13 November 2007.

p. 131   Dubious survey results are described in Cynthia Crossen, *Tainted Truth*, New York: Touchstone, 1996.

p. 134   Costa Coffee's use of Fairtrade as an identifier of those who would spend more on coffee is described in Tim Harford, *The Undercover Economist*, London: Little, Brown, 2006.

p. 137   The report suggesting that Fairtrade is unfair is Marc Sidwell, *Unfair Trade*, Adam Smith Institute, 2008.

p. 137   The report showing that only 10 per cent of the premium for Fairtrade goes to the producer is 'Voting with Your Trolley', *The Economist*, 7 December 2006.

p. 138   The House of Commons committee report pointing out that Fairtrade is not the only ethical brand is *Fair Trade and Development*, June 2007, Recommendation 1, p. 38.

p. 138   The comment that data is not the plural of anecdote is from Robert Park, *Voodoo Science*, Oxford: Oxford University Press, 2002.

p. 140   The New York City Council uniform initiative is described in Tim Harford, *The Undercover Economist*, London: Little, Brown, 2006.

p. 142   The percentage of cocoa and chocolate from developing countries is from Marc Sidwell, *Unfair Trade*, Adam Smith Institute, 2008.

p. 143   The study showing that shipping causes cooling rather than warming is Jan Fuglestvedt et al., 'Climate forcing from the transport sectors', *Proceedings of the National Academy of Sciences*, 105: 454–8 (2008).

p. 144   Information on the potentially misleading nature of the claim that shipping causes cooling is from Catherine Brahic, 'Transport emissions study "misleading" say experts', *New Scientist* news service, 8 January 2008.

Chapter 7

p. 146   Information on Steorn from their website www. steorn.com

p. 147   '. . . electrical energy too cheap to meter' is taken from a speech by Lewis L. Strauss to the National Association of Science Writers, New York, 16 September 1954.

p. 148   The power output of the sun is mentioned in a number of online sources including NASA (http://helios.gsfc.nasa.gov/ qa_sun.html), Wikipedia (www.wikipedia.com) and Nine Planets (www.nineplanets.org)

p. 151   Information on solar electricity generation is from Bennett Daviss, 'Our Solar Future', *New Scientist*, 8 December 2007.

p. 152   The twenty times figure for a solar panel in space compared with the Earth is taken from Dan Cho and David Cohen, 'Plug Into the Sun', *New Scientist*, 24 November 2007.

p. 158   Details of early cold fusion research from Nina Hall and Jonathan Beard, 'Test-tube fusion experiment repeated', *New Scientist*, 8 April 1994.

p. 160   The bubble fusion experiment is described in R. P. Taleyarkhan et al., 'Evidence for Nuclear Emissions During Acoustic Cavitation', *Science,* 295: 1868–73 (2002).

p. 161   The 2007 cold fusion experiment using a polymer detector is described in Bennett Daviss, 'Cold fusion – hot news again?', *New Scientist*, 5 May 2007.

p. 161   Information on wind and wave power from the Sustainable Development Commission website www.sd-commission.org.uk, their report *Wind Power in the UK* (November 2005) and the BBC News website news.bbc.co.uk

p. 163   Figures for US bird kill by wind turbines from National Wind Coordinating Committee, *Avian Collisions with Wind Turbines: A Summary of Existing Studies and Comparisons to other Sources of Avian Collision Mortality in the United States*, 2001.

p. 165   Details of tidal options for the UK from Sustainable Development Commission, *Turning the Tide: Tidal Power in the UK*, October 2007.

p. 166   Details of the Stern Review from the UK government's

website http://www.hm-treasury.gov.uk/independent_reviews/
stern_review_economics_climate_change/sternreview_index.cfm

Chapter 8

p. 170   All information on Swindon Borough Council's waste
disposal and the difficulties faced by councils from an interview with Richard Fisher in March 2008.

p. 171   Details of Kensington and Chelsea's thrice-weekly
rubbish collection from the *Evening Standard*, 27 September
2007.

p. 174   The report showing no impact on health of fortnightly
collections is Cranfield University and Enviros Consulting,
*Health impact assessment of alternate week waste collections
of biodegradable waste*, February 2007, http://www.enviros.
com/PDF/Defra HIA Alternate Week Collections.pdf

p. 179   Details of the Mailing Preference Scheme are available from www.mpsonline.org.uk. The Post Office's opt-out
scheme for unaddressed mail can be requested by emailing
optout@royalmail.com

p. 181   Somerfield's statement about plastic bags is from
their website at http://www.somerfieldgroup.co.uk/index.asp?
sid=15

p. 182   Somerfield's statement on 6 billion bags a year is from
http://www.somerfield.co.uk/ourcommunity/bagforlife/index.
asp

p. 183   The incorrect attribution of 100,000 marine deaths to
plastic bags is described in Alexi Mostrous, 'Series of blunders
turned plastic bag into global villain', *The Times*, 8 March
2008.

p. 183   Information on rubbish disposal from Richard
Girling, *Rubbish! A Chronicle of Waste*, London: Eden Project
Books, 2005.

p. 184   Details of the Lancashire recycling plants from
Rachel Nowak, 'Make Landfill History', *New Scientist*, 20
October 2007.

p. 187   For information on local freecycling opportunities, see www.freecycle.org

p. 188   Information on the study showing disposable nappies were no worse for the environment than re-usables is from Cynthia Crossen, *Tainted Truth*, New York: Touchstone, 1996.

p. 188   Information on the CNW study showing Hummers are greener than the Prius is from Ben Goldacre's blog Bad Science (www.badscience.net)

p. 189   The Environment Agency report on lifecycle analysis of nappies is *Life Cycle Assessment of Disposable and Reusable Nappies in the UK*, Environment Agency http://www.environment-agency.gov.uk/commondata/acrobat/nappies_1072099.pdf

p. 190   The Channel 4 report expressing surprise at the nappy survey assumptions is 'Fact Check: Rash verdict on nappies', Channel 4 News, 16 July 2007.

p. 193   Quantities of water used by dishwashers and showers is from Paul Waddington, *Shades of Green*, London: Eden Project Books, 2008.

Chapter 9

p. 194   Dick Taverne's highlighting of the meaning of the word 'organic' is from Dick Taverne, *The March of Unreason*, Oxford: OUP, 2005.

p. 195   The Soil Association's attribution of the word 'organic' to J. I. Rodale is from *Soil Association Standards*, January 2008.

p. 197   Details of Rudolf Steiner's biodynamics are from Dick Taverne, *The March of Unreason*, Oxford: OUP, 2005.

p. 197   The move of early medicine from a spiritual basis to science is described in Brian Clegg, *Upgrade Me*, New York: St Martin's Press, 2008.

p. 198   Patrick Holden's evidence on organic farming is from House of Lords Select Committee, *Organic Farming and the European Union*, oral evidence Q38, 1999.

p. 199   The assertion that organic fruit and vegetables are up to 73 per cent more expensive in supermarkets than in local organic veg box schemes is from the *Ecologist*, news section, February 2008.

p. 200   Paul Waddington's assertion about pesticide levels in bananas is from Paul Waddington, *Shades of Green*, London: Eden Project Books, 2008.

p. 201   Joanna Blythman's comments on residue levels in food is from 'Toxic Shock', *Guardian*, 20 October 2001.

p. 203   Lord Krebs' comments on the impact of pesticide residues on food are from John Krebs, 'Why Natural May Not be Healthy', *Nature*, 415: 117 (2002).

p. 206   Data for graph of relative cancer risk is from Bjørn Lomborg, *The Skeptical Environmentalist*, Cambridge: Cambridge University Press, 2001.

p. 208   The study by Professor Carlo Leifert and colleagues showing enhanced levels of antioxidants in organic food is described in 'Official: organic is better', *Sunday Times*, 28 October 2007.

p. 208   Information on antioxidants from Ben Goldacre's blog Bad Science (www.badscience.net)

p. 211   Information on integrated farm management from Dick Taverne, *The March of Unreason*, Oxford: OUP, 2005.

p. 212   The organic movement's request to hold off banning copper fungicides is noted in Dick Taverne, *The March of Unreason*, Oxford: OUP, 2005.

p. 213   Energy use comparison for different types of chicken breeding is from Paul Waddington, *Shades of Green*, London: Eden Project Books, 2008.

p. 216   The DEFRA stance on farrowing crates is from the department's website at http://www.defra.gov.uk/animalh/welfare/farmed/pigs/index.htm

Chapter 10

p. 231   Information on soil fertility from Mark Gillingham, *Is*

Organic Farming Sustainable? Unpublished report by a soil scientist for organic farmers.

p. 233   C. S. Prakash's comment on sustainability in the developing world is from Dick Taverne, *The March of Unreason*, Oxford: OUP, 2005.

p. 235   The benefits of cocoa farming in restoring some of the environmental benefits of the rainforest is described in Fred Pearce, *Confessions of an Eco-Sinner*, London: Eden Project Books, 2008.

p. 236   The figure of 15 per cent extra energy for air-freighting green beans is from Fred Pearce, *Confessions of an Eco-Sinner*, London: Eden Project Books, 2008.

p. 236   The figure of air freight producing 11 per cent of carbon emissions from UK food distribution is from the Soil Association website at http://www.soilassociation.org/airfreight

p. 237   Information on sustainable farming using perennial crops from J. D. Glover, C. M. Cox and J. P. Reganold, 'Future Farming: A Return to Roots?', *Scientific American*, August 2007.

p. 239   Information on zero-carbon housing in the UK and the government's plans from a number of online news sites, including BBC and Channel 4.

p. 241   Information on zero-carbon Britain is from the CAT's Zero Carbon Britain website www.zerocarbonbritain.com

p. 247   Jonathon Porritt's remarks on the UK government's incrementalism are from the BBC News website (13 October 2007): http://news.bbc.co.uk/1/hi/uk/7042958.stm

Chapter 11

p. 249   Figures for CO_2 emissions from flights in the US and the UK are from Fred Pearce, 'Why bother going green?', *New Scientist*, 17 November 2007.

p. 250   Michael O'Leary's 2005 comment on environmentalists is from Paul Waddington, *Shades of Green*, London: Eden Project Books, 2008.

p. 250   Andy Harrison's comment that easyJet is greener than a traditional airline was quoted in 'Fact Check: How green is easyJet?', Channel 4 News, 11 May 2007.

p. 252   Details of Virgin's green publicity stunts from Ben Webster, 'Virgin's green idea loses pulling power', *The Times*, 10 March 2008.

p. 254   Figures on runway capacity at Heathrow are from Camilla Cavendish, 'We've fallen for the great Heathrow con', *The Times*, 31 January 2008.

p. 257   Comparisons of flying with Virgin Trains and Eurostar from Fred Pearce, *Confessions of an Eco-Sinner*, London: Eden Project Books, 2008.

p. 258   Figures for cars' emissions from the UK government's Act on CO_2 website at 7 March 2008 http://www.dft.gov.uk/ActOnCO$_2$/index.php?q=best_on_co2_rankings

p. 259   The out-of-town comparison of a Prius with a BMW is from Paul Horrell, 'Me and My Prius', *Guardian*, 29 February 2008.

p. 259   Information on Toyota's diesel technology and reasons the Prius is not based on diesel in an email from the Toyota press office dated 10 March 2008.

p. 260   The response to my concerns about the Department of the Environment website is from a letter dated 11 April 2008.

Chapter 12

p. 264   The negative impact of standards in pollution control is described in M. S. Anderson, *Governance by Green Taxes: Making Pollution Prevention Pay*, Manchester: Manchester University Press, 1994.

p. 267   Information on the timeline of the fuel protests of 2000 is from Special Report: the petrol crisis, *Guardian* http://www.guardian.co.uk/petrol/story/0,,397493,00.html 2000

p. 268   Conflicting information on the fuel escalator at www.petrolprice.com was between the pages http://www.petrolprices.com/fuel-tax.html and http://www.petrolprices.

com/blog/petrol-price-protests-planned-for-this-wednesday-86.html

p. 273   The early idea of green taxes is in Arthur Pigou, *The Economics of Welfare*, London: Macmillan, 1920.

p. 275   The observation that green taxes are not applied uniformly but favour producers, comes from Carsten Daugbjerg and Gert Tinggaard Svendsen, *Green Taxation in Question*, London: Palgrave, 2001.

p. 277   The comparative rates of green tax on industry and the individual in 1997 is from Carsten Daugbjerg and Gert Tinggaard Svendsen, *Green Taxation in Question*, London: Palgrave, 2001.

p. 279   Chris Patten's suggestions for market-based pollution controls are in Chris Patten, 'The Market and the Environment', *Policy Studies*, 11:2, 4–9, 1990.

p. 283   The example showing the Kyoto Protocol requirement costing thirty-nine times more with a tax than permit-trading is from Carsten Daugbjerg and Gert Tinggaard Svendsen, *Green Taxation in Question*, London: Palgrave, 2001.

p. 287   The prices for trading in sulphur dioxide emissions in the US are taken from Tim Harford, *The Undercover Economist*, London: Little, Brown, 2006.

p. 287   The change of heart of US environmentalists over permit-trading is described in Carsten Daugbjerg and Gert Tinggaard Svendsen, *Green Taxation in Question*, London: Palgrave, 2001.

Chapter 13

p. 291   Information on the McLibel trial from John Vidal, *McLibel: Burger culture on trial*, London: Macmillan, 1997.

p. 292   For more on creativity techniques, see Brian Clegg and Paul Birch, *Instant Creativity*, London: Kogan Page, 2007.

Index

acetone 160

actonco2.direct.gov.uk 51

Adam Smith Institute report
   on Fairtrade (2008)
   137–40, 144

Advertising Standards Agency
   205, 254

agriculture 237
   biodynamic 196–7

air conditioning 55

air travel 69, 249–55
   and airport growth 253–5
   budget airlines 250–1
   and carbon dioxide
      emissions 63–4, 249–50
   Virgin's 'green' initiatives
      252–3
   and zero-carbon Britain
      242, 245–6

aircraft
   taking off 2–3
   and weight of passengers
      3–6

airlines, budget 250–1

airports
   growth of 253–5
   use of biometric systems to
      identify individuals 10

Alar (daminozide) 36–8

algae
   as source of biofuels 98–9

Allen, Paul 241, 242, 246–7

Alley, Richard 113

aluminium cans
   recycling of 176–7

American Petroleum Institute
   107

Ames, Bruce 203–4

animal welfare
   and complementary
      therapies 232
   and organics 215–21

annual crops 237–8

Anslow, Mark 24, 25

Antarctic 113

Anthroposophy 196

antibiotics

use of by farmers 209

antioxidants 208–9

apples 36–8

Arcadia Biosciences 49, 51

Arctic ocean 114

asbestosis 21

Asher, Allan 90

astrology

and agriculture 197

astronomy 197

atoms 43

auctions

and carbon trading 68

and pollution permits 255,
264, 286–8

Automotive X Prize 261

Aviva 56, 88–9

BA (British Airways) 85, 254

'balance'

media and biased 18

Balfour, Lady Eve 199

Bali conference (2007) 68

bananas 142, 200–1

Band Aid 81

Banqiao dam (China) 165

barrages 165

BBC 18, 27

Bellamy, David 103, 117–20,
121–4

Berndt, Colleen 139

biased 'balance' 18

Big Bang 43, 118

bills 178–9

biochar 185

biodiesel 93, 95

biodiversity 211, 212

biodynamic agriculture 196–7

bioethanol 93, 95

biofuels 75, 93–8, 252

algae as source of 98–9

and biodiesel 93, 95

and bioethanol 93, 95

in direct competition with
food issue 94–6

energy input into growing
and carbon dioxide
emissions 75, 96–7

political expediency of 94,
97

and United States 94

use of lignocellulose 98, 99

Blythman, Joanna 201

bogeyman

and balance 17–41

Boxer, Senator Barbara 106

BP 77, 85–7, 88

brands 82–4, 99

Branson, Richard 252

British Airways see BA

Brown, Gordon 267

Browning, Helen 209, 220, 221, 223, 224, 225
bubble fusion 160–1
Burger King (Swindon) 179
buses 258
Bush, President George 94, 97

CaféDirect 135
Calder, Nigel 114–15
Cameron, David 80, 278
cancer cases
    clusters of 20–2, 23
cancer risk
    and diet 205, 207
cap and trade *see* carbon trading
car-sharing 64
carbon 41, 42–79
    benefits of 74–5
    essentiality to life 42, 74
    recycling of to make new fuel 74–6
carbon capture 76–9
carbon credits 59, 65
carbon dioxide/carbon dioxide emissions 34–5, 43, 44–5, 46, 47, 48, 109–10, 113
    and air travel 63–4, 249–50
    and BP 86
    and cars 54–5, 255–6, 258, 260, 261
    and flying food from abroad 236
    and global warming 45, 74, 113, 120, 121, 122, 123
    and growing of biofuels 97
    measures of 58–9
    and organic farming 212
    and plants 44
    reducing of food value of crops by increased 73–4
    reducing of through genetic modification 49
    rise of following warming argument 122–3
    taxation on 275
    and zero-carbon homes 240
carbon footprint 42, 43, 51–2
carbon negative 57, 60
carbon neutral 56–9, 79, 240
carbon offsetting 42, 56–8, 59–67, 87
    calculating amount of carbon to be offset 63–4
    and carbon trading 68
    and Gold Standard 63
    issues to consider 59–60
    and 'moral hazard' objection 66
    second-generation 65–6
    and trees 60–2
Carbon Rationing Action Groups (Crags) 69–71, 72

carbon trading (cap and trade)
42, 67–71, 288–9, 296
and auctions 68
and carbon offsetting 68
and Carbon Rationing
Action Groups (Crags)
69–71, 72
and hot-air trading 288–9
impact on the consumer 69
at a personal level 69–71,
241, 242
CarbonNeutral company (was
Future Forests) 62
carcinogenics 37, 204, 263
carrier bags 181–3
cars 54–5, 255–7, 258–62
and carbon dioxide
emissions 54–5, 255–6,
258, 260, 261
compared with trains 255–7
cutting of emissions 54–5
diesel 259
electric 243–5, 261
hybrid 54–5, 258–60
hydrogen-fuelled 245
and taxes 265, 266
Carson, Rachel *Silent Spring*
83–4, 204
Castro, Fidel 95
cauliflower 39
causality 15–16
celebrities 99
green-lifestyle 100

promoting going green 80–2
Center for International
Climate and
Environmental Research
143
Centre for Alternative
Technology (CAT) 229, 241,
242, 290
charity fundraising events 81
Charles, Prince 232
chemicals 204–5, 231–2
in coffee 204
versus natural 12–13, 33–4
Chernobyl 155
chickens 218–19
child mortality
and hunger 94
Children in Need 81
Chilling Stars, The
(Svensmark and Calder)
114–15
Clarkson, Jeremy 52, 244
Clegg, Brian
The First Scientist 22
climate change 18, 57, 103,
106, 120
company resistance to 105,
106–7
and organics 212–14
scepticism over and
arguments against
107–25
see also global warming

climate models 116, 117, 119–20
clovers 229
clustering/clusters 20–3, 71
CNW 188
coaches 258
coal 43
    burning of and carbon dioxide emissions 77
cocoa 142
cocoa plantations 235–6
coffee 203–4
coffee shops 134–5
cold fusion 147, 158–61
Comic Relief 81
Communities and Local Government Select Committee 168
companies
    ignoring of negative aspects of products 105–6
    and illuminated signage 179
    promotion of green status 84–5, 88–9
    resistance to climate change 105, 106–7
complementary therapies and animal welfare 232
composting 228–9
computers 10, 186
congestion charge 270
Conservative Party 278

Converging World organization 65–6
copper sulphate 212–13
cosmic rays
    impact of on climate change 105, 114–15
Costa Coffee chain 134–5
cottage garden 236–7
councils *see* local councils
cows' milk 81–2
Cranfield University 174
Creationists 253
creativity 292–3
crops
    annual 237–8
    and biofuels 93–6
    perennial 237, 238–9
Crossen, Cynthia
    Tainted Truth 131
crystals
    and carbon capture 78–9

D-CAT 259
Daily Mail 107, 119
daminozide (Alar) 36–8
DARPA 99
DDT 83–4
deforestation 96
DEFRA 216
Denmark 277, 278
Department of Transport 260
desalination 192
deuterium 158, 159, 160

diesel cars 259
Dinorwig station (Wales) 164
dishwashers 192
dogs 39
double-blind testing 25–6,
    28–9
Durkin, Martin 110, 115

e-bills 178
easyJet 250–1
eBay 186, 289
ecologic 6–7, 12, 13
Ecologist 23–4, 46
    'Age of Awakening' 12
    'The Gathering Brainstorm'
        24–6
ecology 12
Economist, The 137
electric vehicles 243–5, 261
electricity 242
    hydro 164–5
    solar 150–1
    and wind 162, 242
electrolysis 158
electromagnetic radiation
    20–1, 24, 26–7, 28, 31
electronic invoices 178
electrosensitivity 28, 30–1
emotions 6–7, 12–13, 295
energy 146–67
    and cold fusion 147, 158–61
    and fusion 156–7
    geothermal 148, 154

nuclear 147, 148, 154–6
solar 75, 148, 149–54, 156
sources of 148–9
tides and waves as source of
    165
and water 164–5
wind 161–4, 242, 244
energy companies 89–90, 92,
    99
and pricing structures 90–1
energy consumption 91–2
    metering and monitoring of
        91
energywatch 90
Enron 89
environmental pressure
    groups 276–7
Environmental Protection
    Agency (EPA) 37, 38, 286,
    287
Environmentalist 100
Enviros Consulting 174
Essex University study 25,
    30–1
ethanol 93, 98
Ethiopia 139
European Carbon Trading
    scheme 288
European Union (EU) 68, 78,
    93–4, 97, 208
Eurostar 257
evolution 234, 253
experts 103, 104–25

externalities 269, 272, 273
ExxonMobil 87, 107

Facebook 294
factory farming 213–14,
216–17, 218–19
fair trade 125, 126, 132–45
non equation with green
133–4
Fairtrade 295
Adam Smith Institute
report on 137–40, 144
distortion of market 136,
137
distribution of agreements
139
idea of 133
low-wage avoidance trap
140–1
as marketing exercise 137
and shipping 143–4
using of to identify big
spenders 134–5
Fangmeier, Professor 73, 74
farms
producing of greenhouse
gases 47
see also organic
farming/farms
fertilizers 74, 82, 83, 196
and GM crops 49, 51
and greenhouse gases 51
nitrogen 47, 48

and organic farming 229–30
financial incentives 67
and recycling 176–7
to going green 52–3, 54
Fisher, Richard 170, 173, 174,
175
Fleischmann, Martin 158, 159
160
flying see air travel
food miles 55–6, 236
food poisoning 203
food prices 117
Food Standards Agency 203,
205
FoodFirst Institute for Food
Development Policy 96
fossil fuels 93, 106, 123, 244
free gifts 180–1
free-market approach 142, 144
free-range chickens 218
free-range eggs 218
free-range farming 213–14
free-range pigs 219–20
freecycling 187
Friends of the Earth 276
fuel crisis (2000) 267–8
fuel duty 266–7, 268–9, 270,
271
fuel duty escalator 267, 268
Fuglestvedt, Jan 143
fusion 156–61, 166
bubble 160–1
cold 147, 158–61

fusion reactor 156–8
Future Forests 62
FutureGen project 77–8

Gaia concept 195
genetic modification (GM)
    39–40, 49–51
    and nitrous oxide emissions
        49, 51
    risks of 49
    and Roundup resistant
        crops 50
geothermal energy 148, 154
Germany
    hosting of World Cup (2006)
        59
    and solar/electric panels
        150–1
Gervais, Ricky 81
glaciers 124
global cooling 122
global warming 18, 40
    and carbon dioxide
        emissions 45, 74, 113,
        120, 121, 122, 123
    and cosmic rays 105,
        114–15
    historic 123
    and nitrogen 47
    and peat bogs 46
    and shipping 143–4
    as swindle documentary
        107–10

see also climate change
glyphosate 50
Goddard Institute for Space
    Studies 112
Goethe 196
Gold Standard 63
Goldacre, Ben 26, 27, 28
Golden Rice 40
Gore, Al 110–11, 112, 113, 124
    An Inconvenient Truth
        110–11, 112, 113–14
gravity 148–9
*Great Global Warming
    Swindle, The*
    (documentary) 107–10
green consumerism 99–102
green policy and politics
    278–9
green taxes 265–7, 272–8, 283
    arguments against 280
    basing of on emissions
        produced 273, 274–5
    and environmental pressure
        groups 276–8
    giving money back 279–81,
        283
    making uniform 273–5
    origins 272–3
    and road-pricing scheme
        270–2
greenhouse effect 44–5
greenhouse gases 44–7, 48, 57
    and fertilizers 51

and hydroelectricity 164–5
and methane 46
and nitrous oxide 47–8
producing of by farms 47
reducing by using nuclear
power 48–9
and water vapour 45–6
see also carbon dioxide
greenhouses 45, 56, 73
Greenland ice sheet 112–13
Greenpeace 40, 276

Hansen, Jim 112
Harford, Tim 57–8
Harrison, Andy 250–1
Haughley Experiment 199
Heathrow
third runway issue 253,
254
heating, domestic 52, 242–3
'heavy water' 158
Heeger, Allen 151–2
helium 43
herbicides 50, 200
Highlands and Islands
Enterprise Board 62
Hitchens, Peter 107–8
Holden, Patrick 198
Holt-Gimenez, Eric 96
homeopathy 202
homes
and sustainability 239–41
Hong Kong 141

hot-air trading 288
House of Commons
International Development
Committee 138
House of Lords Select
Committee on Organic
Farming 198
housing, zero-carbon 239–41
Howard, Sir Albert 198
Hoyle, Fred 117–19
hunger 94
Hutton, John 77
hybrid cars 54–5, 258–60
hydrocarbons 74–5
hydroelectricity 164–5
hydrogen 43, 75
hydrogen-fuelled cars 245
hyperventilation 44

Ibiza Ecomotion 259
ice sheets melting of and
rise in sea levels 112–13
Iceland 154
illumination signs 179
immunization
and organics 209–10
incandescent lightbulbs 53
incentives *see* financial
incentives
India 198
insulation 240
integrated farm management
(IFM) 211

Intergovernmental Panel on
    Climate Change (IPCC)
    106, 112
International Passenger
    Survey 72
invoices, electronic 178
ITER 157–8

James, Walter *see*
    Northbourne, Lord
Japan
    and space-based solar
        generation 153
JAXA 153
Johnson, Boris 183
Joint European Torus (JET)
    157
Jones, Steven 159
junk mail 176, 179

Kensington and Chelsea
    borough council 171
Kenya 236
Kenyon, Paul 26–7, 28, 29–30
Krebs, Lord 203
Kyoto Protocol 115, 283

Lancashire
    recycling plants 183–5
landfill 76, 171, 183–4
Latin America 96
lead 31
LEDs 54

legumes 229
light bulbs
    incandescent 53
    low-energy 53–4
lignocellulose 98, 99
Live Aid 81
Live Earth (2007) 80
local councils
    charging for waste
        collection 176
    and recycling 172–4, 183–5
    and rubbish collections
        168–70, 171–2, 174–5
logic
    and emotion 6–7
Lomborg, Bjørn
    *The Sceptical
        Environmentalist*
        115–16
London
    congestion charge 270
    smog 272
London Greenpeace
    organization 291
Lottery 7–9
Lovelock, James 49, 154
low-energy lightbulbs 53–4
lungworm 209, 210
Lyn, Jonathan and Jay,
    Antony
    *The Complete Yes Prime
        Minister* 128–9

McDonald's
  and McLibel trial 291–2
  putting in charge
    experiment 292–7
  root beer fiasco 296
McLibel trial 291–2
magnesium 231
Mailing Preference Scheme
  179
maize 95, 96
manure 228, 229
Marks and Spencer 85
Marr, Andrew 17
'marsh gas' 46
meat eating 242, 245
meat, organic 209
media 17, 22, 32
  and biased 'balance' 18
  habit of pre-announcing 32
  magnifying of dangers 17
  and MMR panic 19–20
  portrayal of wireless
    networks 23–4
methane 45, 46, 58, 184
Mexico
  Fairtrade agreements 139
  food riots (2007) 96
micro-generation 91, 92, 166,
  295
migrants, statistics on 72
Mills, Heather 81–2
microwaves 24
Mitchell, Greg 98–9

MMR (measles, mumps and
  rubella) scare 19–20, 32
mobile phones
  and cancer outbreaks 20,
    21–2, 23
  upgrading of 185–6
Monbiot, George 87, 100, 124
Monckton, Lord 113
Monsanto 50
moon, tidal influence of 149
'moral hazard' 66
Morris, David 291, 292
Mosier-Boss, Pamela 161
'Mothers and Others for
  Pesticide Limits' 37

nanoparticles 34, 35, 232
nappies
  re-usable or disposable
    187–91
NASA 153
National Lottery 7–9
National Society for the
  Prevention of Cruelty to
  Children 215
natural
  as better than chemical
    12–13, 33–4
  equating with safe 34–5
Natural Resources Defense
  Council (NRDC) 37–8
nature 233–4
Netherlands 277

New Age movement 234
New Labour 278
New Scientist 124
New York City Council 140
News Corporation 56
nitrogen 47–8, 73–4, 229–30
nitrogen fertilizer 47, 48
nitrogen-fixing plants 48, 229
nitrous oxide 47–8
  and genetic modification 49,
    51
'nocebo' effect 26
Northbourne, Lord (Walter
  James) 195, 199
  Look to the Land 195
nuclear energy 147, 148,
  154–6
nuclear fission 148, 155
nuclear power 48–9, 147, 166,
  252
Numismata 1, 4

oceans 98, 109, 192
oil companies 86–8, 99
oil prices 116
oilseed rape 39
O'Leary, Michael 250
operational research 5–6, 13
Orange 178–9
Orbo device 146, 147
Orbost (Isle of Sky) 62
'organic' 13
  meaning of 194

organic box scheme 200
organic farming/farms
  and carbon dioxide
    emissions 212
  and nitrogen 229–30
  and potassium 230
  and sustainability 227–33
organic food 194–226
  buying 222–3
  cost of 211–12
  nutritional benefits 205,
    208–10
  and pesticide residues issue
    36, 200–5
  and taste 214
Organic Gardening magazine
  195
organics 35, 194–226, 296
  and animal welfare 215–21
  arguments in favour of 200,
    224
  attitude towards chemicals
    231–2
  'better for the environment'
    argument 210–12,
    212–14
  British groundbreakers
    198–9
  and climate change 212–14
  and composting 228–9
  and immunization 209–10
  and mysticism 197–8
  origins of 195–7

and profit 199–200, 211
rigidity of certification
    process 225
and supermarkets 199, 211,
    223
sustaining of poverty
    232–3
and use of nitrogen 48
variation of standards
    around the world 222
oxygen 44

packaging 180
palladium 159
Panorama 23, 24–5, 26–8,
    29–30
particulates 143–4, 263
Patten, Chris 279
patterns 9–11, 12, 17
Patzek, Tad 96–7
pay-to-drive scheme 270–2
'peak oil' 123
peat bogs
    impact on global warming
        46
peer-review studies 29
Pendolino trains 257
percentages 22–3
perennials 237, 238–9
permaculture 233–5, 239
permafrost 46
permits to pollute *see* pollution
    permits

perpetual-motion machines
    147
personal cap and trade 69–71,
    241, 242
pesticides 56, 196, 200
    and daminozide (Alar)
        36–8
    and DDT 83–4
    plants and containing of
        natural 204–5
    residues in food 36, 200–3,
        204–5
petrolprices.com 268
Philips, Alasdair 27
phosphates 231–2
photovoltaic cells 149–50,
    151
Pigou, Arthur 273, 274
pigs 215, 216, 219–21
Pimentel, David 97
placebo 26
plantations 235–6
plants
    annual/perennial 237–9
    and carbon dioxide 44
    containing of natural
        pesticides 204–5
plastic bags 181–3
politicians 110–11
politics
    and green policy 278–9
polls 126–30
    biased 131–2

pollution 262, 263–90
  and green taxes *see* green
      taxes
  imposition of statutory
      levels 264–5
pollution permits 282–4,
      286–8
  and auctions 255, 264,
      286–8
  and hot-air trading 288
  and individuals 289–90
Polo Blue Motion car 259
Pons, Stanley 158, 159, 160
Porritt, Sir Jonathon 18, 247
Post Office opt-out scheme 179
potassium 230, 231, 232
potassium chloride 213
poverty
  and organics 232–3
Powerwatch 27
Prakash, Dr C. S. 233
pregnancy
  and bananas 15–16
price/consumption equation
      90–2
Prius *see* Toyota Prius
probability 8–9
Proctor & Gamble 188, 189
Public Lending Right (PLR)
      71–2
public transport 64

quantum energy 149

quantum physics 156
questionnaire bias 25

radiation 27, 202
rainforest 98, 233, 235, 236
Rainforest Alliance 139
re-use 185–7
recycled toilet paper 101–2
recycling 167, 170–1, 172–4,
      185
  of aluminium cans 176–7
  of carbon 75–6
  and councils 172–4, 183–5
  and financial incentives
      176–7
  and supermarkets 175
renewable energy sources 148,
      241–2 *see also* solar
      energy; water; wind
      energy
Rey, Eric 49
risk, balancing of 31–2
risk assessment 38
Riverford Organics 222–3
Road Fund Licence 265, 266,
      267, 270
road-pricing scheme 270–2
road transport 31–2 *see also*
      cars
rock phosphates 231–2
Rodale, J. I. 195
Roundup (glyphosate) 50
Royal Society 40, 109

Royal Society for the
  Prevention of Cruelty to
  Animals 215
rubbish 168–93
  and carrier bags 181–3
  charging for waste
    collections by councils
    issue 176
  council collections 168–70,
    171–2, 174–5
  and disposable/re-usable
    nappy debate 187–91
  and junk mail 176, 179
  and re-use 185–7
  recycling of *see* recycling
  reducing packaging 180
  switching to electronic
    invoices 178
Ryanair 250

salt 33, 194, 231
Santini et al. 25
Science 160
Science & Public Policy
  Institute 113–14
Scripps Institution of
  Oceanography (University
  of California) 98
sea levels, rise in 112–13
sea salt 33
Seat 259
self-deception 12, 23
727 plane incident (Munich)

1–3, 4–5
Severn estuary barrage 165
sheep 215, 219, 220
Sheepdrove Farm 225
Shell 87
shellfish 202–3
shipping
  and global warming 143–4
'shock percentage' effect 22–3
showers 193
Sierra Club 49
signs, illuminated 179
SITA 171
60 Minutes (tv show) 37
Sky 56
slash-and-burn 235
smog 272, 273
social conditioning 14
sodium chloride 231
soil 35–6, 50
Soil Association 34, 35, 194,
    195, 198, 199, 201, 205,
    209–10, 222, 231, 232, 236
solar electricity 150–1
solar energy 75, 148, 149–54,
    156
  from space 152–4
solar heating 149
solar panels 149, 150–1,
    152–3, 243
solar troughs 150
Solucar Solar Plant 150
Somerfield 181–2

soot 143
soya 74
space
    and solar generation 152–4
space power stations 152–3
Spanish tomatoes 55–6
'sponsor an animal' 61–2
Star Trek 6
stardust 43
Steady State theory 118
Steel, Helen 291, 292
Steiner, Rudolf 195–7, 198, 199
Steorn 146–7
Stern Review 166
Stern, Sir Nicholas 166
Strauss, Lewis L. 147
Streep, Meryl 37
subsidies 281–2
sun *see* solar energy
supermarkets 134, 217
    and 'basic' ranges 224
    and organics 199, 211, 223
    and plastic bags issue 181
    and recycling 175
supernova 43
surveys 126–30, 131–2
    biased 131–2
sustainability 196, 227–48
    and cottage garden 236–7
    and homes 239–41
    and organic farming 227–33
    and perennial crops 238–9

and permaculture 233–5
and plantations 235–6
and zero-carbon Britain
    (ZCB) 241–3, 244, 245,
    246–8
Sustainable Development
    Commission 165
'sustainable living' 239
Svensmark, Henrik 105
Svensmark, Henrik and
    Calder, Nigel
    The Chilling Stars 114–15
sweatshops 140, 141
sweetcorn 39
Swindon Council 168–9, 171,
    172–3, 174, 175
sylvinite 213
Szpak, Stanislaw 161

Taleyarkhan, Rusi 160–1
tariffs 141–2
Taverne, Dick 194
taxes, green *see* green taxes
taxing by route 270–2
TEQs 242
Tesco 85
Tesla, Nikola 97
Thatcher, Margaret 111, 279
Three Mile Island 155
tickets, reselling event 284–6
tides
    as source of energy 165
tobacco industry 105, 106

Today 32
toilet paper, recycled 101–2
'tokamaks' 156
tomatoes, Spanish 55–6
touts 285
Toyota Prius 54, 188, 258–60, 261
trade barriers 141–2
trading
    carbon *see* carbon trading
    and pollution permits *see* pollution permits
trains 255–7
transport
    and buses 258
    road 31–2
    and trains 255–7
    see also air travel; cars
trees 76
    and carbon offsetting 60–2
trial statistics 29–30
Turner & Newall 21
2001: A Space Odyssey 153

UK Environment Agency 189–90
Ultimatum game 13–14
UN Climate Change Conference (Copenhagen) (2009) 247
United States 68–9, 94
    and biofuels 94
    and climate change 107
and fusion 157–8
pollution permits for power generators scheme 286–7
universe, origins of 118
University of California, Los Angeles (UCLA) 78, 79
University of Hohenheim 73
uranium 155
US Atomic Energy Commission 147

V1 (speed of last resort) 2, 3
veal calves 216
vegetable oil
    and biofuels 93, 98
vegetables, soil on 35–6
'vehicle to grid' idea 245
Virgin 252–3, 257
volatile organic compounds 263
Volkswagen's Polo Blue Motion 259, 260
Volt electric/petrol car 243–4, 258
Voodoo Science 138
Voyager trains 257
VR (rotation velocity) 2

Waddington, Paul
    Shades of Green 200
Wakefield, Dr Andrew 19
Wall Street 80

water 202
  consumption 191–3
  and energy 164–5
water vapour 45–6
waves
  as source of energy 165
West Antarctic 112
wheat prices 117
Wi-Fi (wireless networks) 20,
  23–31
  article on in the *Ecologist*
  23–6
  double-blind trials on 28–9
  and Essex University study
  30–1
  and *Panorama* 26–8
wildlife
  impact of wind turbines on
  163–4
wind energy 161–4, 242, 244
wind farms 162–3
wind turbines 65, 161, 162–4

wireless networks *see* Wi-Fi
Wirth, Tim 106
wood, burning of 263
wood ash 232
wood chips
  used for domestic heating
  243
World Glacier Monitoring
  Service 124
World Meteorological
  Organization 106
Wunsch, Professor Carl
  108–10

X Prize Foundation 261

zero-carbon Britain (ZCB)
  241–3, 244, 245, 246–8,
  289, 290
zero-carbon housing 239–41
Ziegler, Jean 94, 95

Also From
Eden Project Books

Shades Of Green

A (mostly) Practical A-Z for the Reluctant
Environmentalist

by Paul Waddington

ISBN 9781905811007, £10.99, paperback

HOW MANY OF us only ever want to eat what's in season and grown locally? Or can realistically give up the car for good? Or summon the ready cash and the motivation to become self-sufficient in electricity?

And yet as fears about the food chain, climate change, plummeting biodiversity and the sustainability of our current lifestyles take hold, wouldn't it be good to be clear about our range of options? And wouldn't it be great to discover that sometimes what is best for the planet is not what we might think? In fact the easiest, most readily available, cheapest or most-maligned option may even be the greenest.

Whether you are pondering bicycles or baths, holidays or heating, pets or pasta, washing dishes or wine, *Shades of Green* sets out your choices on a scale from 'completely green' to 'not even a little bit green'. No preaching. No finger-wagging.

Because being green is never black and white.

> 'Paul's books will inspire even the most
> reluctant among us.'
> DARINA ALLEN

The Meaning Of The 21st Century

A Vital Blueprint for Ensuring Our Future

by James Martin

ISBN 9781903919866, £8.99, paperback

WE LIVE AT a turning point in human history. Ahead is a century of massive change. Either we learn to manage this change, or we allow it to control us and face devastating consequences. James Martin explains with clarity and precision the nature of the challenges we face, from global warming to famine, religious extremism and technological advance, and then defines the thinking that will provide us with solutions for the future. Far from doom-mongering, his book is an extraordinarily optimistic and empowering argument for transition on a global scale: a ringing call to arms and a pragmatic blueprint for action. It is essential reading for everyone.

'On rare occasions a special book introduces a
vital new idea into the public consciousness.
This is one of those books.'
SUSAN GREENFIELD,
DIRECTOR OF THE ROYAL INSTITUTION

A Good Life

The Guide to Ethical Living

edited by Leo Hickman

ISBN 9781903919897, £16.99, paperback

MORE AND MORE of us want to try to do the right thing. We know that somehow we must reduce our demands on the planet's resources, but ethical living is about more than environmental concerns. It is also about achieving positive change by improving our relationships with those around us – be it our friends, family or neighbours, or those we never even meet but who make the products we buy.

Leo Hickman's guide to the ethics of everyday life, with its invaluable directory, has already established itself as a bestselling resource for the twenty-first century. Now updated and expanded, it is quite simply a must-have book for all.

'The ideal book for anyone who wants guidance
on making choices that will benefit them, their
family and the planet.'
COUNTRY LIVING

The Final Call

Investigating Who Really Pays for Our Holidays

by Leo Hickman

ISBN 9781905811069, £7.99, paperback

CLUBBING IN IBIZA; cruising in the Caribbean; luxuriating in Dubai; skiing in the Alps; backpacking in Thailand . . . We are all keen tourists. But what is the true cost of our trips away? And is it even possible to have a 'good' holiday?

Travelling the world, from theme park to golf course, from sunlounger to ecolodge, Hickman tells us what they don't reveal in the glossy brochures. Acknowledging that few of us are going to stop travelling, he offers solutions to the problems he uncovers, giving us the wherewithal to make informed decisions about our holidays, wherever the destination.

'Excellent. One of the clearest and most sobering
analyses I've ever seen on the environmental, social,
and economic damage done by tourism.'
PHILIP PULLMAN

Sea Change

Britain's Coastal Catastrophe

by Richard Girling

ISBN 9781903919781, £8.99, paperback

THE SEA DRIVES our economy, our lifestyle and our politics. It affects what we eat, how we travel, our use of the land and how we relate to our continental neighbours. Our love affair with our coastline inspires myth and legend, and influences our literature, our music and our art.

Yet we abuse and despoil our native waters as if we imagine they are infinitely resourceful and forgiving. Our once-grand seaside resorts now embrace some of the poorest neighbourhoods in Europe, while our management of our seaports is so inept that we bring chaos to our roads. And all the time our reckless consumption of fossil fuels pumps out greenhouse gases that accelerate climate change and guarantee a future of ever more violent storms, rising seas and destruction.

With passion and rigour, Richard Girling examines the history and consequences of the issues that confront us along our coastline. Outraged, bemused, despairing, he is also compelling and irrepressibly entertaining as he sifts for solutions along the sands.

'A passionate and blackly witty exposé of
the problems that face us.'
SUNDAY TIMES

Confessions Of An Eco Sinner

Travels to Find Where My Stuff Comes From

by Fred Pearce

ISBN 9781905811120, £7.99, paperback

THE ROAD TO eco-hell is paved with good intentions. Ever wondered what chucking Kenyan beans out of your shopping trolley might do to the poor farmers who grow them? Or whether the women in Bangladeshi sweatshops really want you to stop buying the clothes from their sewing machines? When you bought your mobile phone to stay in touch, did you think you could be funding rebel warlords who press-gang child soldiers into mines? This book travels the world to tell you the hidden story behind all our everyday things, and provides a moral compass through the minefield of modern consumer choices.

'Sometimes frightening, always enlightening, it
will teach you more about other people's lives than
you ever thought possible.'
NEW SCIENTIST